Health Care Civil Rights

The publisher and the University of California Press Foundation gratefully acknowledge the generous support of the Anne G. Lipow Endowment Fund in Social Justice and Human Rights.

Health Care Civil Rights

How Discrimination Law Fails Patients

———

Anna Kirkland

UNIVERSITY OF CALIFORNIA PRESS

University of California Press
Oakland, California

Suggested citation: Kirkland, A. *Health Care Civil Rights: How Discrimination Law Fails Patients*. Oakland: University of California Press, 2025.
DOI: https://doi.org/10.1525/luminos.226

Library of Congress Cataloging-in-Publication Data

Names: Kirkland, Anna, author.
Title: Health care civil rights : how discrimination law fails patients /
    Anna Kirkland.
Description: First edition. | Oakland, California : University of
    California Press, 2025. | Includes bibliographical references and index.
Identifiers: LCCN 2024044573 (print) | LCCN 2024044574 (ebook) |
    ISBN 9780520416109 (paperback) | ISBN 9780520416116 (ebook)
Subjects: LCSH: Medical care—Law and legislation—United States. |
    Patients—Civil rights—United States. | Discrimination in medical care—
    Law and legislation—United States. | Right to health—United States. |
    Health facilities—Law and legislation—United States.
Classification: LCC KF3823 .K57 2025 (print) | LCC KF3823 (ebook) |
    DDC 344.7304/1—dc23/eng/20240920

LC record available at https://lccn.loc.gov/2024044573
LC ebook record available at https://lccn.loc.gov/2024044574

34   33   32   31   30   29   28   27   26   25
10   9   8   7   6   5   4   3   2   1

CONTENTS

ACKNOWLEDGEMENTS

I wrote this book within a community of intellectual and personal support. I'm deeply grateful to the people who granted interviews about their healthcare workplaces, their medical insurance struggles, their political and civil rights activism, their patient care, and their work in government. My research informants talked about difficult situations because they want to make things better for others. Danielle Jahnke was my first research assistant for this work before I had any funding, supported by Michigan's Undergraduate Research Opportunity Program. The National Science Foundation funded the grant that launched this project, with both the Law and Science and the Law and Organizations divisions collaborating to support it (award number 1654645). The NSF funding allowed me to hire a team of brilliant graduate student research assistants to launch the interviews nationwide: Mikell Hyman, Angela Perone, Danya Lagos, Eli Alston-Stepnitz, and Elias Lawliet. Rebecca Warren helped me make research contacts across the state of Michigan.

I had just started my term as director of the Institute for Research on Women and Gender (IRWG) at Michigan when this research began in 2017. My predecessor in the directorship, Sarah Fenstermaker, helped me to see how I could combine leadership and research for feminist aims and provided near-daily guidance while I was her associate director. Abby Stewart and Carol Boyd were always there when I needed support. Working at IRWG gave me the opportunity to do my scholarly work in a truly team-based setting for the first time with colleagues Heidi Bennett, Terrence Crimes, Nicole Perry, Tammy Culler, Jocelyn Stitt, CristiEllen Zarvas, Lisa Parker, and Rebecca Irvine. When I stepped down as director, I felt lost in the push to finish the book in the swirl of political events and data that seemed overwhelming. Elizabeth DeWolf was a stellar developmental editor, helping me to see a coherent structure for my narrative at a time when it was a jumble.

A Michigan Humanities Award gave me the time to do the work of shaping this manuscript. Laura Portwood-Stacer's advice was always a guide for the publishing process. I'm grateful for funding from the University of Michigan through my collegiate professorship, which kept this project going after the NSF ran out. Being able to name my professorship after my friend and mentor Kim Lane Scheppele was a tremendous honor. Shauhin Talesh agreed to collaborate with me to research health insurance discrimination, and his insights are reflected throughout this book and in our collaborative publications with Angie Perone that came before it. My partnership with Leverage Global Consulting started after I searched in vain for a reasonable way to study health insurance plans at scale and heard from one of my research contacts that Christine Ferguson had a database. Along with her team at Leverage, especially Dharma Yechuri and Ashok Seshadri, Christy agreed to partner with me for research access and collaboration that has made years of my work possible. Jim Dupree, Jane Kitaevich, Karra Greenberg, Sarah Burgard, Stan Panis, Siddarth Chaudhari, Sitara Murali, Kate Castle, Luca Borah, Stephanie Lee, Chyanne Laldee, Asha Hill, and Rosemarie Steffen were critical collaborators in this insurance plan research at Michigan. I'm grateful to Michigan's Institute for Healthcare Policy and Innovation for supporting medical student members of our research team through their summer fellowship program. Rianna Johnson-Levy's research trip to the LBJ Presidential Library and her thoughtful memos on the documents she found give this book its detail of the hospital desegregation process. Rory Peters created the index and gave the manuscript a detailed fact and citation check, and any errors that got through are mine. The students in my law school seminar on health discrimination were brilliant interlocutors across all the issues in this book.

Conversations with treasured colleagues over the years have shaped this research considerably. I'm grateful to Elizabeth Chiarello, Carol Heimer, Oliver Haimson, Joanna Wuest, Colleen Grogan, Liz Sepper, Jennifer Reich, Amanda Hollis-Brusky, Josh Wilson, Kate Redburn, Doron Dorfman, Marie-Andrée Jacob, Jonathan Metzl, Simone Chriss, Jim Dupree, Lilia Cortina, Andrea Bolivar, Angie Perone, Gary Harper, Sandra Levitsky, Elizabeth Armstrong, stef shuster, Carla Pfeffer, Kristi Gamarel, Megan Lane, Daphna Stroumsa, Alison Dundes Renteln, Katharine McCabe, Zach Kapner, Mitchell Travis, Chris Dietz, Jennifer Piemonte, Nicholson Price, and many generous anonymous peer reviewers who gave insightful feedback in the journal and book review process. I benefited from generous audiences, discussants, and co-panelists at the University of Leeds School of Law, the 2021 Consumer Law Scholars Conference, the UC Irvine Socio-Legal Studies Workshop, the UC Irvine School of Law Faculty Development Workshop, the

University of Massachusetts Department of Pediatrics, the Penn State University Bioethics Colloquium, Hackensack Meridian School of Medicine, the Program on Women's Healthcare Effectiveness Research within the Michigan Medicine Department of Obstetrics and Gynecology, the Center for Racial and Social Justice at the William and Mary Law School, the National Clinician Scholars Program at Michigan Medicine, the University of Michigan Science, Technology, and Society Program, the Michigan College Executive Committee, Dean Anne Curzan, and Associate Deans Tim McKay, Barb Meek, Gregory Dowd, and Tricia Wittkopp, and the annual meetings for the Law and Society Association, the American Sociological Association, the American Society for Reproductive Medicine, and the American Political Science Association.

Michigan has talented staff who graciously helped me with grants administration, IT support, hiring my research assistants, and reviewing my IRB applications for this project (HUM00120522, HUM00130154). Michigan librarians, especially Meredith Kahn, have always been exceptional problem solvers and collaborators. I appreciate her help in learning about and figuring out the open access publishing world, an important ethical as well as dissemination goal for this research. An award from the University of Michigan Library, the College of Literature, Science, and the Arts, and the Office of the Vice President for Research, along with the commitments of the University of California Press, made the open access publication of this book possible. I thank Associate Dean Gregory Dowd for his help in securing those funds in the rush of publishing deadlines. Maura Roessner, my editor at the University of California Press, has been an inspiring supporter of this book. Sam Warren and Francisco Reinking expertly guided it through the publishing process and Tim DeBold and Michelle Black provided the final polish in copyediting and cover design.

Some sections of this book draw directly or indirectly on my previously published work. I thank and acknowledge the following publications for reprint permissions: *Law and Society Review* for "Health Insurance Rights and Access to Health Care for Trans People: The Social Construction of Medical Necessity" with Shauhin Talesh and Angela Perone in vol. 55, no. 4 (2021): 539–62 and "Civil Rights as Patient Experience: How Healthcare Organizations Handle Discrimination Complaints" with Mikell Hyman in vol. 55, no. 2 (2021): 273–95; *Social Science and Medicine* for "Dropdown Rights: Categorizing Transgender Discrimination in Healthcare Technologies" in vol. 289 (2021); *Transgender Health* for "Transition Coverage and Clarity in Self-Insured Corporate Health Insurance Benefit Plans" with Shauhin Talesh and Angela Perone in vol. 6, no. 4 (2021): 207–16; *New England Journal of Medicine* for "Health Coverage and Care for Transgender People—Threats and Opportunities" with Daphna Stroumsa in vol. 383, no. 25 (2020): 2397–99; "Physicians as Political Pawns—The Texas Directive on Gender-Affirming Care and Other Moves" in vol. 386, no. 16 (2022): 2161–64; and

"Protecting Care for All—Gender-Affirming Care in Section 1557 and Beyond" with Megan Lane and Daphna Stroumsa in vol. 387, no. 21 (2022): 1916–18.

Caregivers' labor, especially during COVID school shutdowns, made it possible for me to keep doing research and writing. I'm grateful to the leadership and staff of the Ann Arbor Jewish Community Center, especially Marlowe Susselman, for their learning supports during that time. And for always, my friends and family have my love and gratitude.

Introduction

The Hope of Health Care Civil Rights

Sam (not his real name) arrived at a major university hospital emergency department with his boyfriend, experiencing intermittent and severe bouts of abdominal pain.[1] Sam is a transgender man, meaning he was assigned female at birth but has a male gender identity. His electronic medical records had been updated with his correct gender identity as male. Sam told the triage nurse he was "a transgender man . . . [that] he had previously used testosterone, as well as hypertensives, both of which he had discontinued because he'd lost his insurance coverage."[2] He had not menstruated in several years and tested positive for pregnancy that morning with a home test, though "he wondered whether it was a false positive." The triage nurse "assessed him to be a man with abdominal pain who had not taken his prescribed blood-pressure medication" and "obese."[3] She classified his case as nonurgent, so he waited hours to see an emergency room physician.

However, the emergency department physician shifted the understanding of the situation, recognizing Sam as a pregnant person experiencing dangerous complications, such as possible preterm delivery, placental abruption, or preeclampsia. She paged the obstetrics team who examined him and found that Sam had a prolapsed umbilical cord. When an umbilical cord slips down through the cervix when water breaks but before a baby is born, it can be squeezed tightly enough to cut off blood and oxygen. Sam's baby was stillborn. He had not known he was pregnant, but he was nonetheless "heartbroken and had a major depressive episode."[4] An official case report concluded that a cisgender woman presenting with the same symptoms and history would "almost surely have been triaged and evaluated more urgently for pregnancy-related problems." Sam "should have received the same treatment," an interdisciplinary team found, and earlier detection might have prevented fetal death.[5]

I knew Sam's story from the interdisciplinary team's case report, which was written with Sam's permission and input. My use of quotes from the report is based on an understanding of the publication as a careful collaboration to present a painful situation so that others can learn from it and as one in which Sam had agency over the telling. As I was gathering the interviews for this book, more than one person who worked at this hospital told me this story. It had happened recently, and people were upset. They understood the injustice of Sam's case as a harm of misrecognition leading to poor provision of care. One interviewee explained that staff "[felt] awkward about language, what to say, where to touch, how to acknowledge that this is a man that they're providing obstetric care for." They felt unprepared for "providing, you know, vulvar care for someone bleeding after a delivery or putting in a Foley catheter." Sam's story became a tale of organizational failure to recognize and provide for a trans person's medical needs properly.

Sam's story is an example of the kind of incident that should be prevented by Section 1557 of the Patient Protection and Affordable Care Act (ACA), the antidiscrimination clause of the landmark health care law that prohibits discrimination against patients on the basis of race, color, sex, national origin, language spoken, disability, and age.[6] When the ACA passed in 2010, all the other protected categories besides "sex" had been linked to healthcare settings already through other discrimination laws. The inclusion of the antidiscrimination clause in the ACA resulted from coalitional civil rights organizing to support LGBT rights in healthcare reform and the health rights of transgender and other gender-nonconforming people in particular. Democratic presidential administrations have interpreted protection from sex discrimination in health care to include gender-identity protections for trans people. I use the term "trans" to refer to those whose gender identity differs from the sex they were assigned at birth.[7] I use the term "health care" to refer to the context of or interactions between a care giver and a person seeking care or the act of care, and the term "healthcare" to mean the healthcare system and institutional structures.

The foundational concept of gender-identity discrimination in Section 1557 is discrimination as failure to treat a trans person the same as a cisgender person. That is, it would be wrong to withhold some form of care from a trans person just because they are trans if a cisgender person would be able to access it, such as a hysterectomy or hormone treatment. Any differential treatment or denial of care must be for a legitimate, nondiscriminatory reason that is not based in animus or bias. Section 1557 also requires recognition of one's gender identity: placing a patient in a room with other patients of the same gender (a transwoman with a cisgender woman, not a cisgender man) as an inpatient and using the proper pronouns to address a trans person. Electronic medical records should record a patient's correct sexual orientation and gender identity. Section 1557 extends health care discrimination law to health insurance coverage, prohibiting categorical exclusions of gender-affirming care. The vision of health care civil rights grown from the

ACA calls for the appropriate *recognition* of gender identity so that proper *provision* of health care can follow.

When I asked one prominent trans-rights policy advocate about their hopes for the law, they replied:

> [Section 1557] should mean that transgender people are no longer afraid to get health care. You know, our US transgender survey that we conducted in all fifty states saw nearly a quarter of transgender people said that they avoided getting health care when they needed it in the last year because they were afraid of discrimination. So, you know, ideally, trans people would know that they weren't going to face discrimination, that they would know that their gender identity would be respected by healthcare providers, they would not be subject to harassment, that healthcare providers and their management wouldn't tolerate harassment from their other staff or from anyone else, of patients, that people would have access to facilities like restrooms in a healthcare facility consistent with their gender identity, and that people wouldn't face discrimination in health insurance.

Putting these ideas together through Sam's case reveals that implementing Section 1557 well is organizationally complex; that is, it requires attitudes and knowledge throughout staffing levels and systems of knowledge and recording about patients and their bodies so that Sam's situation can be understood, respected, and treated with speed and attention. It requires changes throughout the health insurance industry and in employers' relationships to their sponsored benefits. Fundamentally, it requires political and legal acceptance of the idea that gender identity is a rightly protected category, that people bring a range of gender identities to healthcare settings that come with legitimate health care needs, and that these identities and their needs are important and deserving of legal protection.

But Sam's experience of gender-based discrimination occurred years after the passage of Section 1557. Achieving successful implementation of Section 1557 has been hard at every level. Trans people consistently report discrimination in medical care, including insurance denials or exclusions for gender-affirming care, such as surgery and hormone therapy, harassment by care providers such as being called the wrong name or addressed as the wrong gender and being outed by these practices, misdiagnoses or nonrecognition of health conditions, such as Sam's case, receiving dehumanizing "freak" treatment through unnecessary questioning, probing, or exhibiting of their bodies, or simply being disbelieved that they are transgender in the first place.[8] Gender-nonconforming people report high rates of poor health.[9] The phrase "transgender broken arm syndrome," or the experience of showing up for care for something entirely unrelated to one's gender identity but having one's care mishandled because of it anyway, comes from an actual case in which a doctor refused to set a trans person's broken arm because he claimed he did not have enough experience treating gender dysphoria.

Experiences of discrimination still drive trans people from care.[10] Anticipating future discrimination makes them stay away. Even when electronic medical records correctly identify their gender identity and sex at birth, trans people may face direct hostility for being trans or the kind of erasure that Sam experienced even though information about him was available. Insurance coverage battles over whether gender-affirming care is medically necessary or cosmetic still make it difficult or impossible for many people to obtain the medications and procedures that can align their bodies with their gender identity even if their insurance plan does not categorically exclude their care. Gender-affirming care for trans adults and youth has become a contentious political issue, with Republican state legislatures passing laws to burden or ban its provision while Democratic administrations have insisted it is a civil rights violation to withhold it. Conservative judges do not recognize gender identity as a legitimate civil rights category, and they do not defer to (and actively block) the civil rights regulations that implement protections in health care for trans people.

There are some other features of Sam's story that reveal additional difficulties in designing a policy solution to prevent what happened to him. Sam was a younger adult (32) without health insurance coverage in a nation with no universal health care. Even with the coverage expansions of the ACA, he still fell through the cracks. Perhaps Sam's whiteness shielded him from some racial discrimination, such as the criminalization that Black women differentially face after pregnancy loss.[11] He was not arrested or charged with a crime. Sam's case looks like weight discrimination, in which his gender identity, body size, and failure to take his high blood pressure medication routed him into the category of noncompliant fat man. Even though weight discrimination is well documented in health care, there is no federal civil rights protection for that category at all.[12] It has been difficult to fully represent the ways that intersectional identities matter in civil rights law and in healthcare settings, but when someone shows up for health care they are already situated in systems of power that shape how they will be treated all the same. Our civil rights laws still capture these complexities only superficially.

We have neither appropriate recognition nor proper provision of health care for so many people in this country. In this book, I argue that such discrimination persists because Section 1557 of the Affordable Care Act is a weak strategy for ensuring equal treatment and access to care. It is weak because it brings a thin, raggedy collection of civil rights policies to bear against an enormous, complex edifice of organizations, financial interests, political interests, religion, professions, and cultures that make up the American healthcare system. These forms of weakness invite absorption and deflection of health care rights within structures such as hospitals and insurance companies, each sites of their own priorities and modes of governance that are not rights friendly. It is also weak because we lack a shared political commitment to both health equity and civil rights, making it easy for conservatives opposed to health care civil rights to simply dismantle them. Rights exist in competition with other rights, and it is possible to defeat some rights (equal health care for trans people) by reframing and invoking others that can trump them (free exercise of religion to withhold care). Rights are malleable political rhetoric for any side of an argument to use. Section 1557 represents the conflicted dualism of the American approach to health and rights: both are highly salient ideologically and politically but in divergent ways that keep the temperature high and agreement at bay. Deeply embedded structures of the American state and private sector also shape this frustrating situation. To understand the well-meant intentions behind Section 1557 and why it is still insufficient, it is critical to first examine common assumptions about health and inequality in the United States.

HEALTH DISPARITIES AS CIVIL RIGHTS ISSUES

Identity matters for living and dying in America today. Poorer health and shorter lives mean that some groups cannot thrive, put their life plans into action, and function as fully as others in US society. Persistent health inequalities sort us into hierarchies by race, gender, income, gender identity, immigration status, disability, and sexual orientation, among other factors. The term *health disparity*, now a buzzword that appears widely (with *health equity*), means a difference between measured outcomes between groups on some measure of health or mortality. A disparity is a difference between groups that is understood to be unfair. The problem of health disparities has become a predominant frame for inequality in center-left politics in Western democracies,[13] including the United States. More robust social justice accounts of how inequality and injustice harm health have never really caught on.[14] "Racism is a public health crisis" and "gun violence is an epidemic" are examples of how we frame social problems in health terms now.

Black Americans on average have a lifespan that is six years shorter than the average white person's lifespan. Black birthing people die from pregnancy-related causes nearly three times more often than white birthing people, even when they are middle class or wealthy.[15] Racism in health care means that the dictum of parity in care (Sam should have been treated just as well as a pregnant cisgender woman) is white-centered and oblivious to the reality that a Black cisgender woman with a pregnancy emergency may face very poor treatment too. Transgender people of all races report that they avoided seeking health care because of past experiences being humiliated, turned away, or dealing with a provider who did not understand their gender identity.[16] Black trans women lead especially precarious lives with high exposure to lethal violence.[17] The coronavirus pandemic laid these inequalities bare, yet we still have not been able to solve this problem. People with disabilities and those living in institutional settings comprised one-third of all US COVID-19 deaths in the first year of the pandemic.[18] Black Americans died of COVID-19 at a rate twice as high as white people in the first six months of the pandemic.[19]

We can locate almost any social problem, from gun violence to poverty to maternal mortality, in a health disparities framework and acknowledge disparate outcomes based on race, gender, and other categories. Everyone can relate to the value of health as a baseline requirement for meeting other needs, for carrying out goals in work and family, and for full participation in society. The moral case for health equality is also widely compelling: no one should consider suicide because living out their gender identity authentically seems impossible. No one should have a shorter life because they were born next to a toxic environmental site or because they are Black. Talking about health disparities is an easier way to talk about race for many white people, perhaps because it offers an account of a problem that does not place blame. Health seems fixable in ways that other social problems, like poverty or crime, do not. We have doctors, vaccines, hospitals, and shiny new innovations in technology and pharmaceuticals that hold out hope. There are health-based movements from both the left and the right that hold up alternative approaches to medically based health based on diet, herbs, supplements, meditation, yoga practice, homeopathy, and many other modalities. Health seems useful and powerful, in other words. It seems like something a person could *achieve*.

Maybe we can use the law to achieve health for more people. It is reasonable to locate the root cause of identity-based inequalities in discrimination and therefore to argue that antidiscrimination law, in the form of civil rights, is an important way to address such inequalities. By civil rights, I mean statutory protections against mistreatment based on one's identity or status as well as for inclusion in mainstream institutions regardless of identity or status. Civil rights laws typically apply to identity categories like race, sex, religion, disability, age, national origin, gender identity, sexual orientation, veteran status, and other traits. Most civil rights statutes at the federal and state levels contain a list of such characteristics and require that the person claiming a right make an argument that their rights were infringed "on the basis of" one or more of these traits. Law professor Craig Konnoth argues that there are many reasons why making civil rights claims linked to medical status is appealing: invoking medical status can confer material benefits like insurance coverage, it can offer comforts like giving meaning to one's suffering or entry into a community, and it recruits the prestige of medical and scientific expertise in its defense.[20] If civil rights are the solution to inequality, then bringing them to bear on the idea of health as a driver of inequality via laws like Section 1557 seems like a powerful solution.

CHALLENGES TO A CIVIL RIGHTS APPROACH TO HEALTH INEQUALITY

There is, however, a string of assumptions connecting the ideas that health disparities are the result of illegal discrimination and that the law can fix them. Those assumptions include knowing what causes health disparities, knowing that the cause is a discrete type of policy, action, or omission that can be described as a legal wrong, and that there is some remedy that antidiscrimination law can offer to address it. There must be agreement that protecting people from harm based on an identity trait (like being trans or non-binary) is a good thing to do (as opposed to trying to change them or label the identity as deviant or confused). Health morality, once invoked, may not stay cabined in the way one hoped, or it may not be so powerful against other moral formations from religion, for example.

Unfortunately, there is little reason to think that measuring inequalities and framing them in terms of health makes them easier to solve or less likely to provoke animus and backlash. As political scientist Julia Lynch demonstrates, Western democracies have been focused on solving inequality through health, or medicalizing inequality as she terms it, for several decades, while measures of health disparities have only gotten worse.[21] Indeed, medicalizing inequality makes health equity even more elusive, she argues, because framing inequality through health makes it easier to individualize it, because it sidesteps more obvious ways to blunt inequality like income redistribution and market regulations, and because the solutions are very difficult to implement. Lynch points out that we often think of health inequality as caused by lack of access to health *care*, but the link between medical care and health is not as tight as it might seem. There are no straightforward, evidence-based interventions that show much promise for solving the "wicked problem" of health inequalities. Health inequalities are closely linked to relative economic inequalities in societies, which have grown dramatically. We have excelled at measuring health and inequality by, for example, operationalizing race as a variable and breaking out subgroups understood as vulnerable in datasets. But as political scientists Jamila Michener and Tiffany Ford point out, those measurements alone cannot get us what we really need, which is an understanding of and ways to intervene in interlocking systems of oppressions, their cumulative effects across spheres like health, employment, and housing, and the power relations that allow structures and institutions to perpetuate inequality.[22]

The promise of medicalizing inequality has failed to remove it from moral debates. I've argued that civil rights frameworks have not been able to alleviate anti-fat bias and discrimination, even as obesity has become more medicalized in supposedly sympathetic ways.[23] There are multiple causal stories about why any given health disparity found in population-level data exists, and the moralism cuts different ways.[24] A health disparity can be explained by prejudicial stereotypes about group behavior (laziness, gluttony, and lust leading to fatness and sexually transmitted infections). Indeed, the racial history of what we now call health disparities reveals that many group-based differences in health outcomes were regularly attributed to an out-group's filthy habits and derelict morals. Emphasizing COVID-19's racially disparate impacts, for example, can backfire if those who hear about the disparities conclude that they must have come from Black people's vulnerable racial biology or bad habits.[25] Conservative religious opponents of trans health care rights deny the very existence of the category proposed for protection, characterizing the problem as "gender confusion."[26] They blamed Sam for what happened to him when he went to the hospital.[27] Health and wellness remain individual moral imperatives even on the left, where concern for structural inequalities sits uncomfortably with embrace of lifestyle conceptions of health as a lifelong project.

Meanwhile, civil rights may not be particularly effective at addressing health disparities because of well-documented weaknesses in rights as a tool for ending oppression. Legal rights and antidiscrimination law have long been a disappointment to the feminist and critical race scholars who have carefully assessed its legacies. Legal rights against discrimination are often narrow remedies for individual bad conduct that is hard to prove, and often one must present as an appealing victim who did everything right to win. Antidiscrimination law has often been criticized for conceptualizing wrongdoing overly narrowly by focusing on the one bad perpetrator, leaving it conveniently unable to address structural harms built up by decades and even centuries of inequalities and violence that play out today. When antidiscrimination laws try to address unequal outcomes that are not the result of a bad actor but have harmed a protected group nonetheless (termed disparate impact discrimination), these potentially stronger versions have been cut back at the Supreme Court or foundered because it is difficult to pinpoint one policy that caused an unequal outcome. Inclusion, conceptualized as civil rights protections against individual acts of wrongdoing and inclusion in mainstream institutions such as marriage and military service, cannot "truly address and transform the conditions of premature death facing impoverished and criminalized populations," trans legal scholar Dean Spade insists.[28]

Activists and social movements in the United States have long mobilized around health as an issue of justice in feminist, queer, and anti-racist terms not centered around law or the state.[29] The turn from reproductive rights to reproductive justice, led by Black feminist activists and scholars, is a paradigmatic example showing how merely securing the now-lost constitutional right to an abortion is a meager part of the full picture of reproductive freedom and social justice.[30] Abortion rights as personal choices to use one's resources to acquire something without too much state interference is no grounding for protections against racist practices in prenatal care or traumatic family policing visits, which half of Black children and families now experience.[31] Reproductive justice offers a fuller positive vision of a world in which all parents and children are valued and safe, and thus has been a model for rethinking the narrowness of rights.

Abolishing or stepping out of oppressive state systems, not bringing in more law, has been the solution in these lines of research, including in the new and growing field of trans studies. Trans and non-binary people, especially trans women of color, suffer poorer health and shorter, more violent lives because they are targets of violence by the state through incarceration, policing, and immigration detention. Activists and scholars have advocated for collective, community-based responses based in mutual aid and what Hil Malatino calls "trans care" that are not part of any state apparatus.[32] These critiques from the left refuse to contain injustice to the narrow terms offered by an individual health focus or a civil rights focus. They reinterpret both recognition and provision, turning away from what the state and the law offer to those who meet its definitional categories.

A focus on health care civil rights in this book indeed means that two powerful institutions—medicine and law—already delimit the possibilities for opening up who the subject of trans rights is and what the meaning of care and justice is.[33] We know that injustice in health is much more complex and multifaceted than mere bad actors taking discrete actions based on prejudice against a sympathetic figure, which is the form of injustice our civil rights laws most concretely make illegal. Pulse oximeters do not work as well on darker-skinned people's fingers, giving inaccurate readings. They have been allowed to be designed that way, but no one specifically intended that outcome (or thought much about it).[34] Limiting trans patient rights by requiring a comparison to what cisgender people can obtain keeps the cisgender body and experience at the center of the definition of proper care. These two examples show how whiteness and being cisgender can be built into the basic infrastructure and foundations of health care. Our entire edifice of health insurance—the gateway to care and the primary way of paying for its high costs—sorts people into different care and costs based on what kind of job they have, their immigration and citizenship status, how old they are, what state they live in, and how much money comes into their household. Addressing these injustices would require confronting the complex, systemic ways that whiteness, heterosexuality, cisgender status, wealth, citizenship, and other factors confer advantages to some patients over others and influence care.

Health care civil rights have adapted to these challenges in some important ways. It may be, as Dan Carpenter has argued, that health care is different.[35] The politics of health and health care offer pathways in law and policy that are somewhat more expansive than those in the employment context. The expansions in health insurance under the Affordable Care Act and the implementation of Section 1557 have indeed improved health equity already,[36] and there are more possibilities for how law might address discrimination in more complex ways. For example, the Biden administration used Section 1557 and Title VI of the Civil Rights Act of 1964 to address environmental racism in an Alabama community where Black residents lived with raw sewage in their neighborhood.[37] Legal claims based on multiple categories—the best version of intersectionality theory available—are at least intelligible in court and affirmed in civil rights regulations, including the Department of Health and Human Services regulations for Section 1557. Section 1557 prohibits the use of patient care decision support tools such as algorithms in health care that discriminate based on race, color, sex, national origin (including language), gender identity, disability, and age, a potentially far-reaching innovation that goes far beyond the bad actor model of discrimination to try to reach "baked in" bias.[38] The Joint Commission, a major accrediting body for hospitals, requires that someone be in charge of addressing health disparities, that organizations measure patients' "health-related social needs," and that they identify health care disparities "by stratifying quality and safety data using sociodemographic characteristics" of their patients.[39] We now have version 10 of the International Classification of Diseases or ICD-10 Z codes designed to capture social determinants of health in patients' medical records, billed as a "data journey to better outcomes."[40] Physicians use these Z codes to document diagnoses, symptoms, and procedures for billing to insurance, and now providers have codes for things like illiteracy, food insecurity, or toxic exposures. Will health care be different because it can more successfully ground rights that both recognize properly and provision adequately? Will it be different through its other ways of knowing, tracking, measuring, and managing disadvantage and discrimination? What is it to code for something that a physician cannot fix? Whether different means better or worse is, as we shall see throughout this book, also open to question.

Although I understand the critics who eschew tinkering with liberal legalism, I choose not to follow them outside the laws and institutional structures of healthcare and the state in this book. Mutual aid within groups of like-minded and bonded people has been a source of health care prior to the establishment of the welfare state, and conservatives still celebrate turning back to communities to meet the needs of the vulnerable rather than expanding government's reach.[41] But the history of American health care security shows that taking care of one's own in segmented private groups, like workers or mutual aid societies, leaves too many people out.[42] Large scale interventions to combat health inequalities are matters of government policy, with all the messiness and compromise that entails. Staying in the bounds of what these powerful structures can offer may predictably disappoint, but as I'll argue throughout the conclusion, it still gives me many concrete suggestions that could make people's lives better.

REFRACTING CIVIL RIGHTS THROUGH HEALTHCARE

Health care civil rights in the contemporary United States have been made weak, while healthcare institutions have been deliberately allowed to be strong. Civil rights in these institutions are thin and raggedy first because they are not written out and explained in the laws that Congress passes. They lack a robust legislative history and a strong political consensus that sets out a vision of equality these laws should defend. There is no argument or explanation from Congress about why protecting anyone, including trans and non-binary people, from health discrimination is important. That is because the ACA itself barely squeaked by and its antidiscrimination clause received no attention at all. Powerful majorities or near-majorities oppose health care civil rights, and sometimes they have squelched or nearly defeated them. Health care civil rights are also weak because they follow a path set out by previously enacted civil rights laws, which were themselves hobbled by politicians determined to make sure they were not strongly enforced.[43]

In addition, health care civil rights are weak because the organizations they regulate can construct what these rights mean for themselves. Organizations such as hospital systems turn these rights to further their own organizational goals rather than to enact justice for patients.[44] Health care civil rights regulations spell out prohibitions on discrimination but give over the meaning of compliance on the ground to health care professionals with more pressing compliance concerns such as the next accreditation. Health insurance companies can be required to remove exclusions but continue to find ways to make using health insurance for gender-affirming care difficult. Finally, weak civil rights are no match for right-wing religious mobilization against gender-identity protections, which has forcefully pushed back against trans health rights.

In the last decade or so, we have seen both the largest expansion and the largest contraction in trans rights protections. These shifts are possible because of the civil rights and healthcare landscape in the United States, which come together in a fractured federal system of uneven laws and contentious politics. Private companies and religious groups share the job of securing us against illness and unbearable financial costs with the state and federal governments in a patchy system designed to further many other interests before patient well-being. Vulnerable people suffer on this landscape, and the solutions we have in civil rights law fail to meet the challenge of easing their suffering most of the time. Both recognition and provision in discrimination law fail patients in different ways, in other words, and they fail because of systemic flaws in both our healthcare system and our civil rights system. We only see this clearly by looking at both together in an expansive and detailed way.

Because the United States lacks systems to support the delivery of health care civil rights, I argue that civil rights get *refracted*, meaning transformed, turned, diminished, weakened, and distorted, as they come up against our healthcare system and other more powerful structures. Refraction causes light or sound to change direction or separate when it goes through water or glass. The image on the 1973 Pink Floyd album cover for *The Dark Side of the Moon*, one of the most recognizable album covers of all time, shows a glass triangle refracting a beam of white light, which comes out on the other side at a different angle in rainbow colors. I mean refracting in the breaking apart sense, unfortunately. This book explains what happens to civil rights when they refract through existing healthcare, legal, and political frameworks. *Refracted rights* are diverted and changed as they encounter transformatively powerful entities. Sometimes rights cause transformations too, but in my research, I found that the mutual refractions were uneven and more clearly on the side of rights refracting against healthcare and political structures.

When civil rights are refracted through health care encounters and the health-care system, they undergo reframing. They skid off to one side, they look different, or they no longer seem to work. Sometimes they are outright vanquished, but usually the process is more subtle. Social scientists have long used the terms *frames* or *framework* to talk about how we sort and make sense of our experiences in the social world.[45] The idea is that to answer the question, What kind of problem is this? or, Is it discrimination that is happening here? we bring initial frames of understanding and sorting that make it possible to see it one way or another. Frames can become more than individual lenses for perception when they are the norms of a profession (giving a diagnosis, judging a case) or the rules for managing problems within an organization (selecting a type of problem from within a drop-down menu in patient grievance management software).

Throughout this book, I use the concept of frames in this organizationally and legally thick sense. Civil rights in health care are sufficiently ambiguous and contested that is not always clear that a problem in a healthcare setting is a civil rights problem. Most of the time health care problems are not seen as civil rights problems, even when they involve people saying they have been harmed because of who they are. Even when advocates argue that an injustice in health care is a civil rights problem, there are other competing frames, such as religious liberty or medical necessity, that also have power in that context to dislodge that frame in favor of another. Seeing a problem through a certain frame tends to dictate what the proper response should be. When the civil rights answers seem to fade away, break apart, or become blocked and diverted, I argue that they have been reframed in the refraction into healthcare systems and health care interactions.

Professionalization—the training and socialization into a field of work that confers a sense of ownership over a problem—is a big part of transforming rights into other things. For example, if a cadre of professionals who manage patient complaints or safety compliance are already in place across hospitals, we might expect the work of patient civil rights problems to be routed to them. We can understand gender identity through a frame of medical expertise, in which the tools of diagnosis and treatment by expert medical professionals position trans people as patients who deserve the care that their doctors recommend. Seeing gender identity as a civil rights problem through a medical expertise frame connects trans people seeking care with powerful groups like physicians and medical societies who defend gender-affirming care as medically necessary, recommended treatment for a diagnosis called gender dysphoria. Obtaining a diagnosis is the typical path to securing medical treatment for that condition under a health insurance plan. Physicians maintain control over gender identity as a medical problem and resist giving it over to those who would reframe it as a moral or cultural problem.

But a medical expertise frame can be knocked aside by a religious freedom frame. A religious frame for gender identity—and the main one operating in the United States today is a conservative evangelical Christian or conservative Catholic frame, specifically—sees biological men and women created by God to complement each other sexually and by nature as the only reality, rendering any other forms of sexuality or gender identity as confusion in the face of this reality or as revolt against God. Shifting or proliferating gender identities are then not the proper subject of discrimination claims or medical expertise but a cultural problem to be solved by religious authorities. Religious authorities operate large parts of the US healthcare system. A religious employer does not have to include gender-affirming care in their health plan and a religious hospital may not have to provide it. The doctors who work there do not have independent judgment over trans health care; they are bound by their religious employer's guidelines. In that case, one right has lost to another in a direct competition between them. As I'll explain, these contestations happen in court but also reverberate through the professions and organizational cultures of healthcare.

While the medical expertise frame may be helpful for trans and non-binary people seeking care, it also positions medical experts as gatekeepers who have the power to grant or withhold medical services and coverage. It does not allow trans people themselves to define their identities and needs and to be experts themselves. This book makes competing frames visible and explains what is at stake as they clash or come to dominate in a context. The messy interaction of different frames that draw their power from different professional structures, economic incentives and policies, forms of legal protection, and political formations helps explain why health care civil rights cannot solve problems of health inequality.

LAW IN ACTION FROM THE HOSPITAL TO THE COURTROOM

I understand health care civil rights through a theoretical framework that decenters their formal specifications in law and considers them instead as law in action, or as ordinary people make sense of them in their lives as patients, hospital administrators, billing clerks, health information technology workers, doctors, and lawyers. Therefore, research for this book is grounded in the assumption that what law really means is what it means to the people who claim it, use it, work with it, implement it, and resist it. These moments unfold within complex structures and according to existing frameworks that shape what rights are. Health care civil rights unfold within a political and legal economy of healthcare that sets up conditions of inequality and spins them out in new ways. My approach moves across and around distinctions between public law and private law, statutes and the Constitution, and religion and economic interests. This approach enables me to explain what happens to health care civil rights across contexts, allowing all the complexity of healthcare professions, organizations, laws, politics, and economies to flow through my story.

I focus on trans health care civil rights and gender-affirming care throughout the book as vivid sites of rights contestation and meaning-making. My analysis would look different if I had studied the refracted rights in another legal category that has also been a major policy focus in the development of Section 1557, such as national origin (with a focus on those who speak languages other than English) or disability. Some chapters are more focused on the site and details of trans health care civil rights than others because that is how the evidence unfolded in the research path I chose. At some points lived experiences drive my narrative, and at other points I argue that impersonal institutional structures and legacies of past decisions from law and politics have explanatory power.

What health care civil rights are, where they come from, and what they mean is a complicated set of questions that requires investigation at multiple levels and with different research tools. My research team and I used multiple methods to triangulate the story of health care civil rights and gender identity. The story is about both a legal category and lived experiences, with disjunctures, erasures, and highlights creating an always-inaccurate assemblage of who is in the category and what is happening to them. There was not much to start with. Section 1557 is an ambiguous law. It has no legislative history. To construct its origins, I conducted in-depth interviews with twenty-one activists and government employees who wrote the original clause in the Affordable Care Act, guided its enactment and regulations, and worked to implement it. They helped me understand why the clause is written in such a bare and unelaborated way, why the process to implement it took so long, and what they hoped the law would accomplish. The lawsuits, judicial opinions, and administrative rulemaking about Section 1557 from its passage to the present can help us to understand what the category was supposed to do in the formal legal sense and how what it means legally has been partially dismantled, mangled, and put back together repeatedly.

To understand the impact and path of Section 1557 from the perspective of the regulated, my research team and I used multiple qualitative methods and data sources that capture both the detail and change of the formal law and rules and also their meanings and use in the everyday professional settings they govern. The professional settings include not only the hospitals and clinics where discrimination may be likely to occur but also the administrative settings where disputes over insurance coverage happen and in lawsuits over the meanings of health care civil rights. The analysis in this book proceeds in levels, from micro- to meso- to macro-, starting with the closest encounters one would have as a patient raising a problem about her treatment in a healthcare setting and proceeding up and out to insurance settings and finally to courtrooms. It is not that the microlevel is more real or experienced while the higher levels are more legal and abstract, though. Every level is a site of rights refraction, category and systems work, and lived experiences. This arrangement shows how health care and healthcare systems matter for civil rights: health shapes rights conceptually, organizationally, technologically, bodily, and politically all the way up and down. If we want changes in the power of our civil rights laws, we can look to health to diagnose their limits and point to possible changes.

On the ground (at the microlevel), the right to gender identity nondiscrimination under Section 1557 was initially supposed to be enforced through a grievance procedure that every healthcare entity taking federal funding with more than fifteen employees had to put in place. Under implementing regulations promulgated by Presidents Obama and Biden, each site had to name a Section 1557 coordinator to handle patient civil rights claims. (President Trump's alternative regulations temporarily withdrew this requirement.) Every hospital and clinic in the United States whose federal funding comes from billing Medicare or Medicaid or from assistance in transitioning to electronic medical records should have named such a person in 2016. My interviews for this research began in 2017 and continued until 2020. These are all the typical settings where one would seek health care, perhaps encounter something unpleasant or discriminatory, and where one might ask for help or try to file a complaint. Who are the people who receive these stories, and how do they perceive and process patient problems? What are the implications for placing new healthcare civil rights in their hands? My research method started from the entry point for patient problems to emerge within the organizational setting. I did not find lawyers doing the bulk of the rights work in healthcare settings. Of course, hospital attorneys would handle formally filed cases and, as I found, keep a close eye on some categories of clinical problems that look risky. But contrary to the image of hyperattentive and defensive medical-legal practice that has gotten so much popular attention, rights work in healthcare is enacted through professionals like patient experience administrators. These grievance handlers, as I call them, are central actors in the law because of ways that healthcare is regulated and incentivized that are not primarily about civil rights or group identities.

The next level (the mesolevel) is one step further from experiences in health care: the health insurance carrier and the employer-sponsored plan. We like to think we get health care from doctors and nurses, but most of the time our health plan dictates what is covered and therefore accessible. Most working-age people in the United States get their health insurance from their employer, who may buy a plan for all their employees or act as their own insurer. The employer may be a public employer, like a state government, or a private corporation, or a religious employer. All these factors make a difference for the reach of the law into these health care arrangements. Civil rights provisions can regulate what health insurance companies must offer in their plans, but depending on the type of antidiscrimination law and the type of insurance, they may not always apply. The ACA directly prohibited a lot of what used to be perfectly legal health discrimination in insurance through its structural rules, such as refusing to issue any coverage at all to people with preexisting conditions or refusing to cover maternity care.[46] These are nondiscrimination provisions, but they are not part of civil rights law. Section 1557 added identity-based civil rights protections to these already-enacted health insurance discrimination protections but without defining what counted as health discrimination.

This may be confusing, but we are just getting started. Health insurance in the United States is an incredibly complex set of private and public offerings, utilization management techniques, regulations, and protections. I analyze health insurance as structure beyond the experience of the insured because much of the exclusions, barriers, and discrimination take place out of sight within private entities. Indeed, researchers cannot even gain access to decision-making within insurance companies. I developed an industry partnership with Leverage Global Consulting, a healthcare consulting firm specializing in insurance plan data and analysis, to gain access to their repository of health plan documents. The discussion of health insurance in this book draws on my data collection and content analysis of 1,496 health insurance plan documents, scrutinized for details of gender-affirming coverage and exclusions, among other details. I also interviewed trans and non-binary people who had recently used or tried to use their coverage for gender-affirming care and some of their care providers. Their stories reveal the rights work to be done to use the health insurance one supposedly has. Doctors, therapists, and their office administrative staff members take on the roles of advocates with insurance companies, in effect behaving like lawyers arguing a case with the insurance company. Sometimes all this work results in care, but sometimes the barriers at this level are not surmountable.

The final and highest level of health care civil rights refraction considered in this book is the Section 1557 gender-identity discrimination litigation, state legislative actions both against and in support of gender-affirming care, and the advocacy from social movements, religious leaders, and politicians (the macrolevel). States can pass laws requiring their state Medicaid plans to cover gender-affirming care, for example, and states have also banned such care under their Medicaid plans. Religiously affiliated hospitals and professional groups have conducted impact litigation (bringing strategic lawsuits to establish policy through court decisions) to broaden religious liberty protections so that they do not have to comply with gender-identity nondiscrimination and even to stop the Department of Health and Human Services from enforcing the gender-identity protections of Section 1557. To understand this story, I gathered and analyzed documents from rulemaking and litigation, including public comments on the Section 1557 implementing rules, the rules themselves, opinions in major cases about Section 1557, and briefs and filings from both sides. Collectively, these three levels—the patient experience, the insurance plan, and the courtroom and legislative body—form the reality of what Section 1557 has been able to be and will become.

I'll admit to some misconceptions when I came up with the methodologies for the study that would become this book. I approached health care civil rights implementation from a framework of social movement contestation and political disagreement. There would be pushback from hospitals and healthcare structures in conservative areas while implementation in liberal areas, well on their way to embracing transgender rights, would proceed more smoothly. What I did not fully realize is that healthcare structures are far from an open field for rights disputing, and the path dependence of many other unrelated policy outcomes and professional practices would constitute the grounds for rights claiming. State-level policy differences and political environments did not produce the variation I was expecting. The grounds for rights claiming (or not) are already deeply carved out by previous changes in the business, ethical, professional, and organizational structures of our healthcare system that do not map onto political positions about trans rights or any other type of rights for that matter. I also failed to appreciate how health insurance is the most difficult part of so many people's use of and path through health care. Health insurance problems surpass the interpersonal civil rights violations I imagined I would hear about as interpersonal events of exclusion, degradation, and harm.

My own positionality in this research, particularly my cisgender identity and whiteness, shapes the research and analysis here. There is a rich and growing literature detailing the health care discrimination that trans people experience, much of it written and researched by trans people themselves.[47] There are trans people at every level and institution in this book. They are people seeking care, they are doctors and therapists, they are scholars and researchers, they are hospital and medical records company employees, and they are attorneys. Trans and nonbinary people seeking health care are a diverse group of people with varied experiences and needs who have already explained many of their painful experiences to us.[48] When I designed the study that would become this book, I chose to turn the research focus first onto institutions and onto mostly cisgender actors in the legal and health fields. This book is not primarily grounded in my representations of trans experience, in other words. I leave that work to other very capable advocates and scholars who have considerable theoretical and methodological expertise in doing so.

Instead, I first turn my analysis on the actors in the health care settings who do rights work, because it is appropriate and necessary to make this work about them and because my research confers sufficient authority for me to talk about them. I pivot to these frontline rights workers in hospitals because they are critical to making trans health rights what they are, and thus they are worthy of being the central characters in my story. When anyone raises a problem as a patient in a health care setting, these are the people one meets first. I found mostly cisgender middle-aged white women working in this sector of healthcare administration and constructing the meaning of health care civil rights for trans people. Likewise, the arguments doctors have with other doctors at insurance companies help determine care access, and the political and legal disputes at the state and national levels will have deeply personal impacts in real people's lives. The lawyers and politicians—like the doctors, typically cisgender and white—at the national level have also profoundly shaped what health care civil rights can be for trans people.

My feminist research ethics is grounded in a never-easy, never-finished balancing between my own scholarly authority, my assessment of the power dynamics that are inevitable in gathering data from people and drawing conclusions from it, and the hope that my work might help improve people's lives. This book is an open-access publication so that I can remain in conversation with the people who helped me understand what I study but who may not have a university library login. I aim to maintain the critical focus on the fact that cisgender people overwhelmingly determine rights and health care for trans people. My first scholarly article was addressed to cisgender feminists and it is about trans people in court cases.[49] I asked people like me to think with me and about *themselves* differently through greater understanding of the trans litigants' positions. This book addresses anyone who cares about health and civil rights by talking primarily about the people who have some power to determine what those rights look like for others and by making failures vivid by showing how civil rights have often failed trans people.

I have both taken direction from trans people's own expertise and directed attention about rights that impact trans people's lives in ways that I see as innovative and important. Insurance denials and discrimination are top research priorities for trans people, so I increased the focus on that issue in my research program.[50] I suspect it was easier for someone like me to talk to cisgender people in healthcare organizations than it would be for a scholar who is not white and cisgender. I grew up with parents in the medical and healthcare fields, tagging along to our rural county hospital. I'm comfortable and curious in those settings. Research work as a subject or an investigator can be psychologically taxing when the topic is the mistreatment of people like yourself.[51] After experiencing a harrowing child protective services investigation in my own family, I have never considered researching anything in that topic area because it is too upsetting.[52] But my identity and presentation helped me to connect with hospital administrative staff, and I was able to absorb and analyze their awkwardness and even antipathy to patients' stories.[53]

"Studying up" is notoriously difficult.[54] To study up is to do research in more elite or powerful, closed-off settings, where organizational priorities rarely include openness to interview requests or observation. Different levels of analysis in this book call for different methods and data, some of them hard to access. Health care settings are particularly tough because not only are they large, bureaucratic, and tend not to empower the people who answer the phones to be forthcoming, but privacy laws prevent sharing many details or letting researchers look at their data systems. Employees are uncomfortable answering questions about problems and discrimination in their organization, though I found that simply defining frameworks for problems was incredibly revealing of the structures that matter for civil rights claiming. The internal deliberations and processes within health insurance companies about rejecting claims are difficult to access in any authentic way. I have represented those conflicts from one perspective, that of the trans or non-binary person and the care team, both because that perspective matters most to me and because the barriers to uncovering insightful information from within insurers are so high. My collaboration with Leverage Global Consulting has enabled my fascination with reading insurance plans (not a common interest even among professors) to develop into this book and hopefully to bring insurance more fully into discussions about health rights and equality. Legal and political arguments matter because they define public stakes and outcomes, and these are available for study because the documents themselves are publicly available. Since conservative opponents of health care civil rights have delineated their arguments at length, I rely on those documents to represent their views. I decided against a deep dive into the play-by-play of specific legal cases and their outcomes.[55] Instead, you'll find an account of the major players and arguments at stake and my assessment of why arguments get traction or not. This more supple understanding of the debates will last longer and reveal more about the law and political economy of health care civil rights.

THE PLAN OF THE BOOK

Chapter 1, "Health Care Civil Rights: Set Up to Fail," explains the political and historical apparatus under each word in the phrase "health care civil rights." I argue that health care civil rights are a weak patchwork of other rights that have been set up to fail for many reasons. But to understand why health care civil rights start off from such a poor position, one must understand how *rights* function generally in the American political and constitutional structure, how *civil rights* laws (legislatively enacted antidiscrimination provisions distinct from constitutional rights) have been enacted and changed in the modern era, and the fragility of *health* rights in the United States. Then we can understand the concept of *health care civil rights*, enacted in Section 1557 of the Affordable Care Act, as a residual product of this legal and policy jumble.

Chapter 2, "How Health Care Civil Rights Became Patient Experience," reveals what happens to health care civil rights on the ground in hospitals and clinics. They are refracted through preexisting professional and institutional frameworks and wind up scattered, unrecognized, and lost within a jumble of other problems that the healthcare organization is much better prepared to solve. I take you to the microlevel of rights refraction, which is the workplace of the people who are tasked with handling patient complaints. The patient experience frame, as I term it, is how individual-level rights claims are absorbed and refracted in healthcare. Patient problems, when and if they are even raised, go into a complaint system managed by patient experience professionals whose job is to assuage patient annoyance so that satisfaction survey scores remain high. Recent changes in healthcare law and reimbursement mean that low patient satisfaction scores cost money. Institutions are highly attuned to those implications. Being attuned to low patient satisfaction is not the same as caring about civil rights violations, however, though it is also not necessarily antipathy or prejudice.

In chapter 3, "How Insurance Companies Broker Health Care Civil Rights," we move to the next level of struggle over health care civil rights: insurance discrimination. I explain how health insurance refracts civil rights law at a critical mediating level: above the physician-patient relationship and above the clinic or hospital level and within a complex market system that is unevenly regulated. About sixty percent of nonelderly people in the United States have private health insurance through their employer. Medicare (for those sixty-five and older, about nineteen percent of the population) and Medicaid (for some lower-income people, also nearly nineteen percent) are major publicly funded sources of health coverage. Private insurance companies administer many Medicare and Medicaid managed care plans with public funds, however. The Indian Health Service covers members of federally recognized tribes, and veterans get coverage through TRICARE and the Veterans Administration, also publicly funded. The ACA-regulated marketplace plans are somewhere in the middle of public and private. These plans fill in the gap for about ten percent of the population such as the self-employed and those who do not qualify for any other health insurance. These marketplace plans are sold by private insurers with government regulation that makes it difficult to turn people away from coverage.

Insurance is an odd object for discrimination law because one aim of insurance is to discriminate—that is, to charge differently situated people different amounts of money and give them different services based on their actuarial risk. Yet Section 1557 and other civil rights laws explicitly regulate health insurance discrimination because patient care is mediated by insurance coverage nearly all the time, so health care access effectively means health insurance coverage. In chapter 3, "How Insurance Companies Broker Health Care Civil Rights," I explain why health insurance is so important yet very difficult for most people to use through the case of trans and non-binary people who have employer-based health insurance and have tried to secure gender-affirming care. Even when that care is ostensibly covered under their policy, they confront a medical necessity frame that our current civil rights laws do not dismantle. Even when nondiscrimination is required, health insurers can still deny care that they determine is not medically necessary. This chapter draws on interviews with trans and non-binary people about using their health insurance coverage as well as those who help them navigate health insurance problems (surgeons, office administrators, and health care navigators). It is also based on my analysis of the gender-affirming-care coverage elements in nearly 1,500 employer-based health insurance benefit plans.

Erica, one of the civil rights coordinators I interviewed, worked at a hospital that had just been bought out by a Catholic hospital system. As I waited in the lobby to speak with her, workers were hoisting up the signage with the new name. She told me that much of what Section 1557 required her to do for trans patients was "kind of against the Catholic religion." Indeed, religious opposition to Section 1557 anti-discrimination requirements, though slow to get started, has been vigorous and effective in state legislatures and in conservative legal mobilization. In chapter 4, "How Conservatives Oppose Health Care Civil Rights," I trace these mobilizations against health care civil rights for trans people through primary source documents, including pleadings, briefs, comments submitted about nondiscrimination regulations, and court rulings. Health care civil rights at the national level are refracted through a social movement landscape and a federal court system that advantages the conservative opposition. Path dependencies from previous decades of antiabortion policy (multiple federal laws protecting freedom of conscience) and the long history of religious participation in our rapidly consolidating healthcare system also contribute to this favorable environment. Conservatives draw on religious frameworks about gender and sexuality, political opposition to the administrative state, and defenses of religious freedom to oppose gender-identity nondiscrimination and the provision of gender-affirming care. They also attempt to rebrand religious arguments when they seem too extreme or when they need credible expert witnesses to counter the mainstream consensus in favor of gender-affirming care. I describe what happens to health care civil rights as they are refracted through these major divisions in our legal and political system, arguing that these divisions are deep enough we cannot build thoroughgoing national protections against gender-identity discrimination in health care.

Despite the grim picture described at three levels by this point in the book, chapter 5, "Realizing Health Care Civil Rights," reorients the story to acknowledge that my research found significant moments in which health care civil rights broke through. That is, they were clearly recognized, provided for, enacted, and defended successfully in ways that achieved social change. Analysis of these moments is important to show why and how rights were successful and helps set up the conclusion by anchoring some of the possible solutions in the evidence from my research. I draw on the data at all three levels in the book: accounts of civil rights successes on the ground in hospitals and clinics, expansions in health insurance coverage for gender-affirming care, and national-level legal victories for gender-identity nondiscrimination frameworks. I argue that these victories are impactful and meaningful, although too scattered, contingent, and easily undercut by the powerful frameworks described in chapters 1 through 4.

A book that is largely critical must pivot to answer the question, Well, what do we do? In the conclusion, I remind the reader of all the reasons why health care civil rights have failed at the three levels (the hospital, health insurance, and the legal and political battles). Refracting rights has resulted in absorption, deflection, and sometimes defeat. And yet there have been some clear victories at each level that show plausible paths forward. I argue that we should not remain within what political scientists call the "Overton window" of policy plausibility (that is, policies with a real chance of being enacted under current conditions) as we consider what different options might accomplish, but rather spell out what it would take to achieve a significantly different world for health care civil rights. This final chapter describes the range of solutions suggested by other scholars and in my own evidence and arguments, showing what they might accomplish if implemented and what it would take to achieve them.

Health Care Civil Rights

Set Up to Fail

Peggy, an older white woman trained as a nurse, has worked at the same rural Michigan hospital for twenty-nine years. Her primary role is patient and family advocate, handling patient complaints. If health care civil rights violations emerge from discriminatory experiences with care providers, and if patients complain about them, health care staff like Peggy are the first people to hear about these experiences. What they do to frame, manage, and respond to the complaint shapes what health care civil rights are and could be. I wanted to understand how these frontline grievance handlers sorted problems and how they saw discrimination as a problem (and, indeed, if they did). The conversation turned from general questions about Peggy's job day-to-day to her responses to civil rights mandates at her hospital. When the interviewer asked Peggy about using patient scores to pinpoint possible dissatisfaction in protected civil rights categories such as sex, she pivoted immediately back to the need for high scores on patient satisfaction surveys to avoid financial penalties:

> [On this general patient satisfaction survey, have you ever calculated, like, men rate patient care more highly than women, or things like that?] You know, we can. We have the ability to do that. Right now we go by our top box score, which is the, you know, always the nines or the tens. Anything less than those do not qualify and Medicare takes back money from us at the end of the year. Every hospital, that's what they do. So they drive organizations to provide the most best customer service and care, because if you don't, then they're going to be taking back, you know, money.

Peggy is referring to provisions in the Affordable Care Act (ACA) that increased pressure on healthcare organizations to pay attention to patient satisfaction by tying patient satisfaction survey outcomes to Medicare reimbursements under its Hospital Value-Based Purchasing Program.[1] Hospitals do indeed face losing money if patients give low ratings in these satisfaction surveys. The survey in Peggy's hospital is the Hospital Consumer Assessment of Healthcare Providers and Systems. The Centers for Medicare & Medicaid Services publishes the results on a website called "Hospital Compare."[2] Physicians are also evaluated using a similar survey for their outpatient work, and scores impact performance evaluations and pay.

In her first response, Peggy denies the relevance of any civil rights categories because every patient who responds to the satisfaction survey matters to the organization in the same way—as a respondent whose unhappiness can result in financial loss. Peggy put up antidiscrimination notices and updated them when Section 1557 was enacted because she needed to do that for the hospital's accreditation under the Joint Commission.[3] She explains that the hospital is located in an overwhelmingly white rural area, and they do not do any specialized "gender-change surgeries or anything like that," so she does not really see discrimination complaints. But moments later, she described using their scoring history to pinpoint problems using age. They found among pregnant patients in the obstetrics ward, the "really, really young patients, [who were] not educated and, you know, no prenatal testing, no insurance, no prenatal support, and we looked at that and found that we really needed to spend more time educating and talking and encouraging the younger patients."

Peggy carefully follows "the nines and tens" in the satisfaction surveys, and sometimes a dip in the numbers could point to problems caring for a particular subgroup. In the case of the very young pregnant patients, the surveys helped her hospital see that these patients were particularly vulnerable and needed more support. In other words, the organizational requirements and legal structures that comprise Peggy's everyday working reality are primarily determined by healthcare regulations and practices that are not primarily about civil rights or discrimination. She saw a problem in a group of patients with certain characteristics using the survey data but not as a problem of structural vulnerability for these young people giving birth without resources. Civil rights issues and discrimination problems are certainly present in the hospital regulatory regime, but they are surrounded by and interpreted through more compelling problems, practices, and procedures in the operation of Peggy's hospital. Possible civil rights problems are refracted through these policy pressures for measuring quality of care, for example, which is related to discrimination but not always the same thing.

How did we get here? As recently as the 1960s, hospitals were considered private entities beyond reach of federal antidiscrimination law.[4] Southern hospitals segregated patients by race even as facilities popped up across the rural landscape in one of the largest postwar structural investments in American healthcare history. Federal dollars built those hospitals, but the federal government permitted racial segregation to continue. Peggy's hospital was constructed during those boom years. The Civil Rights Act of 1964 and the new Medicare and Medicaid programs enacted in 1965 put a stop to hospital segregation as courts and the Johnson administration agreed that accepting federal funds meant healthcare facilities could not discriminate. Medicare billing remains the major tie between healthcare and civil rights, but legal enforcement has significantly lagged.

New incentives arose instead. Interest in measuring patient satisfaction dates to the 1980s, and the Affordable Care Act in 2010 was a major effort to incentivize high-value, safer, more patient-centered care. The patient safety movement increased professionalization and bureaucratization in health systems around patient issues with the rise of the patient experience or "PX" professional in the last decade. Hospitals have lawyers on staff, of course. But problems filter through this other bureaucratic compliance side of the healthcare system, in which patients trying to articulate a rights violation are lumped in with all possible problems and complaints and treated as part of a cascading mishmash. All these shifts—in the application of civil rights law, in the understanding of the patient experience, and in the ways financial incentives shape these interactions—have their own roots and histories, combining unevenly over time according to a reactive, volatile American health politics that has never been able to support a unified account of what health care civil rights are and why they matter.

HEALTH CARE CIVIL RIGHTS
IN THE AMERICAN RIGHTS TRADITION

This book analyzes civil rights in health care in the contemporary United States. But civil rights are usually understood to be about voting, education, and employment, not health care. Scholars of civil rights have mostly studied them in the workplace, theorizing how rights can assist social movement mobilization but also reinscribe inequalities and ratify ineffective organizational practices that fail to produce much social change.[5] What do civil rights look like when refracted through the lens of American healthcare, a massive and complex web of public and private relationships, laws, regulations, institutions, professions, norms, and financial arrangements that comprises one-fifth of the US economy? What rights are there in US healthcare, anyway? What would a nondiscriminatory health benefit plan look like? We are famously a country that lacks an explicit right to health. And yet our US healthcare and welfare systems offer a range of entitlements, protections, rules, and supports for health insurance, so much so that Christina Ho argues that we already have some rights to health that we fail to see as true rights.[6] So then what is a civil right in health? It turns out that seeing rights through health is different in important ways than seeing them through other contexts like employment.

By rights in general, I mean an obligation either to provide something beneficial or to refrain from doing something harmful on the part of the state, which is owed from the government to an individual. A typical top-down exploration of legal rights would begin with the rights in the US Constitution. This approach gives us little understanding about health care rights, however, because there is simply very little in the Constitution, particularly as it is interpreted in the federal courts right now, that supports health care rights. Our Constitution is notable for being one of the shortest, oldest, and most limited constitutions of any that currently governs a large democratic society. Over sixty-seven percent of countries have a right to health of some kind specified in their national constitution, but we do not.[7] Our Constitution contains mostly *negative* rights, that is, the right not to have the government take some harmful action (like quartering soldiers in civilian homes or infringing the right to keep and bear arms), which envision an empowered individual who primarily needs forbearance from the state to enjoy his private property unencumbered.

Health rights are really only meaningful as *positive* rights: a right to be provided with something good, not simply the right to have the government refrain from doing something bad. From clean air and water to untainted food to emergency surgery, sustaining health requires the regulation and provision of resources through laws and government as well as collective and individual action. Finding a right to health in our Constitution would mean interpreting other broadly written clauses to include it or amending the Constitution to add it (a very burdensome process that is practically unusable). The Fourteenth Amendment's due process protections, both procedural and substantive, offer some protections from having entitlements from the state withdrawn or for the exercise of personal freedoms, such as freedom from sterilization and the ability to use contraception without it being criminalized by the state. Similarly, the Fourteenth Amendment's equal protection clause could be construed to prevent any state action that treats certain groups worse than others without adequate justification (such as denying health care to transgender people that is extended to cisgender people), and indeed attorneys have vigorously made these arguments in court filings.[8]

It is conceivable that in some alternate universe in which many political events had unfolded quite differently in the United States, we could now enjoy interpretations of our constitutional rights that guaranteed the kind of provisioning—positive rights to health—that we would need to promote the thriving of our citizens much more widely and equally that we have now. One could argue that to enjoy rights of self-governance, due process, and equal protection of the laws secured in the post-Civil War United States, we need conditions for freedom such as universally available high-quality education, basic income, and health care for all. But this vision is unimaginable under current interpretive conditions for the US Constitution to compel (and not politically realistic to hope for from Congress, either). Our Constitution has serious structural flaws that have permitted and strengthened minority rule, particularly in the presidency (because of the electoral college that permits a candidate who has lost the popular vote to win), the US Senate (because each state gets two senators despite wild population variation), and the Supreme Court and the lower federal courts (because justices and judges are nominated by the president and confirmed by the Senate, thereby doubling down on minority power).

Instead, conservative, Republican-appointed judges dominate our federal courts and hold a conservative supermajority at the Supreme Court, where interpretive ambiguities in our constitutional text become policy outcomes in particular cases. Republican policy preferences often oppose civil rights to help minoritized groups or positive rights to health. After the 2022 *Dobbs v. Jackson Women's Health Organization* decision that abortion rights are no longer included in constitutional protections, all previously protected rights that relate to health, privacy, reproduction, and sex and gender discrimination protections are on much shakier ground.[9] Republicans do not support policy proposals widely understood to promote health and health care access, such as greater health and welfare support spending, environmental protections, universal health care, better education, and health care civil rights. The growth area for constitutional rights in the present is in greater individual access to firearms of all kinds and in religious protections from duties not to discriminate based on conservative interpretations of evangelical Christianity and Catholicism. Both Republican-supported constitutional rights expansions are antihealth in profound ways, as firearms are now the top cause of death for children in the United States, and religious rights ground denials of health care from abortion to HIV medications to gender-affirming health care.

Civil rights is an ambiguous term that we use to refer to a collection of rights that can mean different things.[10] It can mean legal protections from racial discrimination established during the civil rights movement of the 1960s (and indeed when we say someone is a "civil rights icon," that usually means a prominent leader for Black civil rights to equal voting, public accommodations, and education during that period). This period featured major legislation as well as constitutional rulings to promote racial equality, and in that sense *civil rights* refers both to statutes such as the Civil Rights Act of 1964 as well as to constitutional law. People sometimes use the term *civil rights* to mean all rights related to equality, including constitutional rights or human rights, and critically, employment rights that apply to private companies. In this book, I use the term *civil rights* to mean the statutes that protect rights based on a named trait or set of traits in the contemporary US legal system. As we will see, civil rights in health care must apply to many private actors as well as the government, since employers, private insurance companies, and governments work together to provide health care in the United States. I distinguish civil rights from constitutional rights, which are the rights either spelled out in or interpreted by judges as grounded within the US Constitution or state constitutions. Sometimes these are nearly the same thing; sometimes they are not. This book is focused on the transformations of the Affordable Care Act and its interventions into civil rights, which start in the statutory and administrative realms. Arguments about the meanings of discrimination and equality for trans and non-binary people rage across all these legal and governmental levels and within private companies and organized religious groups, and to understand how they unfold it is helpful to keep these basic distinctions in mind.

Often the impulse behind civil rights legislation is to require treating a person from a historically minoritized or stigmatized group the same as a member of a favored group: hire them, rent an apartment to them, and so on, as if the stigma attached to their identity did not exist or does not matter. But the laws are written to apply to anyone on the basis of the trait, so laws against racial discrimination protect white people and laws against sex discrimination protect men, for example. Usually civil rights claims are individual-level disputes over specific discriminatory decisions or practices rather than over the fact, for example, that entire school districts may be neglected and underfunded, that there is little affordable housing available, or that there are no jobs nearby that are compatible with raising a small child. These kinds of problems or harms are harder to tie to a bad actor doing discrimination on the basis of a protected trait to a specific person or group. The term *civil rights* can just as easily be applied to conservative causes such as anti-affirmative action (as discrimination against white people) and has indeed been successfully deployed for many different ends.

The health-based rights that I focus on in this book are the civil rights or anti-discrimination laws that apply to patients, protecting them from discrimination on the basis of race, sex, age, disability, and national origin or language (and depending on the jurisdiction, a few other traits). Health care civil rights laws, such as the nondiscrimination clause of the Affordable Care Act, Section 1557, Title VI, prohibiting racial discrimination in entities such as hospitals receiving federal funds, and state-level insurance nondiscrimination laws, often function in this list-driven way.[11] I use the term *patients* (and *people seeking care*) but I also mean health care consumers and holders of health insurance policies, since these laws touch many encounters in the healthcare system beyond the provider-patient interaction. Health care civil rights can be a right to be treated equally, respectfully, and in accord with one's gender identity, including having providers use the correct pronouns. It can mean being able to communicate with your health care provider no matter what language you speak, for example. It can be a right to be provided with publicly funded health care or specific health insurance coverage or terms of coverage. Health care civil rights are both rights of proper recognition and of sufficient provision. More specifically, one can be affirmatively provided with something such as health insurance coverage for pregnancy or gender-affirming care. Or one can be entitled to restraint or nondisclosure in a healthcare setting, such as the Biden administration's regulation that tells healthcare providers that they cannot provide private health information about reproductive health to law enforcement if, for example, officers are investigating whether someone left a state where abortion is illegal to obtain a legal abortion at their facility.[12]

FEDERAL SPENDING AND HEALTH CARE RIGHTS

A person could have a health right in many ways. In the United States, we have them in fairly thin and fraught ways. What that means is that health rights do exist, but they are often contingent on being able to actualize them with additional resources and power, and access to those resources and power is not guaranteed and is regularly denied. Health rights mean a wide range of things in practice, and they appear across a lot of different laws, attach to different contexts, uses, and statuses, conflict with each other, and are not grounded in any overarching political commitment based on a shared understanding of why health rights are good and necessary. One could have an entitlement right to be provided with something like a health benefit. In practice, being provided with a health benefit may simply mean having the right to buy health insurance that covers a certain scope of care, to be charged the same rate as others, or not to have one's coverage cut off. It may mean actual provision of items one needs to live and thrive, such as home health visits for someone living with a significant disability or kidney dialysis treatment for someone with kidney failure. There are rights to procedures, such as being given notice and an opportunity to object before one's benefits are terminated. The provision one has a right to could be merely information, such as being mailed a copy of the employer health benefit plan.

Most of what counts as health care rights and healthcare regulation comes from statutory law passed by Congress or in the states and administered within the agencies of the federal and state governments. Outcomes that support health and equality have been driven by major federal spending programs that did not have civil rights as a core aim and were instead universal social welfare and health benefit programs, such as Medicare (universal after age sixty-five, that is). The basic social and health welfare structure of the United States is shaped by structures of federalism and policy commitments over time to age-based relative generosity for older people, legacies of racism, and a commitment to employer-based health insurance. We have a federal government with considerable power to spend money and regulate commerce under the Constitution, which means that there is strong national government power to shape healthcare systems and care delivery. But powers for health and welfare devolved in many important ways to the governments of the states, where policy variation is permitted, and have long been shared with private groups like businesses, unions, and religious organizations.

In healthcare, rights are typically legislative enactments because the federal government has used its power of the purse, or Constitutional spending power, to make requirements of any entity that accepts federal funding. Acceptance of federal funding in healthcare means billing to Medicare, for example (as well as other forms of federal support for health clinics, the Indian Health Service, and technology grants). So even health care or services typically provided by private individuals acting as providers, private companies such as insurers, medical groups owned by a group of physicians, or nonprofit or for-profit hospitals and clinics can come under the tent of government's power to create obligations to do something or refrain from doing something. Federal health care rights are thus potentially very far-reaching.

Congress and the president showed significant political will at midcentury to solve the problem of poverty for older Americans through Social Security and Medicare, which are the most popular and transformative social policies in American history that provide cash income and health coverage to people who reach the age threshold. In effect, older Americans are entitled to a basic income and universal health care. Everyone else lives under a patchwork system of employer-based health insurance coverage, poverty-linked Medicaid health coverage, poverty-linked benefits such as food stamps, Temporary Aid to Needy Families, and the Child Health Insurance Program, or any other services a community, state, religious group, or private organization wishes to provide, disability benefits, health insurance policies bought from somewhere other than an employer such as on the state exchanges, or going without any health insurance. There is no right to an income source per se. These health and welfare programs, even the nonuniversal ones that are not age-based entitlements, reach deeply into the middle class and are used by millions of Americans. Medicaid pays for over forty percent of births in the United States today, for example.[13] All these programs have qualification rules, applications procedures, and are typically administered at the state level with a mix of federal and state funding and with state-level political prerogatives to be more or less generous. In California, Medicaid covers nonparent or noncaregiver adults with incomes at or below 138 percent of the federal poverty line, while in Florida, nonelderly adults who are not parents or caregivers are not covered no matter how poor they are.[14]

The reach of the federal welfare state, limited as it may seem compared to other countries, is also the key to protecting civil rights because taking federal funding is the means to require compliance. But it was not always the case that health care civil rights could use this key of federal spending to enable civil rights. The federal government had to shift from explicitly supporting white supremacy and the southern racial segregation system in healthcare to opposing it with the spending lever. After World War II, President Harry Truman hoped to establish national health insurance along with significantly increasing spending on hospital construction and public health. The legislation that emerged did not include national health insurance, but the Hill-Burton Hospital Survey and Construction Act of 1946 led to the building of 7,750 hospitals and clinics with $3.7 billion sent out to the states.[15]

As historian Karen Kruse Thomas explains, "The Hill-Burton Act was debated in Congress and passed into law at the height of the South's paradoxical status as the nation's neediest yet most politically powerful region."[16] Southern congressmen made sure that Hill-Burton's nondiscrimination provisions preserved racial segregation in health care by allowing "separate but equal" facilities (termed "like quality" for "separate population groups") and by specifying that hospitals were private facilities under state rather than federal regulation.[17] Framing hospitals as private meant that their segregationist policies, widely practiced throughout the South, were not state action under the Fourteenth Amendment's equal protection clause and deprived the Department of Health, Education, and Welfare (the precursor to today's Department of Health and Human Services or HHS) of jurisdiction over their internal policies, such as racially segregating patients by room and ward, maintaining "white only" and "colored" waiting rooms, and denying privileges to Black physicians and nurses.[18]

Hill-Burton spending was need based and focused on rural capacity building. Southern states received ninety-three percent of the early Hill-Burton appropriations (by 1950) and benefited from a funding formula that funded the poorest states at a per capita rate 3.56 times higher than the formula for the wealthiest states.[19] This pattern, in which southern states most hostile to federal policymaking draw disproportionately on federal healthcare support, was entrenched in the architecture and care structures of the American landscape through Hill-Burton spending. This pattern continues in policies such as our current federal Medicaid reimbursements to states in which wealthy (on a per capita basis) Connecticut gets just fifty percent of its expenditures back while poorer Mississippi gets back seventy-eight percent.[20]

The Supreme Court's declaration in the school desegregation case of *Brown v. Board of Education* in 1954 that separate but equal public schools were inherently unequal and unconstitutional made segregated hospitals insecure.[21] Public schools are clearly state run and thus part of state action, which tethers them to constitutional guarantees. Private entities, such as the many private schools that sprung up across the South to avoid admitting Black students, were not and thus were allowed to discriminate. The same legal idea sustaining racial segregation in healthcare settings, that hospitals were private and therefore not subject to antidiscrimination requirements even though they were built with federal dollars, held on for nearly a decade longer until 1963. Dr. George Simkins Jr., a Black dentist in Greensboro, North Carolina, and a local NAACP leader, led a class action lawsuit in 1962 against the segregated hospitals that barred both Black practitioners and Black patients. Dr. Simkins and the plaintiffs argued that the racial segregation violated the US constitutional guarantees of equal protection under the Fifth (due process) and Fourteenth (equal protection) Amendments. These arguments underlie the notion that when the federal government or a state is sufficiently supportive of an entity that is otherwise private (such as providing funding), that is enough to bring its operations under the doctrine of state action, meaning that the entity must protect constitutional rights too. The plaintiffs initially lost their case in federal district court on the grounds that the nonprofit hospitals were private, free of constitutional duties, and could discriminate.[22]

The US Commission on Civil Rights issued a sharp report in October 1963, pointing out that federally subsidized racial segregation in health facilities was unconstitutional under the school desegregation decisions and should not continue. The *Simkins* doctors and patients appealed with Justice Department backing. The millions of federal dollars that had gone to building these Greensboro hospitals and the state of North Carolina's role in managing the projects was more than enough for the federal appeals court to find for the *Simkins* plaintiffs in November of 1963. The majority on the Fourth Circuit Court of Appeals noted that, "Racial discrimination by hospitals visits severe consequences upon Negro physicians and their patients."[23] The Supreme Court did not take up the case and the Fourth Circuit's holding stood in that jurisdiction, finally extending the constitutional protections against racial discrimination to hospitals as (at least partially) state actors. Soon after *Simkins* was decided, and propelled by its successful linking of federal funds and nondiscrimination in health, Title VI of the 1964 Civil Rights Act passed, which prohibits race discrimination by entities receiving federal funding in healthcare and other areas such as education.

The contemporary period in which civil rights laws apply to health and healthcare begins with Title VI the Civil Rights Act of 1964 and the legacy of pushing back against white supremacy in healthcare settings. It provided a pathway for federal enforcement of health care civil rights using the carrot and stick of federal dollars. The Civil Rights Act of 1964 is probably better known for its employment protections under Title VII on the basis of race, color, national origin, sex, or religion, but patients are not employees.[24] Title VI statutorily prohibits racial discrimination by recipients of federal funding, the same funding affirmed in *Simkins* as conferring constitutional duties not to discriminate in healthcare facilities.[25] The Hill-Burton funding was a large and attractive source of federal dollars, but hospital construction would not go on forever. Title VI turned out to be an effective tool for dismantling racial segregation in health care facilities, but it took another part of President Johnson's expansive agenda plus considerable organizing around the South to make it happen.

Hill-Burton would soon be eclipsed by the most far-reaching spending and civil rights promotion tool ever enacted: the Medicare program, passed in 1965. Medicare would become the most important federal lever for civil rights compliance, perhaps ever.[26] Medicare payments for care provided to the elderly brought nearly every hospital under the aegis of Title VI and its nondiscrimination requirements by its implementation date of July 1, 1966, though there was a considerable fight to make it happen. Medicare legislation came in 1965 after Title VI had passed in 1964, but exactly what that meant for segregationist hospitals that anticipated receiving Medicare payments was not discussed in Congress. Senator Robert Byrd of West Virginia, a prominent segregationist, asked the Department of Health, Education, and Welfare for clarification about whether Title VI would apply to hospitals under Medicare as the bill was near to passage. Labor and civil rights leaders opposed to segregation also wanted to know. If the Department of Health, Education, and Welfare did not think Title IV would apply to Medicare, liberals in Congress would want an antidiscrimination clause in Medicare to get the same result. Johnson administration officials and their allies in labor and civil rights groups worried that adding an antidiscrimination clause to the Medicare bill would risk southern support and divide the Democratic coalition needed to pass it. The decision was to work closely in Congress "to avoid any amendments being offered and to keep the whole thing as low keyed as possible" while affirming administration support for Title VI's reach into Medicare.[27] It is worth remembering how hard it is to pass a healthcare bill with an antidiscrimination clause in it. Section 1557 was also kept "as low keyed as possible" in the Affordable Care Act passage.

Once Medicare passed with hospital segregation still widespread across the South, there was no avoiding the fight. Hospitals had separate "white" and "colored" facilities for everything from waiting rooms to beds. The Johnson administration's hopes for a successful launch of Medicare ran directly into the persistent practices of white supremacy in American southern hospitals. During the time between Johnson's signing of the Medicare law on July 30, 1965, and the July 1, 1966, start date when hospitals needed to be certified to participate in Medicare, civil rights activists and administration officials worked hard to dismantle the racial segregation that was standard in hospitals across the South. Civil rights advocates filed hundreds of complaints to put the spotlight on illegal racist policies in facilities. The Public Health Service dispatched investigators across the region to see for themselves if desegregation had really been achieved. Three months before the deadline, only forty-nine percent of hospitals overall and only twenty-five percent of southern hospitals were in compliance.[28] Johnson was caught between his two major initiatives: wanting Medicare to launch successfully with near-universal coverage for the elderly and civil rights progress. The formula to achieve both was to push hard at the local level, keeping lists of every hospital and its compliance state day by day as the July 1 deadline approached, combined with strict enforcement by threatening to withhold funds.

In the final days leading up to desegregation compliance in hospitals, officials placed National Guard helicopters on standby in case historically all-white hospitals refused to care for critically ill Black patients. The plan was to fly them to military hospitals or Veterans Administration facilities.[29] The Office of the Surgeon General set up a twenty-four-hour phone line for physicians to call if a non-compliant hospital refused admission to one of their Black Medicare patients.[30] The helicopters were not used; the large-scale push for compliance with Medicare payments hanging in the balance worked. For a few more decades, Title VI litigation against racist practices in health care continued with some success against practices such as disproportionately certifying only a few beds for Black Medicaid patients.[31]

Black and white people sharing the intimacy and vulnerability of a hospital room had been a huge sticking point in the desegregation effort. Decades later, some of the first claims under Section 1557 were from trans women placed in the wrong inpatient room with a man instead of with a woman. But the enforcement environment has entirely shifted. Title VI became, as Dayna Bowen Matthew points out, "one of the most underutilized tools in the fight to protect equal access to healthy, pollution-free environments and to health care for marginalized communities."[32] Title VI lost most of its power in 2001 when the Supreme Court limited its claims for individuals to intentional rather than disparate impact discrimination. HHS can bring impact-based agency enforcement, but its budget and staffing are rarely up to the task. To implement nondiscrimination in rooming by gender identity, for example, HHS does an investigation and instructs the hospital to room transwomen with other women, but only on a case-by-case basis, not at all during several years when one federal judge blocked HHS enforcement, and without much realistic threat of withholding federal funds. The Supreme Court held that the provision of the ACA that required states to expand Medicaid or face denial of federal Medicaid funds for their whole program was too coercive,[33] and officials are reluctant to withdraw federal health funds in ways that might hurt the patients they want to help. On top of all that, conservative religious groups claim that conscience and religious protections mean that religious hospitals and employers do not have to recognize trans people at all, in rooming or pronouns or provision of care, even with federal funding. Removing explicit racial segregation in hospitals was a comparatively straightforward policy to implement and monitor compared to the ongoing multidimensional health inequalities that law has been unable to solve. The rest of this book is focused on the present and the recent past, but this history can reveal the past policy choices that structure what is currently possible in health care civil rights as well as some paths not taken.

HEALTH CARE RIGHTS AS A PATCHWORK

The federal push to end hospital racial segregation through Title VI enforcement with the threat of withholding Medicare funds was a singular campaign. We have not seen such an effective and coordinated effort against such a clear target since then. Congress has intervened with federal legislation to stake out important protections in health care and insurance since Title VII and prior to the Affordable Care Act in 2010, though unevenly and in reaction to specific crises and constituencies rather than with a comprehensive approach to equity in health care. In other words, political conditions as well as mobilizations around specific diseases through social movements have profoundly shaped health care civil rights since the first and only major push for health care civil rights by President Johnson in 1966 with Medicare implementation and racial desegregation. This haphazard growth creates a patchwork of health care rights that lack any unifying explanation or rationale but have instead been prompted by their own unique histories of activist mobilization and political responsiveness.

For example, in 1972 Congress added specific, singled-out coverage for chronic renal disease to the Social Security Amendments, extending Medicare to nearly everyone with chronic kidney failure. Many circumstances combined to produce this distinct benefit right for one very expensive and devastating disease, including dramatic testimony before a congressional committee from a sympathetic white father on kidney dialysis and political interest in testing out national health insurance through a few catastrophic test conditions.[34] Those circumstances shifted and no national coverage emerged, but national coverage for that one disease became part of the patchwork of health care rights. This unusual example nonetheless shows how patchwork rights get made from political calculations and mobilizations that fit within general hostility toward broad-based health reform in the United States.

The disability rights movement has significantly transformed the legal landscape of rights over the last half century. Disability-based health care civil rights reach into all the areas of law and policy discussed in this book, though full and equal participation in society for all disabled people is far from achieved. Section 504 of the Rehabilitation Act, passed in 1973, protects against discrimination on the basis of disability in federally funded programs or activities, which include hospitals, educational institutions, and government buildings and programs (but not private sector employment or public places that are privately owned, like theaters and hotels, later reached by the Americans with Disabilities Act of 1990).[35] The terse language in the statute needed regulations to spell out what these protections would mean, but they had been blocked and delayed.

In 1977, a coalition of disability rights activist groups occupied a San Francisco federal building to protest that regulations had not been finalized. The 504 sit-ins, which lasted twenty-five days, yielded regulations that same year. Section 1557 brings in disability through mention of Section 504, and 1557 regulations (the first of which took six years to be proposed and implemented by the Obama administration in 2016) expanded disability nondiscrimination in health care with specifications about unlawful disability discrimination in insurance benefit design, telehealth, communication, and clinical decision tools such as algorithms (such as those used to ration care under crisis conditions).[36] The Office for Civil Rights in HHS issued a bulletin in 2020, at the height of the COVID-19 pandemic, reminding hospitals that civil rights remained in effect during the crisis and that "persons with disabilities should not be denied medical care on the basis of stereotypes, assessments of quality of life, or judgments about a person's relative 'worth' based on the presence or absence of disabilities or age."[37] Some crisis standards of care policies were updated during the pandemic to incorporate disability rights perspectives (such as removing categorical exclusions from lifesaving care based on having certain disabilities) and updates continued to include more disability and racial justice-focused provisions than pre-COVID versions of policies.[38]

Another set of significant influences on the patchwork of health care civil rights came from social movements around diseases such as HIV/AIDS and breast cancer. Activist mobilization for resources to fight AIDS in the 1980s and 1990s transformed institutions such as the FDA and secured major legislation to fund HIV/AIDS research and treatments.[39] HIV/AIDS is also considered a disability under antidiscrimination laws. Women's health activism in the 1980s and 1990s also resulted in changes to federal laws about the conduct of clinical trials for health research so that women would no longer be excluded from studies. Requirements to include "women and minorities" are now part of all federally funded health research, but as Steven Epstein has pointed out, they have also cemented ideas about race, ethnicity, and sex as biologically distinct and meaningful that obscure the social and political factors that constitute vulnerabilities around these categories.[40] Breast cancer activists successfully secured not only greater federal funding for research but also mandates for insurance coverage for breast reconstruction after mastectomy with implants (previously not covered because it was deemed cosmetic). Trans health rights advocates point out that this federal legal requirement is gender-affirming care for cisgender women since it addresses the distress one would feel as a woman appearing in public and intimate life with no breasts.[41] Civil rights protections based on pregnancy and the need to pump milk at work are also important examples of the ways that cisgender women's health concerns have gained some formal traction in the law.[42] Perhaps the most emblematic law of the sad patchwork that is our healthcare system, the Emergency Medical Treatment and Labor Act of 1986, guarantees a right to stabilizing treatment in a Medicare-participating emergency department regardless of ability to pay. It stops hospitals from screening out and dumping poor people who have nowhere else to go.

As I pointed out above, the overall context for this patchwork of rights is the fact that national health insurance coverage for everyone is a political impossibility in this country. Health care civil rights related to insurance coverage fracture because different health insurance market segments (the people and policies that are grouped together based on how people get their coverage and who pays for it) are regulated differently and sometimes lightly. Access to public health insurance, such as Medicaid, Medicare, the State Children's Health Insurance Program, the Indian Health Service, or TRICARE for veterans, depends on meeting the eligibility criteria based on age, disability, income, tribal membership, or military service. Federally funded community health clinics are also a critical part of our healthcare system for many people with lower incomes. These structures are publicly funded care to which civil rights laws apply. The next-most public insurance plans are the ACA-regulated health insurance plans, which are offered for the individual and small group markets by private insurers but with considerable government requirements and subsidy. These plans are mostly purchased by people who work in small firms (with fewer than fifty employees), which are not required to offer health insurance benefits, or by individuals who are self-employed. Section 1557 antidiscrimination protections apply to all these public and what I call semipublic plans because they directly receive federal funding and/or are run by the Department of Health and Human Services.

Once we leave the world of the most clearly federally funded forms of health insurance and health care, things get more complicated. It becomes more difficult to define what is private and what is public and who is playing what role with what responsibility for discrimination. The workplace is a particularly high stakes site for health care rights because most nonelderly adults in the United States get their health benefits, in the form of health insurance, through their employment. Most of these benefit providers are private firms (or two private companies: the employer and the insurer). In other words, private companies are acting as health care providers (or at least as conduits that make accessing care possible by providing health insurance), but they are obviously not hospitals or clinics themselves. Is the private employer, like Target or General Electric, a recipient of federal funds for healthcare under Section 1557? The answer has been consistently no, both because they do not receive federal funds and because their business is not principally health care. But this decision is a political choice that could be otherwise. As Colleen Grogan rightly points out, even supposedly private health insurance from employers receives considerable but hidden public subsidy in the form of tax breaks for employers (that is, businesses are exempt from taxation on any money they spend on employee health insurance).[43] Supporting employer-sponsored health insurance costs the federal government over three-hundred billion dollars per year in tax expenditures (forgone revenue) and is the single biggest item in this category.[44] Even so, there has not been an interpretation of Section 1557's tie to federal funding that brings in the tax benefits as a form of federal financial assistance that would apply to all private employers, which would acknowledge that employers are the primary way that nonelderly Americans receive health care and that we divert a lot of money to help them do it. Nonetheless, health benefits are part of employment discrimination law. Title VII of the Civil Rights Act of 1964 prohibits discrimination in employment on the basis of race, color, sex, national origin, and religion, and that explicitly includes health benefits as a "term or condition of employment" that cannot be discriminatory to the employee. But such discrimination protections would not apply to the employee's family as beneficiaries of the health plan because they are not the employee.

Even if the company, like Target or General Electric, is bound by employment law but not health care civil rights law, the health insurance carrier that they work with is in the business of health care. The carrier receives federal financial assistance in the form of payments, subsidies, or some other benefit, probably because some part of the carrier's business involves selling plans on the ACA marketplace and accepting advance payments of the premium tax credit or cost-sharing reduction payments or offering Medicare Advantage plans or Medicaid managed care plans and accepting a set amount per beneficiary. Under the most recent Section 1557 regulations, offering these plans would bring an insurer's whole operation into Section 1557 coverage. That clearly includes all the health plans that the carrier designs and sells to employers as fully insured group coverage. The carrier uses the premium payments from the employer to cover the costs of claims and to turn a profit. But what about when the insurer acts as the administrator for a plan that has been designed within a private company that self-insures its workers' benefit plan?

Self-insuring is a way for private employer-sponsored health insurance to become even more private. By that, I mean it seems to be even more wholly within the firm and more out of reach of regulation (remember to forget about that big tax subsidy). Self-insuring means that a company takes the risk of paying its own employee health insurance claims out of its own reserves. Insurance is mostly regulated at the state level under the McCarran-Ferguson Act.[45] Many states have enacted antidiscrimination protections or mandate coverage for certain things in health insurance, like infertility, based on the states' powers to regulate the business of insurance generally. The major benefit for companies in self-insuring, however, is that they do not have to comply with state insurance laws and instead they are very lightly regulated at the federal level. This route has been popular, and more and more companies are self-insuring, even smaller firms. An insurance product called stop-loss insurance, through which the firm insures itself against having to pay more claims than anticipated, helps buffer the risk for smaller firms to self-insure. Twenty-four states plus the District of Columbia have banned gender-identity discrimination in insurance,[46] but if a corporations' plans are self-insured these laws do not apply. Self-insured firms in states that mandate in vitro fertilization coverage do not have to offer plans that include it, either.

How could an employer doing business in a state sidestep that state's insurance mandates and insurance antidiscrimination law? To understand this situation, we have to take a brief tour of an important law most people have never heard of: the Employee Retirement Income Security Act of 1974 or ERISA.[47] This law was passed to put up guardrails to protect workers' pensions and other benefits when private companies provide them. The concern was that retirement pension funds, back when they existed widely, were being mismanaged and abused. The law was not designed to address health care as an employee benefit. It contains a preemption clause that allows ERISA to supersede state insurance laws for employee benefit plans that are health insurance as well as pensions.[48] That means that ERISA federal law applies, and state laws do not. Employer-sponsored health benefit plans are still federally regulated throughout the patchwork because legislation has sprinkled in some federal health care protections explicitly, and other federal laws are not preempted.[49] But ERISA is mostly a deregulatory vacuum, not a health regulatory regime. The federally enacted right discussed above to have breast implant reconstruction covered after cancer applies to these self-insured plans, for example, along with federal requirements that mental conditions be covered on par with physical conditions. Title VII employment discrimination protections are also not allowed to be preempted under ERISA, so those protections remain as well, at least for the employee. (Section 1557 is a federal law and thus not part of ERISA preemption of state laws either, but remember that private businesses that are not healthcare related are not covered by it.) Courts have held that exclusions for gender-affirming care in employee health plans are discriminatory under Title VII.[50]

The catch is that employers who self-insure do not want to be a health insurance carrier in addition to being say, Target or General Electric. The company hires a health insurer to act as their administrator for the self-insured plan, called a third-party administrator or TPA. The TPA is typically a large commercial insurer, but they are providing this other service, not the plan itself. The TPA processes all the claims for the sponsoring business. Those carriers are the same entities discussed above (already in the health insurance claims processing business) that are not allowed to discriminate under Section 1557, likely because they sell Medicare Advantage plans or marketplace plans. That means that they cannot administer discriminatory plans even if employers wish to hire them to do exactly that. If Section 1557 works the way its 2024 regulations spell out, even employers who want to draw up their own discriminatory health benefit plan will not be able to find a TPA willing to administer it in violation of civil rights law, and that's how Section 1557 will succeed despite the rise of self-insured health plans.

If this sounds confusing, it is because it is. Complexity is good for creating billable hours for lawyers and profits for corporations but not for people seeking care. Health care civil rights laws are really a patchwork upon a patchwork upon a patchwork, with state laws, federal laws, and private employer and insurance decisions making up the reality of what discrimination protections and benefits exist in health insurance in any particular case. That is because our health care landscape generally is a mix of public and private health care in a federal system and because private employers play such a big role in the American provision of retirement and health care. Section 1557 of the ACA is the newest health care civil rights innovation in this patchwork context. As I detail below, Section 1557 is simultaneously broad but vague and thin. It gestures towards what it wants to protect rather than spelling out those protections forthrightly. It was passed without much notice when a flurry of other things seemed more important. It uses the worn paths of previous laws but also extends health care civil rights in some bold ways. Its combination of ambiguity and boldness has meant that it has attracted controversy at the same time it has been watered down in practice.

HOW SECTION 1557 BECAME PART OF THE PATCHWORK

The patchwork of health care civil rights described above still permitted a lot of exclusions and discrimination in access to health insurance. People who did not work for an employer that offered health insurance could not afford or were shut out of the market for individual health plans. There was no market solution for them. President Obama made health care reform his top priority, and the ACA squeaked through in 2010. Its cryptically short antidiscrimination clause provides that, "[A]n individual shall not, on the ground prohibited under title VI of the Civil Rights Act of 1964 (42 U.S.C. 2000d et seq.), title IX of the Education Amendments of 1972 (20 U.S.C. 1681 et seq.), the Age Discrimination Act of 1975 (42 U.S.C. 6101 et seq.), or section 794 of title 29, be excluded from participation in, be denied the benefits of, or be subjected to discrimination under, any health program or activity, any part of which is receiving Federal financial assistance." The text of the law simply lists other preexisting civil rights laws for its coverage (such as Title VI for race, the Age Act for age, and Section 504 of the Rehabilitation Act for disability), and its reference to Title IX ushered in sex. The other laws already reached healthcare settings, but the addition of sex discrimination in healthcare was new. There is no other language announcing or explaining what a right to nondiscrimination in health care is. There is no legislative history.

Why were health care civil rights so unelaborated in the ACA? As one health policy advocate explained to me, "Writing it that way through those cross references was a way politically for members of Congress who were drafting this version to signal to their colleagues that this shouldn't be really this controversial because they were just extending principles that were already well established in federal law." Recall that the innovation of Medicare and Medicaid came without their own statutory nondiscrimination clause and without playing up the implications of Title VI's ban on race discrimination on purpose because of concerns that it would create opposition from white supremacist senators like Robert Byrd of West Virginia. When I asked all the administrative insiders and advocates about the process for getting the nondiscrimination clause into the bill, everyone said some version of the same thing: it was relatively unnoticed and noncontroversial in the chaos of getting the ACA as a whole passed. The extensive conservative and religious opposition to nondiscrimination that exists today did not yet exist. "To our knowledge, there wasn't anybody out there lobbying against passage of 1557," this advocate said.

The major transformations of the ACA mandated insurance coverage in some nondiscriminatory ways in its regulated markets. It intervened in the smaller section of the health insurance market to stabilize and prop up options for individuals and small businesses that otherwise could not operate at the edges. Everyone else kept their Medicare or employer-sponsored plans. Participation in ACA marketplace coverage reached its highest levels ever in 2024, but that share is only a little over six percent of the US population. These changes did not require use of Section 1557 because they were part of the other structural provisions. The ACA changed the rules for insurance companies in the individual and small group markets, telling them that they could not refuse to extend a policy because of someone's preexisting condition, for example. This new "goodie" could be called a right or a benefit or protection from health discrimination, but instead it carries the boring bureaucratic name of "guaranteed issue." Before the ACA, a person with a preexisting condition or even someone over a specified weight with no other health conditions would simply not be able to buy health insurance on the private market at all.

The ACA-governed plans also had to provide maternity care and newborn care as an essential health benefit without charging women more. Before the ACA, some insurance plans would not cover pregnancy and birth or charged women more because they might incur these costs. (The Pregnancy Discrimination Act of 1978, an amendment to Title VII, had partially alleviated this problem but not entirely.) The National Women's Law Center ran a campaign in support of the ACA with the slogan "Being a woman is not a pre-existing condition" to highlight the problem of gender discrimination in health insurance. Breastfeeding support and supplies, including breast pumps that cost around $500, were included in the ACA as maternity and newborn care. These new ACA structural provisions had a powerful equalizing force because discrimination based on pregnancy and other preexisting conditions had excluded people from accessing any coverage or resulted in them being charged more. Critically, this provisioning was achieved through changing the structural rules of the game for insurance companies and through national legislation, not through creating a civil right that individual patients would have to claim and fight for within an organizational culture.

Advocacy groups mobilized around these new rights as the ACA rolled out. Much like Section 504 disability rights, the rights in Section 1557 were so abbreviated that they would need regulations to spell out what they meant even though technically the Office for Civil Rights (OCR) began enforcement upon enactment. Advocates turned their attention to getting people signed up for care. Out2Enroll, an LGBT-health advocacy group, started in 2013 in anticipation of the ACA marketplaces opening up. LGBT people were more likely to need health insurance coverage, and Out2Enroll wanted to help enroll people with targeted messaging and training for LGBT health concerns. They worked with the more than five thousand enrollment assistants in every state working on the frontlines to sign people up for marketplace plans. The assistants who received Out2Enroll training got a rainbow icon next to their name in the search website for people looking for help signing up for their ACA plan, so that the person buying insurance could select someone informed about the issues that LGBT people faced when trying to buy a health plan. For instance, it was common for a trans person who had changed their name at the state level to be listed in the marketplace with their previous name.

Another big problem for LGBT access to health insurance in 2013 and 2014 was confusion and barriers due to marriage inequality for same-sex couples. The *Obergefell v. Hodges* ruling to protect marriage rights for same-sex couples would not create a federal right to marriage until June 2015.[51] A same-sex couple would complete the process on www.healthcare.gov, but then the insurance company handling the policy would reject it, saying they do not offer a family policy for two men or two women, even if they were legally married in their home state. "It wasn't explicitly 1557," one Out2Enroll advocate explained, "but what HHS ended up doing was putting out guidance saying if you offer family coverage to heterosexual couples you also have to offer family coverage to same-sex couples, and trans people need to be able to change their name on their marketplace profile." This equality requirement for insurance pre-*Obergefell* was anchored not in 1557 but in the guaranteed issue part of the ACA for individual and small group plans, telling insurers that they must issue a policy regardless of health status, age, gender, or other predictive traits.

Advocates continued to see discrimination in the ACA rollout, however, and kept pushing the Obama administration to do more. They wanted strong implementing regulations. The health discrimination problems most prominently encountered by cisgender, heterosexual, and child-bearing women had been addressed in the structural rules about maternity care and essential health benefits including contraception, but there were forms of gender-based health discrimination that were not captured in the ACA structural provisions. Subsidized plans under the ACA with essential health benefits that no longer excluded gender dysphoria as a preexisting condition could have been immediately beneficial to trans people, but nearly all states had explicit exclusions for gender-affirming care (often called "sex changes" or other outdated terms) in their benchmark plans. Even free preventative services under the ACA—say, a mammogram—would be denied because the person's gender marker did not match the service, and insurance would not pay.

Rights that apply to everyone may falter in practice and thereby showcase the unique vulnerabilities for some people, who then are understood to need trait-specific civil rights elaborations. HHS put up a website to help trans healthcare consumers navigate these problems, which Out2Enroll advocates would point to and say, "Guys, the federal government has a page on transgender health—the government sees you." HHS issued an FAQ in 2015 explaining that sex-specific services needed to be covered without cost sharing regardless of gender identity and sex listed on documents as part of the ACA preventative services requirements. These developments came before the first formal regulations implementing

Section 1557 were published in 2016, showing how advocates used the general benefits and rights under the ACA to amplify trans health issues in particular. The 2016 final rule from the Obama administration implementing Section 1557 included a ban on explicit categorical exclusions for gender-affirming care in insurance and a requirement that care be given with parity, that is, if a cisgender person would be able to get a prostate screening or a mammogram, then a trans person who needs it must also be able to receive that care.

It initially seemed that Section 1557 could have major impacts throughout the healthcare system. Both the ACA generally and these specific rights promised expanded access to health insurance and health care, and advocates hoped that the well-documented patterns of discrimination, stigma, and abuse of transgender and gender-variant people in health care settings would become recognized and possibly eased along with health disparities based on other categories such as race.[52] Business-side lawyers appeared to agree that there could be a lot more litigation pressure on insurers and healthcare providers for discrimination claims of many kinds. One healthcare attorney called Section 1557 "the future of healthcare discrimination litigation" and the "legal side of health equity," warning clients that the private right of action and access to disparate impact claims made Section 1557 "a powerful tool in the hands of a private plaintiff."[53] Moreover, health care *is* different: it is more complicatedly regulated than other domains, highly specialized and segmented into many professional subgroups, significant in its impact as a sector of our economy, and also part of highly personal experience for many people.[54]

Indeed, Section 1557 protections started off strong under the Obama presidency. The Office for Civil Rights (OCR) at the Department of Health and Human Services (HHS) began taking complaints to enforce it when the ACA passed in 2010. Implementing regulations for Section 1557 issued in 2016 required all covered health care entities with fifteen employees or more to appoint a grievance officer and establish a process to hear claims, to notify the public about these requirements and options, and to provide all health care services equitably to transgender people (among other things).[55,56] There were therefore several new and potentially significant features of this new healthcare rights law (the provision itself combined with the implementing regulations): (1) it added sex to the list of protected categories in healthcare; (2) it required that at least part of someone's job be focused on civil rights in nearly all healthcare settings in the United States; (3) it required a grievance process on site about civil rights claims; (4) it gave patients a private right of action to file a lawsuit without waiting to go through that internal grievance process; (5) it embraced gender-identity and sex stereotyping as part of sex discrimination, thereby explicitly elevating transgender health care concerns; (6) it made it illegal for a covered health plan to have a categorical exclusion for gender-affirming care; and (7) it expanded the scope of legal remedies to include disparate impact claims.[57] The basic principle was parity: if a form of care would be available to a cisgender person, such as cervical cancer screening for cisgender women, that same service cannot be denied to someone because he is a transgender man (but may still have a cervix). Importantly, the 2016 rules did not include a religious exemption from the duty not to discriminate. A former Office for Civil Rights employee who worked on the Obama rule described the impact of the Section 1557 implementing regulations to me as transformative, especially the ban on categorical exclusions for gender-affirming care in ACA-regulated insurance plans.

There were not many complaints filed at the Obama administration's Office for Civil Rights (OCR) about gender identity between 2010 and 2016 (my Freedom of Information Act request yielded eighteen, another study with a slightly later time frame yielded thirty-four, and OCR has estimated between fifteen and twenty per year).[58] The remedies OCR imposed were limited to nonpunitive solutions such as trainings. The Obama-era administrative responses aimed at critical drivers of transgender mistreatment in health care settings: misgendering, humiliation and stigmatization, and denial of care. OCR admonished hospitals for misgendering trans patients by rooming them with patients of the other gender, delaying their care, denying their same-sex relationship status, refusing them care that would have been granted to cisgender people, mocking a (presumably cisgender) man for coming to the ER after a domestic violence incident at the hands of his girlfriend, and for sending bills to a (presumably cisgender) woman's husband rather than to her, even though she had her own job and health insurance. These judgments were well publicized, and I found they had made their way into training slides and legal advice prepared for healthcare organizations.[59]

The surprise election of Republican Donald Trump to the presidency in November 2016 slowed this clear expansion of health care civil rights for transgender people as he took control of the administrative agencies in charge of civil rights, health, education, and more. President Trump took significant steps against transgender rights and in favor of evangelical Christian and Catholic conservatives, rolling back Department of Education guidance protecting transgender students' access to bathrooms that match their gender identity and banning transgender soldiers from serving except under their sex assigned at birth. Trump's director of the HHS Office for Civil Rights, Roger Severino, created a new Conscience and Religious Freedom division in the office to protect the rights of religious conservatives to avoid participating in care or subsidizing care that they objected to. The conservative legal movement had mobilized against Section 1557's gender-identity protections before Trump's election, however, filing lawsuits to stop HHS from enforcing Section 1557's gender-identity protections.

Before getting into some of the legal details that set the stage for the rest of the story in this book, it is worth reprising why Section 1557 became so legally contentious. The biggest political reason is that it was the first time in federal civil rights law that trans people's health concerns and rights to be recognized with dignity were significantly advanced by the federal government. More doctrinal legal reasons added ambiguity. First, the way it was written cobbled together other statutes and lacked a freestanding statutory text and fact-finding that would have given it independent grounds beyond those stilts of the other listed statutes to hold it up. That meant the relationship of those listed statutes (and each one's own legislative history, judicial interpretation, implementing rules, and remedies) to Section 1557 cases was up for debate in the courts. Could plaintiffs rely on any of the remedies listed in any of the referenced laws or only the ones linked to the particular trait that law had been cited for in Section 1557? Recall that "sex" came into Section 1557 linked to Title IX, so the question was whether all subsequent interpretations had to remain under Title IX doctrines only. Some federal courts have held that Title IX bans transgender discrimination as sex discrimination, but the Supreme Court has not decided that issue. Title IX otherwise permits a lot of sex-based differentiation (on sports teams, in single-sex dormitories, and so on) and draws on biological differences between the sexes to justify differential treatment. Title IX also has its own religious exemption. How much influence would these different civil rights statutes from other realms have on Section 1557 in healthcare?

Second, what legal rights did the clause on its own confer, distinct from the 2016 rules that elaborated them? Lawsuits continually target the implementing rules as an overreach of the administrative state, but the clause itself is still there. Republicans have failed to repeal the ACA despite claiming it is a top priority. Even if judges do not have to defer to the HHS interpretation of what the clause means, the clause remains for judicial interpretation on its own terms. A judge who regards Section 1557 as enacting its own distinct new health care civil right would interpret it as uniting all the prior civil rights traits under a clause that then had its own independent legal force and health-specific raison d'être. It should be read within the goals of the ACA, which were to broaden health care access and intervene in discriminatory market behaviors that hurt people. This approach is a maximizing view that would expand civil rights remedies in health care by bundling them together, essentially.

A judicial minimizing approach would take apart the bundle, limit the sex discrimination provision to only what is provided under the referenced Title IX, amplify the essentialist gender-binary-focused elements of Title IX, deny that Title IX interpretations should be influenced by other civil rights statutes such as Title VII (thereby limiting remedies and definitions, most importantly the *Bostock v. Clayton County* ruling that Title VII protects trans employees), refuse deference to HHS's interpretation in its regulations, and grant generous religious exemptions. There are long-standing statutory protections for conscience exemptions in medical care, but religious groups resisted the idea that if they provided a hysterectomy in medically indicated cases for cisgender women, they would have to provide it for a transman, for example. Will religious exemptions be allowed to swallow the duty not to discriminate entirely? Each of these questions mattered a lot as lawsuits against Section 1557's transgender-inclusive interpretations unfolded. They continue to define the debate over gender-identity protections in the ACA today.

In the first major salvo, the Becket Fund for Religious Liberty, representing a group of conservative Christian physicians and dentists, several states, and a Catholic hospital association, sued the Obama HHS over the 2016 regulations in August 2016, arguing that the rule required them to perform abortions and gender-affirming care or face penalties for discrimination on the basis of gender identity and termination of pregnancy and that their religious freedom was violated, among other claims.[60] They filed their case in a federal district court in Fort Worth, Texas, with only one active judge, Judge Reed O'Connor. Judge O'Connor is a well-known and reliable conservative judge, consistently ruling against LGBT rights and the ACA itself, and by filing there the plaintiffs would be assured he would hear their case.[61] Judge O'Connor issued a nationwide injunction against HHS on December 31, 2016, to stop them from administrative enforcement of the transgender and pregnancy-termination protections in the newly enacted Section 1557 implementing rules.[62] When Trump assumed the presidency a few weeks later, his HHS would not appeal the ruling against its enforcement powers.

The clause in the statute itself remained since Republicans were not able to repeal the entire ACA under Trump. Section 1557 gives individual plaintiffs a right to sue on their own, so even when HHS was enjoined from enforcement, lawsuits could continue. Other federal judges declined to follow Judge O'Connor's injunction, noting that the statutory language has supported transgender inclusion all along by reference to sex discrimination.[63] Katharine Prescott sued Rady Children's Hospital in San Diego under Section 1557 after staff repeatedly used feminine pronouns for her teen transgender son, Kyler, when he was an inpatient for extreme psychological distress due to gender dysphoria. Kyler died by suicide a few weeks after his hospital stay. Even though the O'Connor injunction was in place, the federal judge ruled that his mother's Section 1557 claims on Kyler's behalf could go forward because the clause itself covered gender-identity discrimination. Ms. Prescott settled with the hospital in 2019.[64] This case is an example of the pro-health care civil rights "bundling" approach to Section 1557 that would not be limited by the injunction on the Obama or Biden implementing regulations. As a matter of formal law, any covered entity could still be subject to a lawsuit from a patient making this argument throughout the time that I was researching this book, though I found most people on the ground barely knew about any of these litigative details.

The Trump administration attempted to define sex in federal law as either male or female, unchangeable, and fixed at birth through new Section 1557 regulations issued in 2020 to replace the 2016 Obama regulations (and will surely do so again). The Trump regulations took out all the gender-identity protections from Section 1557 and ten other regulations, stripped other protections from LGBT people and those living with HIV, limited application of the clause, and offered broad religious exemptions.[65] The Trump regulations also removed the duty to post antidiscrimination notices and to designate someone to be the 1557 coordinator. The Supreme Court was deciding a case that term, *Bostock v. Clayton County*, about whether Title VII's employment protections extend to gay, lesbian, bisexual, and transgender people under that statute's ban on sex discrimination.[66] Trump officials must have expected the conservative court to limit sex discrimination coverage in similar terms (such as to only biological males or females on the basis of sex at birth), which would have further supported the conservative roll-back of LGBT rights under sex discrimination law across the federal government that Trump's administration had begun.

Instead, the Supreme Court opinion in *Bostock*, written by Trump appointee Neil Gorsuch, held that discrimination against an LGBT person was necessarily sex discrimination in the *employment* context. LGBT health and advocacy groups immediately filed five different lawsuits challenging the 2020 Trump regulations as arbitrary and capricious (given well-documented problems of transgender health discrimination, especially under pandemic conditions) and untenable after the *Bostock* ruling that transgender discrimination is sex discrimination.[67] Favorable decisions in those cases affirmed that, indeed, the Trump 2020 rules were contrary to the law of *Bostock* and should not have been issued without considering the outcome of that case.[68] The 2020 Trump regulations for Section 1557 were then also placed under injunction and many of their provisions did not go into effect.[69] The Biden administration then turned policy around again, enacting new 1557 regulations that affirmed gender-identity protections in care settings and health insurance coverage. Just two days before those new regulations were set to go into effect in July 2024, a conservative district court judge placed them under preliminary injunction yet again.

It is a dizzying story, with health care civil rights that protect gender identity whipping back and forth between judges, presidents, and the Supreme Court. Some branches of the federal government wish to protect gender identity as a nondiscrimination category while others are much more hostile, and commitments shift depending on elections and judicial nominations. The statutory versus constitutional settings for trans rights matters, too, as does state versus national politics. Notably, there is no Supreme Court ruling about gender-identity protections under Section 1557 as this book goes to press. A Fourteenth Amendment equal-protection ruling about trans rights that fails to protect them from state action, such as bans on gender-affirming care for minors, would preserve those bans on care but would not reach Section 1557 itself. The conservative justices in the majority on our Supreme Court would likely prefer to halt transgender-inclusive interpretations of Section 1557, but with *Bostock* as such recent precedent it would be tricky to find a way to say so. One way would be to deny that Title IX's ban on sex discrimination is the same as Title VII's ban on sex discrimination and to distinguish them. That would mean a finding that health care discrimination and educational discrimination against transgender people is permitted but employment discrimination against them is not. States could ban care that federal civil rights regulations say must be provided without discrimination against trans people. Conservative legal organizations like the Becket Fund and the Alliance Defending Freedom are busy serving up lawsuits and amicus briefs in preselected jurisdictions to supply all the legal reasoning the conservative Court majority will need to select the policy it prefers.

The easiest way to defeat Section 1557 trans health care civil rights has likely already happened in the Supreme Court's overturning the so-called *Chevron* deference in *Loper Bright Enterprises v. Raimondo*, however. That's because the ruling allows the judicial branch to brush aside the regulatory process that yielded the detailed Section 1557 rules (or any other regulation) and substitute another understanding of what an ambiguous or brief clause requires.[70] This route steers interpretation back to Title IX (because of its reference in the clause itself) and its acceptance of seemingly biological essentialist accounts of gender in defense of sex exclusion in education, as in fraternities, sororities, father-son or mother-daughter activities, and beauty pageant scholarships. Indeed, this reasoning underlies the most recent injunction against the HHS rules from Mississippi federal judge Louis Guirola Jr. that there is no deference to the agency's interpretation of Section 1557, and instead the best understanding is based on ideas about sex from 1972 when Title IX was passed.[71] Title VII protections for gender identity under *Bostock* cannot simply move over into healthcare, he found. The spending clause requires that Congress direct its intentions more clearly, Judge Guirola held, so if Congress wants sex discrimination to include gender identity it must say so explicitly.

The Trump administration and the actions of Trump-appointed judges certainly thwarted some implementation and enforcement of Section 1557's protections, though it is not clear exactly how much. One of the biggest impacts of Section 1557 was the large-scale removal of categorical exclusions of gender-affirming care from ACA-governed health insurance plans.[72] As I explained, the 2016 Obama regulations prohibited covered entities from having or implementing these categorical exclusions.[73] Almost half the states also banned categorical exclusions in their state insurance laws. Exclusions for gender-affirming care had been common prior to the ACA, but an analysis by Out2Enroll, the LGBT healthcare advocacy group formed at the launch of the ACA, found that ninety-five percent of insurers had removed transgender-specific exclusions from their 2017 silver ACA marketplace plans.[74] This significant social change persisted despite Judge O'Connor's quick injunction against HHS enforcement of the gender-identity protections in Section 1557. In 2018, the same analysis found that ninety percent of covered insurers continued to offer silver marketplace plans without trans care exclusions.[75] Moreover, courts continue to find that Title VII employment discrimination law protects trans employees from discriminatory health benefit plans that exclude their needs. Major insurers sell plans nationwide in many markets and would be reluctant to rewrite them every few months or to guess how the litigation over gender-affirming care would finally conclude. Importantly, the individual right to sue under Section 1557, serving as another form of enforcement, remained and could still pose a legal risk to organizations. I found that generally, large corporate entities like insurers and hospital systems took steady actions towards transgender rights expansions and treated the Trump administration's rollback as temporary, though Out2Enroll found that discriminatory exclusions increased slightly in 2023 and 2024.[76]

Almost no one at the patient-care level, including the more informed Section 1557 coordinators, even knew what Judge O'Connor's injunction was. Among the management-level people I spoke with who knew about it, there was total disregard for it and a determination to forge ahead with gender identity as a health care civil right, at least as they understood it. A senior diversity manager at a hospital system was explaining everything his system did in 2016 to respond to Section 1557, including systemwide trainings, getting a new electronic medical records system that would properly gather the correct name, a wristband with the correct name, and so on. I asked whether the injunction would have any effect on their plans. "So to your point about the injunction put there by the judge," he responded, "we're saying, okay, we get that, but we believe that the law of the land will ultimately say, yes, you have to include [transgender people] and you need to do whatever accommodations for that." Another interviewee in state-level leadership put it more bluntly: "We're going to just continue acting like 1557 isn't enjoined until somebody who's my boss tells me otherwise." Federal district court judges can issue preliminary injunctions against enforcing the gender-identity protections in Section 1557 regulations, which is certainly one way the law fails in the face of conservative legal mobilization against it. But then managers on the ground in organizations could simply ignore those injunctions.

I've argued that the American system of civil rights and rights generally includes negative rights that are unhelpful for health, a sphere in which specific provisions of care are needed for a right to amount to anything. The political misfortunes of our overall approach to health policy refract health rights, breaking them up into disparate, measly provisions for the poor and vulnerable through unpopular spending programs like Medicaid and blocking anything like a national healthcare system that would provide everyone with a reasonable baseline of care. Instead, we may end up with a genuinely weird situation in which trans employees have the right to nondiscriminatory employer-sponsored health plans as a job benefit, but trans people *as people seeking health care* are not afforded those protections under a nondiscrimination law in a health care law. The ACA, limited in some ways since it only reshaped the margins of our employer-based health system, nonetheless created structural changes that banned a lot of health discrimination that had been widespread and harmful. Recall that the Johnson administration could not risk a fight about nondiscrimination by race in the final stages of passing Medicare because segregationists might have withdrawn their support. The ACA squeaked through Congress with an antidiscrimination provision, which no one noticed or defended, and which has since come under relentless attack once it became clear that it mattered a lot for trans people's health.

The structures of our federal judiciary also make it possible for conservative lawyers to direct cases dismantling health care civil rights to a single right-wing judge (so-called forum shopping). A powerful and effective conservative legal movement has mobilized to feed cases through the system (concocting injuries that never happened to recruited plaintiffs) and tee them up for the conservative Supreme Court majority. Health care civil rights can fail at this national level of refraction through neglect, lack of political support, injunction against their enforcement, and defanging of real enforcement powers. At the mesolevel of insurance law and regulation, we see that the organization of our health care system into mostly employer-sponsored health insurance further refracts rights through a tangle of state and federal regulation. Health care civil rights refracted through insurance in the United States are strongly influenced by employers' and insurers' own profits and market decisions, such as the option to self-insure and opt out of state antidiscrimination requirements. Some constituencies have won health rights through federal legislation, but overall, we live under a regulatory system designed in the 1970s for regulating retirement pensions that is no match for the modern healthcare economy. Health care civil rights can fail at this mesolevel because of neglectful politics and the autonomy of corporate benefit designs.

Finally, there is Peggy, watching the "nines and tens" on her patient satisfaction surveys. Organizational culture refracts rights at the patient-care level, and sometimes it safeguards them. Some leaders kept complying with Section 1557 in their own organizations even though they knew HHS enforcement power had been removed. Perhaps they will do so again now that civil rights regulation and enforcement have been undercut again, perhaps fatally. But health care civil rights can also fail at their microlevel by refraction through other hospital performance incentives or, even when they are still supported, by being left to enforcement on a voluntary basis. Notice that none of these forms of failure for health care civil rights are about the complexities of health disparities or the depth of the social problems that produce inequality in our country, which is the focus of much important research trying to explain why solving these problems is so hard. Instead, the forms of failure I explain here are driven by the structure of our institutions, mobilized conservative opposition, the political economy of healthcare, and the political decisions we have made over decades. The next chapters elaborate on all the ways that health care civil rights are refracted through these different levels of meaning and enforcement. They are mostly changed for the worse, though not always.

How Health Care Civil Rights
Became Patient Experience

Greg is a grievance analyst who started out in the "Consumer Resource Center," a division of the Patient Relations Department at the large California hospital where he works. He told us about how his experience in retail management prepared him well for his current role:

> The majority of time I've been in retail management. And then I transitioned over into healthcare, just because healthcare has transitioned over to a really customer-focused, a patient-focused organization, as we have most of our survey scores are really tied to reimbursement rates. And so having people with a customer-service background is, you know, when you have doctors that don't necessarily know how to be nice to people. Having that customer service background is helpful, you know, in those types of situations.

Greg's work is typical of someone working in a larger healthcare organization. "Patient Relations is the office of record for all formal grievances and complaints that are related to clinical care issues or any service-related issues . . . or the patient's perception of something that went wrong," he explains. He does the "initial intake" and "document[s] the information to an internal system that we have here." After deciding what kind of problem the issue seems to be, Greg "direct[s] those complaints out, or grievances out, to the appropriate areas to find some resolution." Then he is responsible for communicating back to the person about their problem. If a patient seems to be describing an incident of discrimination, he would "pass the buck" to their Equal Employment Opportunity Office. When we asked him specifically about the Affordable Care Act (ACA) and sex discrimination, he replied that he would send any issues like that to the woman in charge of the sexual harassment compliance and prevention office. Greg is mistaken about the law here, interpreting patient discrimination as employment related. An essential task of his job is recognition and sorting of problems, and he does not seem to recognize health care discrimination as a civil rights issue.

Will is a nursing administrator at an ambulatory surgical center, another type of health care organization covered by the sex discrimination clause of Section 1557. For Will, there is no need for the identity politics of civil rights because the patient care ethic takes care of it:

> And what is in the best interest of the patient, okay. And that's why I keep reiterating the patient. It doesn't matter what the patient is—black, white, female, male, sexual orienta—I mean, all these things that fall under 1557, we don't address those things. All we're addressing is the patient, and what is in the best interest of the patient. I mean, we're in healthcare, we're in to help people. It doesn't really matter about the rest. I mean, it's kind of like the Hippocratic Oath, it's like I don't understand where the problem lies. Why do we have to have this written down? It's what we do!

Will knows about the legal requirements but pushes them away. Ignoring the law, misunderstanding it, reframing it, or grudgingly implanting it are common ways that health care civil rights get refracted on the ground.

Understanding what health care civil rights are means studying them where they matter most. The first place that health care civil rights matter is within health care settings such as hospitals or clinics where people seeking care may encounter discriminatory treatment. They may be ignored, denied care or specific treatments, harassed, physically mistreated, or arrested or singled out by security, for example. If this treatment occurs because of a trait that the law protects in this context, then it could be illegal discrimination. But for a problem to be seen as a health care civil rights problem, a lot of things need to happen. The person seeking care needs to understand it as wrong and to complain about it. Someone in the organization needs to receive that complaint and understand it as a problem too. The problem needs to be understood as a possible rights violation or a civil rights problem, not some other kind of problem. This process is not at all smooth, and whether it happens or not and in what ways it happens depends on many features of the organizational culture and the frameworks for problem-solving that the people in that setting use to understand what is happening when someone complains. This chapter is about how complaints—also sometimes called grievances—are understood on the ground in healthcare settings.

SECTION 1557 COORDINATORS
AS MICROLEVEL RIGHTS WORKERS

The class of professionals and the bureaucratic workflow that I found managing patient civil rights problems is part of the what Kathleen Sutcliffe and Robert Wears call the institutionalization of the patient safety movement into managerial, scientific-bureaucratic medicine.[1] Moral panic and publicity about medical harms plus concerns for out-of-control healthcare costs helped drive "patient safety" and "medical errors" to prominence in the 1990s and early 2000s. Sutcliffe and Wears argue that what could have been an interdisciplinary and more innovative movement to understand patient safety and harm was diverted into simple, instrumental tools for safety and absorbed within the bureaucratic apparatus of hospital compliance staff. These workers, mostly women with training as nurses, would manage the bureaucracy of safety in lower-status ways, guarding it from incursion by outsiders but also ensuring that "any potentially radical change to improve safety would be stifled, limiting patient safety efforts to small, nondisruptive changes on the margins of clinical work."[2] Computerization of medical records and reporting systems, proceeding along at the same time, was appealing as an implementation modality for this bureaucratic, regulatory approach to safety because it could prioritize the needs of managers, designing out discretion for doctors.[3]

All the pieces of the hospital civil rights administration, such as it exists at all, were already evolving into place before the passage of the ACA in 2010 and its new civil rights mandate. The ACA added incentives for maintaining high scores on patient satisfaction surveys to avoid losing federal funding, fully enmeshing patient satisfaction with patient safety in the healthcare bureaucracy. There was already a required grievance procedure for any entity participating in Medicare. The world into which new patient civil rights came, in other words, was already made up as a reporting and managerial bureaucracy in which mostly women, frequently trained as nurses and responsible for multiple aspects of administrative compliance, sorted, routed, and resolved patient problems using grievance reporting software systems. This is the world I found when I started to ask about patient civil rights.

To find the people tasked with implementing Section 1557 on the ground and to understand what they were doing, my research team and I called the numbers for Section 1557 coordinators between May 2017 and October 2018, asking to speak to those people. If we could not find a named Section 1557 coordinator on the organization website, we called more general numbers and asked to speak with someone who handles patient complaints and then determined if they would indeed be a person who would work on complaints including discrimination. By "handling" patient problems, I mean in the metaphorical work sense but also in the material sense: what did these grievance handlers literally *do*, as in sort, move, and work with these problems? They described a rich world of obligations, pressures, systems, norms, and professional practices from the view of their desk every day. *Grievance handler* is my term for them because it most plainly describes what they do. Sometimes they were called the Section 1557 coordinator, but more commonly they had other titles like patient advocate or patient experience coordinator.

Our team interviewed sixty-four people from the 744 healthcare settings we called.[4] All names and workplaces have been replaced with pseudonyms. Fifty-nine of those people worked handling patient problems, of which forty-three (seventy-three percent) were the primary grievance handler at their facility. The others were people we reached through snowball sampling, asking the first person who else was helping with 1557 implementation and then seeking out those people. Of the fifty-nine implementors, only fourteen had been specifically designated as the Section 1557 civil rights coordinator and knew they had this role. The remaining forty-five grievance handlers were people who would be assigned the 1557 role if the organization had complied, but there was not a named person in their clinic or hospital yet. A majority (seventy-one percent) of interview subjects worked in the domains of patient relations, risk, compliance, and quality assurance. Nursing was the most highly represented educational background (thirty-seven percent), with the rest comprised of a wide range of professional and non-advance-degreed backgrounds. Notably, there were only two attorneys in our sample.

The largest single group of our interview subjects (fifty percent) worked in patient experience roles. What we call patient experience includes a variety of job titles including "patient advocate," "patient relations associate," "patient experience representative," or "customer relations coordinator." Titles sometimes explicitly linked the patient and the customer, as in "patient advocate and customer relations specialist." At larger facilities, our respondents worked exclusively on responding to patient complaints. Among smaller organizations, however, patient experience was likely one of several responsibilities assigned to an individual. For example, at smaller rural hospitals, the patient experience role might fall to the "director of social work and risk management," the "chief quality improvement and patient safety officer," or the "system director of clinical risk management," all titles our interviewees held. At ambulatory surgical centers, grievances were often handled by CEOs or executive directors.

Grievance handlers were mostly middle-aged, white (seventy-eight percent) women (seventy-six percent). A large portion of the professionals working in complaint handling (twenty-one out of fifty-eight, or thirty-six percent) were trained nurses who had transitioned into a patient experience role. For example, Michelle is a nurse and patient advocate who finds that her nursing background helps her to explain medical issues to patients and head off communication problems between doctors and patients. She explains that she deals with "everything from billing to, you know, care issues, to physician issues." "Gosh," she continues, "I mean, it's really been a game of lost items, lost teeth, lost dentures. Lost shoes, I get called. But in order to be able to understand, number one, what the patient is here for, diagnosis, to be able to kind of speak the language, and then help bring it down to their level, is very helpful. So, I just think it's a nice fit to be a nurse."

Compliance officers and risk managers also handled patient problems. Like their counterparts in patient experience, they regarded other regulatory duties as more salient than civil rights enforcement as they did their jobs. Compliance professionals are in charge of making sure the hospital or facility's existing policies and procedures abide by all governing rules, regulations, and professional standards. Possible discrimination complaints are a small part of the myriad compliance obligations they confront. Justin, a program manager in the compliance office of a Michigan community hospital who is also the Section 1557 officer, explains his regulatory world:

> So what we look at, just about everything. We're always looking for HIPAA [Health Insurance Portability and Accountability Act]. We're watching for any sort of Medicare/Medicaid fraud. EMTALA [Emergency Medical Treatment and Active Labor Act], any of the regular regulatory, you know, federal government compliance issues. So our primary focus, oddly enough, the one that has the highest risk, is physician contracting.

He explains that "the civil rights coordinator position had already been attached to the program manager job—it's not looked at as a separate job, a separate job title. It's like our director of medical records is also our privacy officer." Risk management is, as Jackie, director of quality and risk management at a critical access hospital in rural Michigan, explains, "[A]nything surrounding patient safety that could pose a risk for the hospital." As Sheila, a risk manager at a community hospital in a Michigan town, puts it, "When you're in risk management, you're sometimes dealing with people who have really legitimate complaints or want to sue you." These professionals respond based on a differentiated legal consciousness arranged in a hierarchy of importance, with many priorities above recognizing possible civil rights violations.

Most of the grievance handlers we interviewed were not familiar with the civil rights provision of the Affordable Care Act. Widespread noncompliance is not a surprising finding in sociolegal studies, even among professionals tasked with implementation.[5] For example, Justin had never heard of the specific requirements of Section 1557 despite being given the civil rights coordinator title three months before. When asked when he first heard about the legal requirements for Section 1557 he laughed, saying, "When you called me." Another grievance handler, named Jamie, a nurse turned patient advocate, described "a reference binder that I created to become more familiar with all the rules that come with the actual filing grievances for patients." She pulled it out during the interview but could not find any section in the binder for 1557. Even though she had not heard of Section 1557, Jamie had a ready answer for how she would handle a claim:

> If the patient is discharged and they're calling back up to complain about their hospital stay, then I talk to the patient. So if they had a concern regarding the way that they were treated, based off of their gender, sexual orientation, then I would address it like I would any other concern, which would follow the same pattern: I'd listen to the complaint, I would file it according to our Safety First tracking, I would address it with the director or manager. I would wait for their response, and then I would follow up with a resolution letter to the patient.

Here, Jamie makes it clear that she sees no meaningful distinction between discrimination complaints and other kinds of patient concerns. Their Safety First tracking system is the default technological framework for routing patient complaints about "the way they were treated."

Patient grievances pertaining to discrimination consumed little attention. When asked how the frequency of discrimination grievances compared to other kinds of grievances, for example, Barb, a patient safety manager in California, said, "Ten, twenty, thirty times more. I mean we get very few related to discrimination." Twenty-four percent of the grievance handlers in this book reported that they had never received a complaint about discrimination. But when we probed specifically on that point, we found that forty-seven percent of those said they had dealt with a discrimination-related complaint at some point during their tenure in their current role. Interview subjects with legal or compliance department experience were twice as likely to mention an experience with discrimination handling compared to those without those backgrounds. Yet only two of our respondents had practiced law or had formal legal training.

Human resources (HR) also had little role in Section 1557 implementation. HR departments typically manage employment relationships and Section 1557 is focused on discrimination against patients, so lack of HR involvement makes sense. However, it also means that the bank of professional knowledge about civil rights laws in these organizations is functionally separated from this patient experience framework. I found that most organizations did not hire a new person to comply with Section 1557's civil rights coordinator requirement but rather gave these duties to someone who was already handling patient complaints. Participating in Medicare and Medicaid already required a grievance procedure for patient complaints, enacted in 1986, so every facility already had something in place prior to Section 1557.[6] The 2016 implementing regulation for Section 1557 said that covered entities could reuse whatever grievance process they already had in place, even if it was unrelated to civil rights.[7] So while there would be expertise about civil rights elsewhere in the organization (employee civil rights under Title VII, for example, in HR or the legal department), that framework of understanding was not really applicable to Section 1557, while another one—the Centers for Medicare & Medicaid Services or CMS grievance handling process—was already there and ready to pick up.

There was significant variation in awareness about Section 1557 across the organizations we studied, and some of this variation is likely attributable to whom we interviewed and their place in the organizational hierarchy. As would be expected, higher-level administrators at larger hospital systems knew more about the law than frontline staff in smaller care settings. Larger organizations had committees devoted to the new law. As Kathy explains her organization's approach to Section 1557, "We pulled the regulation. Then we created a gap analysis. And this is our standard process with any new regulation or change in regulation. From that gap analysis, we create a work plan. We put together a committee to ensure implementation." Kathy is the senior director of compliance at a large Michigan hospital system and holds an MBA. So while there may have been well-informed administrators in a hospital, our method of contacting the advertised coordinator might still route us to someone who was not very well informed about the new regulations and would turn to other well-worn paths for doing her job with complaints more generally: listening, filing, routing, and so on.

One way to understand Section 1557 grievance handlers is as actors in a typically unresponsive internal complaint process. We know from the Title VII employment context in the United States that grievance procedures at work are likely to be symbolic shows of compliance that protect the employer from liability rather than prevent discrimination.[8] Internal grievance procedures have been widely popular in the private sector for decades,[9] and the civil rights regulators who promulgated the 2016 Section 1557 rules embraced this structure too. "In OCR's [the Office for Civil Rights] experience," the original 1557 rule explains, "the presence of a coordinator and grievance procedure enhances the covered entity's accountability and helps bring concerns to prompt resolution, oftentimes prior to an individual bringing a private right of action."[10] OCR's enthusiasm for grievance procedures is not an evidence-based assessment of these procedures' effectiveness but rather shows how legal regulators "assume the validity of managerialized conceptions of law."[11]

US healthcare provision differs from the employment context in ways that transform health care civil rights in practice. Whereas the discrimination complaints are handled primarily by human resources professionals in the employment context, a wider array of professionals handles complaints in the context of healthcare provision, but the modal complaint handler had a nursing background and was situated in a patient experience department. The professionals who handle patient complaints are attuned to a different set of legal and regulatory demands specific to healthcare. Organizational decisions about *who* in the organization should respond to claims plays an important role in determining *how* complaints will be addressed. Grievances may be about many things, including but not limited to discrimination, and indeed a major question here is whether it is possible to see discrimination in the claims at all.

THE FRAMEWORK OF PATIENT EXPERIENCE

Jennifer is a registered nurse who has been working in the patient experience department of a large Michigan hospital for five years. It is her job to handle patient complaints about discrimination, but she has never heard of Section 1557 of the Affordable Care Act (ACA) where nondiscrimination rights were newly codified in 2010. Nonetheless, Jennifer has a well-developed approach to detecting and handling patient problems. She explains her "concierge" approach:

> Primarily, my focus is to make sure that our patients have everything they need to have the best possible experience, whether it's through communication, whether it's comfort items, whether it's helping their family make arrangements from a local hotel, getting them directions, kind of like a concierge-type program. And then complaint management and resolution. Like anything to do with quality for the patient experience.

Jennifer cares about patient experience and satisfaction, and her professional orientation toward disputes is organized around these priorities. The rise of patient experience as a financial interest in healthcare required improvements in communication to patients, who come into healthcare settings hurt, confused, and adrift in the busy workplace of healthcare in which everyone is busy and knows what they are doing but them. My research uncovered a vast range of patient complaints, from lost dentures to billing problems to delays in waiting rooms to humiliating encounters with providers. The healthcare organizations' view of the patient experience, however, is shaped by what is measured and how.

Healthcare organizations had previously measured patient satisfaction but not in any coordinated fashion. Two Notre Dame professors, Irwin Press, a medical anthropologist, and Rod Ganey, a sociologist and statistician, started a hospital patient satisfaction survey business in 1985.[12] Today Press Ganey is one of the major healthcare satisfaction surveying organizations. Organized national efforts to gather preferences came from the Agency for Healthcare Research and Quality in 1995, which launched the Consumer Assessment of Healthcare Providers and Systems program to study health plan enrollees experiences with their insurance.[13] In 2002, the Agency for Healthcare Research and Quality and the Centers for Medicare & Medicaid Services (CMS) developed the HCAHPS survey for adult hospital inpatients. CMS implemented the survey in 2006, and in 2007 hospitals received a financial incentive for using HCAHPS, enacted under the Deficit Reduction Act of 2005. Nearly ninety-five percent of eligible hospitals implemented the patient satisfaction survey that year.[14] Public reporting of scores began in 2008, and in the 2010 Affordable Care Act (ACA), HCAHPS scores were explicitly keyed to Medicare reimbursements under "pay for performance."[15] By 2013, the CMS Hospital Value-Based Purchasing Program incorporated patient satisfaction scores in total performance scores, and hospitals would stand to earn back more, less, or an equivalent amount that CMS held back from their diagnosis-related group payments for that year. These potential losses from bad scores are what Peggy means when she warns that "they're going to be taking back, you know, money."

What I call the patient experience frame emerged alongside the period of increased healthcare bureaucratization over the last twenty-five years. How patients felt about their care became acutely important within healthcare bureaucracies. Institutionalization and professionalization around the patient experience in healthcare, or "PX" as it is now branded, has proceeded along familiar lines. There are nonprofit organizations devoted to selling the development of the field of patient experience. Jason Wolf founded the Beryl Institute in 2010 as the "thought leadership arm" of the Beryl Company, a business focused on customer service in healthcare.[16] By 2012, the institute had shaped the Patient Experience Body of Knowledge into fifteen domains, setting a path toward further professionalization through credentialing. The *Patient Experience Journal* was founded in 2014. Jason Wolf founded the sister organization to the Beryl Institute, the Patient Experience Institute, as an independent nonprofit arm for professional certification and continuing education. One can become a "Certified Patient Experience Professional" by taking a course and exam.

Several factors in the patient experience frame are critical for shaping the landscape for civil rights. First, the concern is for patient *experience*, that is, the subjectively felt, remembered, witnessed, and reported state of mind of the person receiving health care services. Experiences are obviously important for one's rights as a patient, but there are many moments that are important for justice that are not part of the patient's experience in health care: anything that happens under anesthesia, the process of insurance coverage within the walls of the insurance company, and all provider thought and decision-making that occurs away from or invisible to the patient, such as charting, evaluating, recommending, forgetting, or ignoring. Second, patient experience was first framed around the hospitalized patient and centered the hospital as the regulated target and central setting for health care experience. Surveys would expand to cover outpatient doctor visits too. Vendors, professional organizations, and internal organization within hospitals built the bureaucracy of patient experience within and alongside the structures for patient safety.

Wolf's professionalization project for patient experience has been successful. Patient experience is not always its own job category, especially at smaller hospitals where the title may be shared in one person who is also a compliance officer or risk manager, but it has certainly become a required department and job title in healthcare organizations around the country. What exactly the patient experience is remains harder to pin down, and it remains closely tied to patient satisfaction outcomes.[17] I heard echoes of Wolf's core patient experience concepts throughout my interviews with grievance handlers, especially an emphasis on communication and miscommunication as the primary axis of evaluation and a somewhat nihilistic devotion to "perception is reality." When they discussed patients' concerns that they had been mistreated or that their rights were violated, I heard "perception is reality" while the patient's concerns were treated as invalid or baseless. That is, it was the second part of a story in which the first part was to present doubts about what the patient said but then pivot to "perception is reality" to move on to describing the "blameless apology" one had to issue (apologizing without taking blame, as in "I'm sorry you're so upset"). Better communication was considered the key to managing patient perceptions, and communications failures resulted in unhappy patients for whom perception was reality.

Researchers disagree about what patient satisfaction scores really indicate and whether they are helpful for improving care. After all, there are many inevitable and unpleasant experiences in hospitals. Doctors often must deliver bad news to deliver good care. Creating the hotel-like concierge atmosphere Jennifer describes might please patients and their families but lacks any relationship to the quality of care. Expensive ambiance could drive up costs and create more work for staff but not really improve health. Physicians could be pressured to give patients what they want, such as antibiotics they do not need or other costly interventions to appease them.[18] There is evidence that reported patient satisfaction is related to health care outcomes, like readmission to the hospital after discharge, and to lower mortality rates.[19] These results suggest that patient perceptions about their inpatient care are indeed discerning about underlying quality and not simply concierge complaints about surface-level features. On the other hand, individual providers, whose ratings may dip based on one bad review in the context of overall low response rates, feel burnt out and pressured to appease patients.

In the following sections, I describe the frameworks that structure the work of grievance handlers, shaping their interpretations of patient problems. These frameworks reveal what health care civil rights can be when they are refracted through the professional grievance management structures in the American healthcare system. Within the patient experience framework, grievance handlers have certain tools to help them do their work of constructing responses to problems as they see them. People make do in their lives with the best-honed tools they have; their tools create lines of action for them to do things, and they value outcomes that they can create with those tools. Section 1557 grievance handlers work within a hierarchical medical system in which they occupy a lower status than clinical care providers but in which patient satisfaction levels have financial implications that higher-ups care about. Their professional frameworks both rationalize these hierarchies and elevate customer service practices designed for dispersing interpersonal conflict. They experience law as regulatory pressure and financial incentive on themselves, not as civil rights protection for patients. They use the tools of bureaucratic management and interpersonal conflict de-escalation to manage patient problems, demobilizing rights claims.

The primary task of patient experience professionals is to process patient feedback. These staff receive, classify, track, investigate, and resolve complaints and grievances issued by patients or patient representatives. Their work is organized around two key distinctions: (1) the complaint versus grievance distinction and (2) the clinical versus nonclinical distinction. These distinctions guide how they sort their work into categories for action. These two distinctions are closely related, as we explain below, and hierarchically arranged. They tell handlers what kind of problem they have, what workflow to follow to dispense with it, and whose professional expertise and tool kit are appropriate.

COMPLAINT VERSUS GRIEVANCE: HOW REGULATIONS SHAPE PROFESSIONAL PRACTICE

The first distinction—complaint versus grievance—is a concept that comes directly out of long-standing Centers for Medicare & Medicaid Services (CMS) guidelines for how to handle patient problems. As Evan, the executive director of an ambulatory surgical center, explains, "There's a difference between a complaint and a true grievance. CMS actually dictates a lot of that language for us." Importantly, the legal risks that people care about here come from the regulatory bureaucracy, not from a potentially litigious person. According to CMS, complaints are problems that can be resolved more or less on the spot. Grievances are problems that are not resolved immediately and require documented action: a written response to the patient within thirty days.[20] I focus more on grievances and adopt the term *grievance handler* because most of the administrative bureaucracy is focused on grievances. They are more significant than complaints and have more rules and practices attached to them. The CMS regulations were by far the most common legal framework I heard about on the ground at this microlevel. When interviewees frequently told us, Oh, we're doing all that already (meaning civil rights implementation of the new Section 1557 rule in 2016), they meant that they were responding within these existing structures.

The CMS guidelines matter because violating CMS rules could mean losing the ability to bill CMS for care. Interview subjects explained what these CMS regulations meant on the ground for them as they ranked problems and triaged their responses. "If it's a grievance," said Frances, a former property manager now working as a patient advocate at a medium-sized hospital, "I have to submit it in writing, and if it's a complaint, I can verbalize that with them during the telephone conversation if I wasn't able to close it when they originally called." Like the financial implications of low HCAHPS scores, running afoul of CMS guidelines and losing the ability to bill Medicare is a highly salient organizational risk that arranges the priorities of any CMS-regulated healthcare setting all the way up and down (despite the fact that cutting off the use of Medicare to a hospital is a never-used and practically unusable sanction). The hospital where Frances worked had not yet posted any of the required Section 1557 language on their website nor was she aware of the law despite being the sole person to gather any patient reports of problems. Like Jamie, who had a binder about how to handle patient problems that did not include anything about Section 1557, Frances had no place in her workflow for rights or discrimination as patient problems. The preexisting CMS process completely covers over what might be distinctive about a Section 1557 civil rights grievance.

CLINICAL VERSUS NONCLINICAL: HOW PROFESSIONAL HIERARCHIES MAKE DISCRIMINATION DISAPPEAR

The second concept in the patient experience framework, the clinical versus non-clinical distinction, is closely related. This distinction goes beyond the CMS guidelines and reflects the workplace hierarchy between doctors and everyone else as well as the risk hierarchy that places medical mistakes at the top and interpersonal gaffes or service problems at the bottom. As grievance handlers described it, grievances usually have to do with quality of care (e.g., believing that the patient was discharged prematurely) or billing issues, while complaints usually pertain to the quality of services surrounding care, such as food, wait times, or facilities, such as, "I asked for a turkey sandwich and they brought me chicken," or personal interactions, such as, "I think the doctor was rude because they didn't shake my husband's hand" (examples our interviewees described).

An exchange between the interviewer and June, the compliance manager for a system of Federally Qualified Health Centers or FQHCs, about "customer complaints" illustrates the distinctions drawn between clinical and nonclinical complaints:

> *June:* We work with the Chief Medical Officer (CMO) to figure out what we do with the complaint if the complaint revolves around treatment issues. If the complaint is something like "The organization won't let me bring my service dog," then that complaint usually comes to me. And I try to resolve it [laughs].
>
> *Interviewer:* How come that kind of complaint comes to you?
>
> *June:* Because the CMO wouldn't deal with that. So as complaints get, you know, bumped up the chain, after the site manager says to the patient, "Well, this is our policy and this is why and this is what the law says," if the patient is still unhappy, then I'm the one who will talk to them or somebody at the compliance team.
>
> *Interviewer:* So the CMO would talk about care specific issues and you will deal with everything else.
>
> *June:* Sure. With all the other stuff that's not related to care.

In this exchange, June uses a complaint about bringing a service animal into the organization as an example to illustrate the distinction between more serious clinical problems that get "bumped up the chain" and lower status, nonclinical complaints. June interprets the presence of the service animal as a nonclinical issue ("not related to care"), and perhaps one that is frivolous, judging by her laughter. But what if a person cannot get treatment because they cannot bring their service dog? The provision of care appears to be contingent on the exclusion of the service animal—a disability civil rights issue—but the distinction between what is a clinical or treatment issue that only doctors can address versus what is another kind of problem better relegated to other staff obscures that connection. One implication of the complaint versus grievance distinction is that CMS guidelines erase civil rights regulations. Seeing civil rights violations was supposed to be a new part of someone's job as the Section 1557 coordinator, but it joins the low-status work of handling complaints rather than being brokered over to higher-status recognition that may have come through treating civil rights problems as real legal risks or harms to patient care.[21] "Dealing with" these lower-status patient problems is feminized emotional administrative labor, diminished on multiple dimensions.

As June's explanation suggests, the bifurcation between clinical and nonclinical problems has the effect of diminishing civil rights claims in a few different ways. First, if a complaint involves a physician, it is removed from the purview of grievance handlers. Uniformly, grievance handlers described a hierarchical system in which only doctors disciplined other doctors, who are unreachable by the lower-level administrators who hold these patient experience positions. The chief medical officer, the senior physician who has the power to rebuke other doctors, "wouldn't deal with" a complaint about service dog accessibility or "all the stuff that's not related to care." Not surprisingly, the patient experience framework reinscribes the status hierarchies within the hospital, elevating "care" up and away from the realm of health care rights issues, which are imagined as trying to placate unhappy people, not delivering medical care. The legal department, a separate professional sphere from the patient experience department, is where hospital attorneys focus on risks such as possible malpractice claims from physician conduct. This bifurcation means that rights and harms from clinical care are in another domain away from civil rights issues, as if a clinical care problem could not be a civil rights problem too. The status hierarchy is also highly gendered; nearly all our grievance handlers are women and chief medical officers are more likely to be men. The care labor of soothing grievances is feminized and lower status, enacted as cleaning up the less pressing interpersonal problems of the medical encounter.

Mary, a patient relations manager at a hospital in a small city in Michigan, employs the clinical, nonclinical distinction to pull clinical care almost entirely away from human interaction. She explained how grievances map onto clinical care problems and interactions with patients map onto her domain in patient complaints. "The two biggies are the grievance, nongrievance, and that is the clinical versus the human interaction," she said. "Those are the two big categories." "Human interaction," Mary continued, "would be things like diversity. Like if a patient perceives that their color or their sexual orientation or their religious orientation is being held against them or affecting their care or something, we subcategorize all of those things [in the complaint system] so that we can break them out." "The clinical piece," she continued, "that's where that's where you get into, you know, 'They poked me too many times,' 'The doctor misdiagnosed me,' you know." These distinctions were common among the grievance handlers we interviewed.

This picture of clinical care is odd because doctors have human interactions, misdiagnoses could be the result of discrimination by doctors, and diversity among doctors matters too. The animating idea of Section 1557 was that addressing discrimination in health care could produce better health outcomes. Yet, here we see Mary articulating a division of labor that assigns her "human interaction," which is the domain for which she possesses a tool kit and which is open to her action, unlike the highly regulated and bounded realm of clinical care that she cannot reach or act within. If civil rights violations were perpetrated by doctors, grievance handlers could not manage them, so they respond by conceptualizing rights problems as distinct from the clinical and lump them in with every other type of complaint they hear. Medical malpractice incidents, by contrast, are routed to hospital attorneys through risk management. Even though risk management and patient experience are sometimes professionally close and some people had both of these terms in their titles, they performed a similar sorting that replicated the status hierarchies: doctors could make clinical mistakes that could cause big, important legal problems while patient complaints about their experiences would be handled by almost entirely nonlegal administrative professionals. Their tools—permitting venting, explaining that there was no bad intent, apologizing without accepting blame—work to demobilize possible rights claims.

THE DROP-DOWN MENUS
IN GRIEVANCE TRACKING SOFTWARE

Karen describes the software her large Michigan hospital uses to track problems: "It has very specific drop-downs where any employee can go in at any time of the day and place a complaint, a compliment, into that system." Then the system uses "auto-firing algorithms" to alert people in departments mentioned in the entry. "It's like forwarding an email," she explains. These socio-technical systems sort, alert, and remind grievance handlers as they do the work of moving along and resolving complaints. The software classifies patient problems in two main ways: (1) what kind of problem and (2) where in the organization it happened. These stories are about improving quality and safety by seeing problems and apportioning blame. The first and most important categorical division that tells "what kind," reflected in everything from the software itself to the organization of the professions within healthcare, is between the patient experience side and the clinical or risk side of problem management. Debra, a nurse and patient relations manager at a Catholic hospital in Alabama, explains the bifurcation:

Well, there's two sides to [our] event reporting system. One is the safety side, which would be, like if the patient fell out of the bed, or if patient got a wrong medication dose. Or any type of event that was an unforeseen thing that could impact the patient clinically. The other side of the event reporting system is called the feedback side. And that's my side. That's where you would enter complaints, grievances, inquiries, suggestions, that kind of thing.

Potential civil rights claims fall under the personal, the experiential, and the nonmedical side, which is lower in status and maintained by a cadre of patient experience specialists who are highly responsive yet rarely able to do much of anything to remedy a rights violation. The clinical side is the risk management side, watching for possible medical mistakes that could blow up into lawsuits. The feedback side is most concerned with patient satisfaction scores, while the risk side is most concerned with the law's external and more threatening forces. Civil rights claims thus become demobilized legally, with literally no place in the drop-down menus that most grievance handlers described. A few reported adding an option called Section 1557, but overwhelmingly the categories described have no obvious relation to any civil rights category, identity, or cognizable harm, and as I show, many grievance handlers resisted and denied this use of their system.

Many interviewees mentioned tracking software by RL Solutions, now RLDatix. This private vendor has over 5,000 institutional customers across nineteen countries.[22] It covers seventy-five percent of incident reporting in the UK health system, and in the United States its customers include the Veterans Administration (the largest US health system), the Cleveland Clinic, Mass General, Duke, Johns Hopkins, and New York-Presbyterian.[23] The 2020 RL Solutions brochure tells hospitals to "[u]se your data to prioritize patient advocacy and service excellence initiatives . . . [for] better patient satisfaction scores and lower readmission rates, which drives better healthcare reimbursement." The software reflects the separation of its "Feedback and Risk modules," by offering "integration . . . to minimize rework, for example, if a grievance reveals that an incident took place." An incident is a risk management event that could trigger a fine or a lawsuit, while a grievance may remain simply "Feedback." Nancy told us how she uses their RL Solutions software:

I receive on the average of maybe twelve [complaints] a month. There's predetermined categories. There is a drop-down box in this software that I was talking about that does classify, say, if somebody, you know, lost something, lost an item, then that goes under service recovery. Replace item, whatever. If they call angry and they tell us to do something, I will put that in and close it right away. And service recovery and facilitation. So those are your classifications. [What kinds of complaints are common?] Um, treatment by staff. A lot of it is not giving the medication that they want. Length of wait in the emergency room is a big one. Patients are not wanting to pay their deductible. Wait time and treatment by staff is our two largest complaints.

Federally Qualified Health Center (FQHC) managers were more aware of their patients' vulnerable statuses, such as being low income or trans. However, they were not any more likely to have ways of recognizing civil rights violations set up in their work routines. They also use similar grievance tracking software. June, who handles complaints at an FQHC, describes the categories they use for classifying complaints:

> Was this about a prescription? Was it about an office visit? Is it about the site? Was it about communication? So themes kind of fall in those bigger categories. Did they have to wait too long? Were they treated rudely? So we have lots of themes. [Are there any themes that are specific to Section 1557?] No.

Jan, another FQHC grievance handler, gave very specific details about their complaint categories and also differentiated between "patient concerns, like let's say somebody slipped in the parking lot" and "clinical concerns":

> [Is there any way you could tell me the categories?] Let's see . . . [reading from software interface] For just general patient concerns, it can be categories under access to appointment. Billing. Confidentiality. Clinical care. Delay in referral. Facility. Medical records. Interpreter. Lab diagnostic results. Narcotics. No return phone call. Parking lot. Prescription. Staff discourteous or disrespectful. Telephone system. And the last one is wait time. I believe it's just one general generic policy [to address all these categories].

If a patient were to complain about discrimination in the form of harassment from a care provider, for example, it would become "staff discourteous or disrespectful."

The selection of a category that the problem "is about" is content-free and seemingly neutral. If one is waiting longer, not getting return phone calls, not getting appointment spots, and so on because of one's identity, then that critical detail would be buried in the notes or fall away entirely. We never heard of an "about" category called racism, harassment, misgendering, or anything similar. As we discovered when we probed for the intersection of patient identity data and problem reporting, there is a strong norm against particularizing patient care and satisfaction problems by civil rights identity category. Jessica, a patient relations specialist at a Catholic hospital in Michigan, explains how discrimination complaints fit into the tracking software for problems of all kinds:

> And then so within MIDAS [their tracking software], there are some general categories that things are sort of classified into. So if it's a staff complaint you would mark it as staff, and then you could further delineate beyond that what specifically it is. Is it, you know, a communication issue? Is it a discharge issue? Is it a wait time issue? A lot of those different categories. We do track like a discrimination complaint, or an ADA complaint, or there's also those buckets of lost belongings complaint. You know, food complaints, facility complaints, or is it a complaint made against a person, so a staff member, a clinician, or a physician.

Jessica moves so quickly from "discrimination" to "lost belongings" in her list that it is clear that discrimination is one of many problems in a jumble.

Sorting this jumble is important because it shows where in the organization the problems arise. Distinguishing types of problems (civil rights versus lost belongings, perhaps) is less important than distinguishing places. We asked Karen about how she analyzes patient satisfaction survey data. She explained that they do it "multiple, multiple ways." They create a score card for each unit with aggregated comments for that point of entry. "Did the patient come through the ER, what was that score?" Karen filters their data by CMS patient satisfaction survey results, day of the week, time of day, work shift, diagnosis group, and provider. "There's a number of ways that we, you know, slice and dice the data," she says. The patients are unknowing pointers to spots of poor care, and they matter when there are enough of their complaints (lumped together) to focus in on problematic sites for healthcare administrators.

Grievance handlers care about certain markers of good care that are internally meaningful to the organization but would not be likely to correspond to a patient's description of a civil rights violation. Jamie described breaking up scoring by patient race or sex as "irrelevant" because "as a whole, I need to move those scores." She elaborated:

> [I was just wondering if you guys ever analyze scores on the basis of sex or race or any of these identity categories.] You can run the report and base it off of race, sex, gender. I don't believe there's any like transgender checkbox. But as far as me running a report like that? No, because it wouldn't be, um, statistically significant for the results in the reports I'm trying to run. It's not what I'm looking for. I'm looking for data about how to improve our scores in different domains such as hospital responsiveness, nursing communication, and medication communication. So to break it up by gender or break it up by orientation, it would be irrelevant, because as a whole, I need to move these scores.

We also asked Erica, an African American working at a Catholic hospital in Michigan, if she tracks patient complaints by race, gender, or age. She replied that she usually does not look at them that way because she does not feel that those categories are important. "It's overall care that we provide for the patient, the individual. To me it doesn't matter if it's a woman, male, child, grandmother. It's a patient who came in for help, and it's our job to do that for them," she says.

We saw in the first story that there is no drop-down for problems labelled civil rights or discrimination problems in the techno-bureaucratic practices of patient complaint handling and that the focus is on places that produce a jumble of problems, not distinctions between types of problems that include civil rights violations and harassment alongside lost dentures. Here we see a second story, about how the homogenized individualization of the best care for every patient erases attention to groups who experience more healthcare discrimination. Every patient is the same in the sense that they all need the best care, and thus differentiating by identity categories (are trans patients treated worse?) does not make sense. The

Joint Commission, one of the major accreditors of hospitals, required hospitals beginning in 2023 to do what Jamie and Erica said they did not need to do at the time of our interviews: stratify their quality and safety data by patient demographic characteristics to see disparities by group.[24] Rather than coming in as a civil rights obligation, these ways of seeing health inequality in patient data will come through accreditation requirements.

Most people denied receiving complaints from trans people, which is not necessarily surprising given the small numbers in the population. When someone complained in a way that seemed to mirror the grievance handler's own approach in minimizing conflict, these interactions could be much more valued. Trans people who presented as authentic selves on journeys rather than assertive rights-claimers were able to put the grievance handler at ease, an example of patient impression management.[25] June, a compliance officer at an FQHC in Michigan, described a positive interaction with a transgender patient who "never talked about feeling discriminated against or disrespected," but instead "just said, it would be more comfortable for me if my case manager would refer to me by the name that I prefer." She explained that the patient had been "very wonderful in this situation in explaining why this was so important to them, and where they were in their journey." Describing it as "actually a really good situation," June concludes that "when people have complaints, it doesn't have to be a situation where you become adversaries."

GRIEVANCE HANDLING AS CUSTOMER SERVICE

Grievance handlers are hired, trained, and train others in a customer service model of patient interaction. Seventeen of our interviewees explicitly used the language of customer service, and even those that did not use the term described working with similar aims, tools, training, and organizational structures. (As the language of customer service emerged clearly in the interviews, we asked more follow-up questions about it and elicited more detail over the course of the research.) As Sheila explained, "Handling patient complaints is the ultimate customer service job." She adds that her side job in the hospitality industry, where she has to deal with "crazy things," helps her in her hospital job. When asked how she came to be named the Section 1557 coordinator at her nonprofit Michigan hospital, Erica replied, "Because of the position that I hold as a patient advocate, they felt that patient relations—so kind of customer service personnel—that I should be the one to be the holder of it, because, again, if anybody has any complaints, concerns, or compliments I'm the one they bring 'em to and I address 'em and try to remediate what we can do to satisfy the customers."

As we noted, specific financial and legal incentives drive this patient-as-customer focus in contemporary healthcare delivery. Grievance handlers cared very much about their institutions' HCAHPS survey scores and using their data systems to pinpoint problem areas. These satisfaction tracking tool kits enable them to gather valuable information and alert others to problems that this system can reveal. "We're always trying to improve our patient satisfaction scores," Sheila told us. "And somebody might come to me and say, like, 'Hey, we're trying to do things better on med-surg. So tell me all the complaints from last year about med-surg,' so I can sort it like that and just give them the report for their department." HCAHPS surveys and CMS grievance procedures were overwhelmingly the most salient contributors to grievance handlers' legal consciousness because of their possible financial penalties.

Grievance handlers directly associated customer service and nondiscrimination, as Brenda explained when asked what training was available: "We have an extensive customer service training as far as nondiscrimination." Casey, whose job title is patient relations coordinator at a large hospital in California, also replied that "we did trainings for employees on customer service, patient experience type of trainings." June elaborated how Section 1557 is about both rights and customer service when directly asked. "[So do you see Section 1557 being about rights or about customer service or both or . . . ?] About both. It's about people's rights to get treatment, and it's about the organization's responsibility to provide their customers that service in a way that's meaningful to them. [You mean both to the patients.] To the patients." We asked if there were other model policies that influenced Section 1557 implementation, and it was common to hear that nothing new had to be done. As Alondra, a program manager in a harassment and discrimination response office for a large health system, told us, her hospital has "always been sensitive to this" and that is "covered in Customer Service Standards."

THE COOLING-OUT TOOLKIT

Constructing patient experience problems as customer service issues leads staff to emphasize interpersonal issues and to construct patient problems as communication failures. Many respondents chalked up patient complaints to miscommunication. Glenda, trained as a medical secretary and working as staff safety and customer relations coordinator at a small hospital in rural Michigan, exemplified this tendency when she described communication as the most common complaint she encounters.

> It's most difficult to be able to hear and understand what the individual is saying [because of] human nature. You are always thinking about your one step ahead of the other individual and not slowing down that interaction and truly listening. Because sometimes you're not able to, especially in an emergent situation, you know, you're needing to act swiftly with a patient's life. So a lot of it is miscommunication, misunderstanding, you know.

Carla, working on diversity issues and patient experiences in Michigan, acknowledges that "we all have those biases" but, reflecting on a 1557 issue that she handled around "identity," thought that "it may have been a communication issue, a misunderstanding." Meanwhile, Catherine, a risk management worker at a rural hospital in Michigan, made a similar comment, explaining,

> I believe that many of the complaints come down to communication. The complaint may start out being, you know, the doctor didn't listen to my problem or I didn't get what I wanted. Or it could even be, like, am I being billed for this? Or, you know, I'm being discriminated against because I'm a senior citizen. And no matter what that verbiage that the patient comes with, I find that it's communication skills that have caused the complaint to happen.

Here, Catherine explicitly includes discrimination complaints among those often typically resulting from communication failures.

Grievance handlers typically recognized that their job required a certain performance of concern and trust in the patient's account. Our respondents articulated varying degrees of skepticism towards patient complaints and invoked multiple strategies for how to react to a complaining patient. For instance, Debra described her reliance on what she termed the "blameless apology" to ease patient complaints and accomplish "service recovery," an industry term for resolving patient problems. As she put it, she "lets them spew" and then apologizes but without accepting blame for the hospital. Meanwhile, Sheila exhibited even greater skepticism towards patients. She laughed when describing a patient who had asked for a discount based on a delayed surgery. "So like I had a guy who came [laughing] to me this week and wanted a discount on his bill because his surgery was delayed for three hours and he thinks that no one told he and his wife that there was going to be a delay, when I know that the doctor told them, the nurse told them. I think they were just like so anxious." She described how she performs acceptance of the patient's narrative, while privately questioning or rejecting its validity.

> You have to just treat it as real. Like you, you have to just treat everything like that. I have to treat all kinds of things like those people who insist that nobody told them their surgery was delayed. I mean, I have to sit and listen to 'em. But at the time, when I'm listening to them, I don't know the whole story. Because I still have to go talk to the nurse that was caring for 'em. I have to talk to the doctor. And so I have to listen and then I have to still write an I'm-sorry letter, as if they're right. Because I can't say you're wrong. Like I can't.

Catherine, Debra, and Sheila describe patient perceptions as malleable and inaccurate, something to be corrected in their process with a combination of blameless apologies and soothing redescriptions of intent. Sheila reflected on the emotional work of being a grievance handler in a smaller hospital. Perhaps one of the reasons she was willing to talk extensively about her experiences and feelings about patients even when they were not flattering was because she lacks a professional community to share her own complaints. "In bigger hospitals they have whole teams who deal with those things and you have people to vent to about it," she said.

The previous examples illustrated the way in which grievance handlers diminished patient frustration by letting patients vent and by validating or appearing to validate their concerns. In addition to these tool kit items, grievance handlers also described discursive strategies they would use to help a patient see their experience differently when handling a discrimination complaint. Catherine describes her reframing process in the following way:

> [Y]ou know, that adage, you know, there are three sides to every story. So [laughs], I, you know, in resolving these issues, I really do try to work interpretively, so that one party understands what the motivation of the other party was, and kind of see the conversation through the lens of the other person. So there's a better understanding of what the intent was, rather than how they felt about it. And that goes back to the whole idea of communication, you know. Like being the root of all complaints, how you say something can really change the outcome. And asking the one single question of, you know, is there anything else that I can help you with? Is there anything else you need to know? And giving the patient the opportunity to reflect on that. Their perception of the entire encounter will be different.

Here, Catherine describes a performance of deference that gives the patient the impression that they are in control of the situation. The main goal seems to be to convince the patient that the other person's intentions were benign after all.

This reinterpretation tool assumes that the patient is mistaken in their belief that they have been discriminated against. Debra interpreted patient complaints based on race, poverty, or fatness as misinterpretations, even as she conceded that there was plenty of racial prejudice in Alabama.

> I've heard them say, "Well, you know, it's because I'm so big," or whatever. But those are very rare. More often, you're going to get the "I think it's because I'm Black," or "I think it's because I'm not insured." You know. Or "I think it's because I have Medicaid." But in reality, it's not. You know, we live in the Deep South, and, you know, there's people, there's going to be prejudice, there's going to be people who feel like they're discriminated against. But in reality, I have not seen anything like that. I mean, I know it exists. It's got to exist.

When Debra describes a patient's family member who "felt like the staff was making fun of [the patient]" about his weight (as he was being helped into a car by multiple staff people), she refuses to accept the veracity of the complaint because of her belief that her staff were only trying to help. "One of the directors, he's a very, very kind director, he said something that was misinterpreted and I can't even remember what the comment was. But one of the family members felt like there was some comment that was degrading. But in the end it turned out that that wasn't the case. What it was is they mis—they misinterpreted something somebody said." Debra attributes the claim to misinterpretation by "people that are not particularly educated" when really "it's not as bad as one would think, you know." She concludes that "there's a lot of people that immediately want to scream racial discrimination when there is none."

Because many situations may occur with only the patient and a caregiver in the room, we asked how grievance handlers resolve opposing accounts as they conduct their internal investigation. Karen's approach assumes that conflicting accounts of reality could be true:

> I think it involves really having conversations with all parties who were a witness to that conversation. And trying to understand where each person was coming from. I kind of liken it to, if you've ever seen those pictures, and if you look at it one way it's a witch, and if you look at it another way, it's [something else], right? So I see it one way, you see it another way. It's the same picture though, isn't it? It's depending on how we each view that. And so I think we have to acknowledge and respect that each of us comes to the table with a different understanding of whatever that occasion or that conversation or that encounter was, and try to discern from that what is the truth.

Nearly every person acknowledged, however, that when it was a patient's word against a staff person's with no other witnesses, there would be very little they could do. Evidence that the same care provider has been the subject of multiple complaints could lead to action against that employee, and employees lower on the hierarchy than doctors were more likely to be described as receiving discipline or remedial action. Doctors only receive rebukes from the doctor at the top of the hierarchy, the chief medical officer, and are not subject to discipline from lower-level staff in patient relations.

One cannot let on to the patients that their stories are not credible. Casey from patient relations in an urban California hospital shows how grievance handlers privately disbelieve complaints while outwardly assigning validity to the patient's perception, which still presents a problem for a hospital. "Oftentimes a patient will say they feel like something is based on their race, sometimes on their gender identification. And when we dig down into it and investigate it and talk to people involved, that wasn't, didn't really, come into play. It's of course kind of hard sometimes to prove or disprove. I always take the opportunity as a reminder and a learning experience for everyone involved at how things could be perceived. And whatever the patient's perception is their reality, and so that's how we address it." Jordan, a former McDonald's manager turned patient relations manager at a Michigan hospital, viewed patient perceptions as a reality to be dealt with. "If a person calls me and they said, hey, this happened, and I felt this person was rude and whatever, I let the manager know and they address it with that person. Because the patient's perception is a reality." Casey and Jordan's phrasing, repeated throughout our conversations with grievance handlers, draws directly from Jason Wolf's patient experience professional training materials. "Experience remains beholden to one test," Wolf argues. "It is only as true as the *perceptions* of those having the experience."[26] The patient's perception is reality. The phrase means that the patient's perception is the grievance handler's reality for their rights-work job, not that the discrimination the patient described is reality.

The people in healthcare organizations whose job it is to recognize and address civil rights violations against patients—the Section 1557 grievance handlers—are poorly equipped to do it well. They are passive recorders of what could be transgender discrimination cloaked in other terms like "rude staff" or "miscommunication." Overall, across contexts, grievance handlers use very similar work tools in similar ways. These tools are not designed to obfuscate civil rights claims; they are designed to flag and push along ordinary problems while alerting administrators to legal risk. But they create stories of nonproblems through lack of a place in the drop-down menu, through cooling-out practices, through relativizing and dismissing patient experience, and through the homogenizing story of the best care for every patient regardless of identity. This refusal to consider identity traits as meaningful is an enactment of so-called color blindness, in which doing justice to someone is supposedly accomplished by ignoring their salient identity traits. Under this view, every patient is equally special and none of them are more deserving of specific recognition than any other. Concern for health disparities in subgroups by race or sex completely disappears under this homogenizing logic.

Additionally, the division between clinical incidents that comprise real risks and feedback that endangers patient survey scores forces an awkward division between poor treatment or harassment and the real health damage that can occur, perhaps later on or because the person does not return to care. It is focused on what regulations make important to hospitals, but it does not reflect a coherent view of how discrimination might harm people's health. The hope was that Section 1557 would address health disparities under the assumption that certain groups were receiving worse care or being mistreated and that a rights-based remedy could help undo that. This chapter showed how some commonplace forms of rights denialism that have been well documented in other contexts have unique appearances in healthcare. Rights denialism combines with the dynamics of color-blind racism,[27] encoded and reproduced through the socio-technical systems of problem management in hospitals.

Health care civil rights are refracted through the everyday professional practices of the people who receive patient complaints. The first step toward mobilizing a right is raising the denial of it as a problem. Section 1557 specified particular people to receive reports of those problems and thus to be the first person on the ground to reframe and respond to problems. Healthcare settings are complex sites that already have structures and incentives in place to interpret patient problems, and civil rights violations are not the most important problems there. We already knew that unconscious bias and outright stigmatization were significant problems in healthcare settings, but I have shown that there are other structural barriers to robust understandings of civil rights. These are the outcomes of other policies, such as trying to incentivize quality patient care by centering the patient experience, and they are not self-consciously opposed to trans health rights or civil rights in general. But the patient experience framework becomes demobilizing for rights through its professional norms, priorities, language, software programs, workflows, and status within the organization. The next level is the mesolevel of health insurance plans. This level moves to a more professionalized and remote context for disputes over health care civil rights as trans and non-binary people wrangle with the insurance bureaucracies both on paper and through intermediaries such as doctors and therapists.

3

How Insurance Companies Broker Health Care Civil Rights

Phoenix, a non-binary Michigan resident, described to us how difficult it was to obtain gender-affirming procedures covered by their insurance: "It was I'd say two years before I can finally get [my insurance company] to agree [to pay for surgery]. But it was just continuous letter writing after letter writing after letter writing. I have been suicidal, I have been depressive, and then they finally said, okay, we'll go with it." Why, if Phoenix's surgery was supposed to be covered by insurance, was it so hard to get?

Michigan's laws are formally supportive: state law prohibits exclusions of transgender care in private insurance plans, and state Medicaid policy explicitly affirms coverage. Health care civil rights apply to health insurance coverage and, at least under Democratic administrations, do not allow categorical exclusions for gender-affirming care. A categorical exclusion is a clause in a health plan that broadly excludes whole categories of care, often in vague and outdated language (such as no coverage for "sex changes"). Nonetheless, insurers are still allowed to use management techniques such as prior authorization and the medical necessity standard for coverage, and civil rights laws do not specify exactly what must be covered.[1] Gender-affirming care cannot be broadly denied as experimental or cosmetic, that is, but individuals are not guaranteed to receive specific procedures as a civil right. Denials must be a for a legitimate, nondiscriminatory reason, but lots of techniques for denials are permitted. As Miranda Yaver has documented, insurance denials are a significant and inequitable barrier to health care for many people without the resources to slog through an appeal.[2] So although Section 1557 of the Affordable Care Act (ACA), a patchwork of state law insurance protections, and *Bostock* provide formal legal protections for trans people using health insurance, insurance companies retain power to slow or deny coverage with tools that they are experts at using.

This chapter examines how health care civil rights to nondiscrimination in insurance coverage are refracted through insurance companies. One gets health care in the United States from one's insurance company as much as from a doctor. As I explained in chapter 1, health insurance is a complex mix of public and private support and subsidy that is regulated in a fragmented and shifting way. What I call the medical necessity framework is the primary way that health care civil rights are refracted through health insurance companies' business practices. Tara Gonsalves points out that medical necessity determinations are also "a deployment of medical authority and a classification grounded in normative understandings of embodied gender."[3] One may have a health insurance policy and a right to inclusive coverage for gender-affirming care, but the right still goes through the bureaucracy and business model of the American health insurance company most of the time. Health insurance companies shape gender-identity nondiscrimination rights quite literally, that is, by deciding what surgical interventions are necessary to change faces and bodies. Legal categories meant to protect on the basis of traits such as gender and race always also shape what is acceptable within those categories and then offer protections back to those who fit sympathetically.[4]

My focus here is on the common form of health insurance that working age Americans have, which is a plan sponsored by their employer. Most trans people have some type of health insurance, but they still report trouble using it to get the care they need, and trans people of color report even more barriers to care.[5] Eighty-six percent of respondents to the 2015 Transgender Health Survey had health insurance, with fifty-three percent of respondents reporting coverage under an employer-sponsored health plan.[6] When trans health care civil rights are successful in health insurance, that usually means that there is a law in place that mandates coverage for gender-affirming care or at least prohibits a categorical exclusion.

Health insurance expansion has been the most significant win for trans health care civil rights by far. One review found that ninety-seven percent of plans in a sample of 1,057 ACA silver marketplace options from 161 insurers in thirty-eight states had removed transgender exclusions in 2020, compelled by the Obama administration's Section 1557 nondiscrimination regulations, which banned categorical exclusions.[7] Categorical exclusions had been quite commonplace in health plans prior to the ACA. Access to gender-affirming care in a primary care setting as well as other health priorities like expanded HIV testing and PrEP access improved dramatically after 2014, all attributed to Section 1557.[8] Having some kind of coverage is one thing, but successfully using it turns out to be quite another. A health plan that does not mention gender-affirming care but does not have an exclusion is hard to interpret. Fully-spelled-out affirmative coverage is the best-case scenario, but it can still be hard to use for all one's needs.

This middle range of rights in health insurance is quite different from the patient experience level at the hospital. Insurers responded rapidly and concretely to explicit legal requirements to remove exclusions. When states make gender-affirming care for minors or adults illegal, however, no provider will bill for it in that state. The medical organization level is interpersonal and governed by preexisting norms of managing problems that are difficult to change, but it could also be a site for norms of recognition and respectful provision of care to take hold that may carry on despite the churning law at the national level. Insurance billing requires diagnosis and thus remains tied to medicalization, which is not an encouraging basis for trans rights claiming.[9] Even so, broader access to health care and insurance generally under the ACA and Medicaid expansions—civil rights enforcement aside—has been critically important for lower-income people and those without access to generous employer coverage. Trans and non-binary people need all the same health care that everyone else needs, after all. The point is that insurance cuts different ways. Successes are bigger and "stickier," meaning more permanent, when they come, which is why I argue in the conclusion that nationally available health coverage that includes gender-affirming care should be a top priority.

THE CHALLENGES OF RESEARCH ON HEALTH INSURANCE

We know relatively little about health insurance coverage in the private market because corporations are not required to share details of their employee benefits publicly. There is no law that says that all health insurance products sold in the United States must meet certain standards of transparency, content, or accessibility (though the ACA's requirements for the Summary of Benefits and Coverage for group plans is a notable exception). Benefit plan documents do not have to be uniformly accessible, say, in an open, searchable database that researchers and consumers could use to understand what health insurance looks like across all market segments and types of coverage. State insurance regulators require firms to file their fully insured health plans, but only the plans that they regulate and then often in obscure databases in offices across all fifty states. Many firms and carriers post their health plan documents on their websites voluntarily, but others place them behind a login for beneficiaries only.

There is an opaque federal government form that health plan sponsors with more than one hundred beneficiaries must submit to the Department of Labor, on which they describe in general terms what benefits they offer that are regulated by the Employee Retirement Income Security Act of 1974, but nearly half of businesses neglect to file it at all and many file it late.[10] The form, called Form 5500, does not explicitly ask if a plan is self-insured, so the Department of Labor had to commission an algorithm to analyze the form to make a best guess about whether a company's plans are fully insured, self-insured, or mixed-insured. The Department of Labor estimates that there are about 2.5 million self-insured plans covering 133 million people in the United States governed under the Employee Retirement Income Security Act, but only 81,800 covering eighty-three million participants filed a form at all, and less than half of those indicated offering a health insurance plan.[11] Sixty-five percent of covered American workers have a self-insured health plan.[12] The ACA requires an annual report to Congress on self-insured health plans, and the secretary noted the "limited scope" of data, "complexities involved in interpreting it," and "substantial uncertainty" in its estimates.[13]

Research into health insurance coverage has focused on insurance market segments where documents are available, such as those on the Affordable Care Act marketplaces, Medicare, and Medicaid. Surveys of other private insurance offerings often do not analyze the actual insurance plan (the consumer-facing document), relying on phone calls to insurers and web searches to gather insurance company information.[14] Advocacy organizations such as the Human Rights Campaign (HRC) have been very important in filling the gap of knowledge for LGBT people with their Healthcare Equality and Workplace Equality ratings,[15] but these are self-reported surveys without outside scrutiny of documents. Health services researchers can study patterns of health insurance use through claims databases, but those only reveal instances when the insurer pays a claim and for what, not the actual terms of the health benefit plan or rejected claims.[16]

It is shocking that corporate health insurance plans for employees—the way most working Americans get their health care and for which companies receive billions of dollars in tax breaks—are so poorly regulated that we cannot systematically, publicly analyze what they offer and how well they are financed. There are many sites of ignorance in US policy and government because of federalism, local control of important functions like education and criminal justice, and the way our administrative state evolved. We do not know how many toddlers shoot themselves with guns they find, how many unarmed people are shot by law enforcement officers, or what is in most health insurance plans. Our databases are scattered and unable to speak to each other—for instance, we do not have a national immunization database, but rather ones at the state level that are not interoperable with each other. Researchers have painstakingly built databases to understand seemingly critical questions like what percentage of US children experience caregiver involvement with the criminal justice system. (It is thirty-nine percent overall and over sixty percent for Black, Native, and low-income children.[17]) As I'll argue in the conclusion, we need a fully transparent public data source for all health insurance plans sold in the United States with uniform requirements for clarity, standardization, readability, and accessibility in addition to substantive reforms to make what is for sale equitable and open to all.

CORPORATE SELF-INSURED HEALTH PLANS IN THE CIVIL RIGHTS PATCHWORK

I have described our health care civil rights system as a patchwork layered on top of a patchwork. What I mean is that we have thinly described, minimally enforced, powerfully opposed rights on top of other long-standing structures and practices that are themselves broken across jurisdictions, underfunded, uncoordinated, and technologically behind. None of this is anyone's nefarious plan necessarily. Nonetheless, this patchwork combined with our ignorance about insurance in particular advantages some and disadvantages others, and it makes it impossible to properly understand important costs, harms, and risks in our society that we otherwise misattribute or simply never think about. Critically, it enables blaming individuals rather than structures for problems when we cannot see and understand what the structures—private health insurance, criminal justice, gun laws and liability protections for gun manufacturers—are doing and how much power they have.

My team worked to improve what we know about coverage for gender-affirming care by coding the language of 435 self-insured health insurance plans offered in 2019 by forty major American corporations.[18] I negotiated access to data from a private healthcare consulting firm, Leverage Global Consulting. Leverage has developed a proprietary database that contains insurance plan offerings and coverage from private and public insurance market segments. They have pulled documents from public filings and websites to assemble a picture of health plan coverage for nearly all covered lives in the United States. Health plan enrollees receive a document called a Summary Plan Description from their employer annually. This document is usually very long (more than one hundred pages) and explains what is covered and what is not covered, among many other legally required details. These are the documents my team used to understand coverage. We hand-coded the plans to find what recommended elements of coverage they offered for gender-affirming care and published the results and over 1,400 plan documents with open access.[19]

Some of these corporate health plans excluded health benefits for gender-affirming care entirely, often in outdated language ("sex reassignment") that was probably in the health plans for years. Ten companies out of this group of forty (twenty-five percent) offered at least one healthcare contract with a total exclusion on coverage for gender-affirming care. The companies vary based on their seeming commitment to their exclusion, with some showing the exclusion in one hundred percent of the health plans we found while others seem to exclude strategically, with only certain health plans—perhaps for some groups of employees or some geographic areas—including an exclusion and others lacking it. Health plans also used generic language ("cosmetic, experimental, or investigational") or gave specific gender-affirming exclusions. Most exclusions we found were related to facial gender-confirmation surgeries and hair removal, which are critically important to gender-affirming care.[20] Surgeons cannot operate before hair removal is complete, and for some people, particularly trans women, facial features that do not match one's gender identity can lead to harassment and even attack.

Outside pressure to be an LGBT-friendly company has been important in creating voluntary corporate change, but we wondered if trans-specific interests in health care were adequately recognized in the most important ratings from the Human Rights Campaign (HRC). We compared our category rankings to the Human Rights Campaign's rankings of the same companies on the 2019 Corporate Equality Index. Only half of the companies (eleven of twenty-one) that scored a top score of one hundred on HRC's rankings had clear coverage for all the health plans in our analysis. Others with a perfect score had silent or ambiguous coverage for gender-affirming care in their plans that we examined. Despite earning an HRC score of one hundred, five companies still offered fifteen health plans with blanket exclusions for coverage for gender-affirming care (Macy's, Marsh McLennan, McKesson Corporation, Stanley Black & Decker, and Symantec), and one company (Stanley Black & Decker) *only* offered health plans in our analysis with exclusions. Finally, three companies with HRC rankings of sixty-five or lower offered at least some health plans with clear coverage for gender-affirming care (Avnet, Costco, and Windstream). While the HRC Equality Index provides important information about LGBT inclusivity overall, this research underscores that a perfect score does not always equate to coverage for gender-affirming care. Scoring trans health care needs with other policies that support gay, lesbian, bisexual, and queer employees obscures the degree to which specific health care needs for trans and non-binary employees are well met.

So far I have argued that it is hard to find out comprehensively what is in corporate self-insured health benefit plans and that even outside indicators are not reliable for understanding gender-affirming-care coverage in particular. It is worth reprising what civil rights law applied to these plans in 2019 as a way of reviewing the patchwork of rights. The Obama trans-inclusive Section 1557 regulations were in place, but they only applied to health care entities like insurance companies who took federal funding. Self-insured corporate plans would not have been covered (and still are not covered) under Section 1557's nondiscrimination clause because the company itself is not a healthcare entity. Fully insured plans created by an insurer that also participates in the ACA marketplaces or otherwise takes federal funding would be covered under Section 1557, by contrast.

Because the plans are an employee benefit and because gender-identity discrimination is sex discrimination under the 2020 *Bostock* ruling, it is likely that trans employees would have a strong Title VII case against exclusions for gender-affirming care in their plans. Since our data come from 2019 plans, the strength of a Title VII claim would have depended on the law by jurisdiction but would have still been a strong claim. Federal antidiscrimination laws like Title VII, Section 1557, and the ADA are not preempted by the Employee Retirement Income Security Act of 1974, the federal law that takes away states' powers to regulate employer-sponsored health benefits, and thus some civil rights protections still apply.[21] If the company takes a discriminatory benefit design from a third-party administrator (TPA) and lets the TPA administer it for them, however, that TPA is liable for violating Section 1557's ban on gender-identity discrimination. But if the discriminatory design originates with the plan sponsor—the self-insured company—then it is not covered by Section 1557 even now because that company is not a health care entity.[22]

Many corporations provide quite generous employee health benefits, though, including all recommended forms of gender-affirming care as well as other benefits that are not required, like in vitro fertilization (IVF). Why extend benefits if one has not been legally required to do so? Companies tend to move together towards similar organizational forms, so expanded coverage required by the ACA for some plans has moved the bar for everyone.[23] There is a strong consensus in the medical community that gender-affirming care is medically necessary.[24] Companies may have been responding to extralegal pressures such as the desire to recruit LGBT employees and to earn high ratings from HRC. They may calculate that gender-affirming services will cost relatively little but be worth the progressive image benefit. Their employees and people they want to hire may demand it. Indeed, the long history of success in expanding sexual orientation nondiscrimination in private company policies without a federal law shows that internal employee organizing for benefits can be successful.[25] Transgender advocacy organizations such as the National Center for Transgender Equality and the Transgender Legal Defense & Education Fund counsel clients to approach their employers directly to extend coverage since this strategy may be much easier than litigation or fighting the insurance company. For self-insured plans that the employer controls entirely, this strategy can be the most efficient.

When health care civil rights are refracted through health insurance plans generally, a lot of different things can happen that reflect different regimes of law and policy that apply to different kinds of insurance. We do not have a way of knowing about a lot of what happens because no one can see it except for the person receiving a denial letter, for example. Bans on coverage through programs like Medicaid, which exist in nine states for adults and three states for minors, are devastating for low-income trans people who do not have employer-sponsored insurance. In those cases, the failure of health care civil rights for trans people is starkly apparent. I wanted to understand how a health care civil right in the form of health insurance coverage for gender-affirming care might work in practice for those who have it. This approach helps us see the close relationship between any health care civil rights regime and our huge, complicated, powerful health insurance industry.

REFRACTING HEALTH CARE RIGHTS THROUGH THE MEDICAL NECESSITY FRAMEWORK

Even if one has a civil right to gender-affirming care, they must navigate their health insurance to get it. My team interviewed twenty-four adults who identify as transgender and/or non-binary, had sought health care to be covered by insurance related to their transgender status in the last two years, had some kind of insurance coverage at the time, and were willing to talk about their insurance coverage in some detail.[26] Notably, the trans and non-binary people interviewed for this chapter had health insurance that ostensibly covered gender-affirming care. Not all trans people seek surgical care, but often they do, and not necessarily to move from one place on the gender binary to the other. Not everyone in this chapter was seeking a surgical intervention, either, though many were. Some interviewees did not have insurance for the care they sought because they were subject to an explicit exclusion. As I discuss in depth in the next chapter, Catholic healthcare institutions strongly resist performing any transgender-related care for both theological and political reasons. Joshua's doctors determined that a mastectomy was medically necessary, but he had to change jobs to get insurance coverage that would cover his care because his Catholic healthcare plan denied coverage. So while trans people have a range of needs and experiences, I'm focused here on a particular type of barrier that is still allowed even with health care civil rights laws in place: the internal wrangling over medical necessity for gender-affirming care. Medical necessity determinations can become the primary site of conflict in benefit plans that are on their face inclusive because, as one surgery scheduler told us, "Benefit exclusions are almost futile to appeal from a provider's standpoint. We can't do anything about that." Even if all categorical exclusions for gender-affirming care in every plan in the country were whisked away, these challenges would remain.

The trans people interviewed for this chapter were mostly properly *recognized* under health care civil rights, but the *provisioning* of those rights still needed to be secured. Although insurers have removed most outright exclusions for gender-transition care, health insurance policy language, interpretation, and implementation of what constitutes medically necessary gender-affirming care still makes insurance hard to use. Many of these difficulties would apply to anyone trying to use coverage for a complex or contested condition, but some are specific to trans people seeking gender-affirming procedures. This chapter reveals not just the power of insurance policy language but also how making insurance claims and getting them paid is a socially contested and negotiated process. The definition, discretion, and disputation around what constitutes medical necessity for gender dysphoria (the official diagnosis for billing purposes) is the primary way that insurance refracts health care civil rights.

The same basic definition of medical necessity appears across the patient-facing document in health plans that offer gender-confirming care and those that exclude it. A standard definition of medically necessary services and supplies (from Cigna's 2019 health plan for Stanley Black & Decker) is: "Medically Necessary Covered Services and Supplies are those determined by the Medical Director to be: required to diagnose or treat an illness, injury, disease or its symptoms; in accordance with generally accepted standards of medical practice; clinically appropriate in terms of type, frequency, extent, site and duration; not primarily for the convenience of the patient, Physician or other health care provider; and rendered in the least intensive setting that is appropriate for the delivery of the services and supplies."[27] This plan explicitly excludes "transsexual surgery, including medical or psychological counseling and hormonal therapy in preparation for, or subsequent to, any such surgery." Adobe's health plan, administered by Aetna, covers gender-affirming care. Their plan's definition of medical necessity is not very different from the Black & Decker health plan above, which fully excludes gender-affirming care. Medically necessary care under this health plan also means what a prudent clinician would do according to generally accepted standards of what is clinically appropriate, not just for convenience, and so on. But just as the words of a statute do not necessarily tell us how the law works in practice, we found that these definitions explain very little about what happens when trans people and their professional allies argue for coverage.

TRANS SELF-ADVOCACY FOR COVERAGE

Malik, who is Black and transmasculine, identified medical necessity definitions as the linchpin of health insurance coverage determinations:

> I think one thing that definitely needs to change is how we talk about gender-affirming procedures or surgeries or hormone replacement therapy. And how insurance companies see how these particular things are affecting individuals. Looking at things as medically necessary is super important because that changes how it's written in the policy and how it's talked about.

He continued:

> I think what the problem is now is a lot of the health care that trans folks are seeking is trivialized and thought of as like something that is, you know, quote-un-quote "cosmetic," which is a way for them to say not necessary. And so if you change the language about it, you change how it's talked about and recognized, how these things are medically necessary—and how that affects the lives of trans folk, then that is the initial jumpstart that you need to get things changed within insurances at an

administrative policy level. Because then once the policy is changed, then they have a rule in place that they follow.

Malik was just twenty-two years old at the time of this interview, but he had become an expert on how health insurance works and how rules, language, and administrative power matter for rights. Trans people, even with employer-sponsored health insurance that is supposedly nondiscriminatory, struggled with numerous barriers to gaining coverage. These barriers, operating with this meso-level of corporate insurance business control, are permitted under Section 1557's gender-identity protections because decisions about medical necessity are explicitly left to the insurer.

Even when gender-affirming care was covered, insurance companies demanded people prove themselves worthy of services. One interviewee detailed how after living as a trans man for ten years, his insurance company (Molina) required a six-month period of verification in therapy before it would approve any medications or services. Merely being in counseling for six months was even rarely sufficient for coverage to start. For Phoenix, who is white and non-binary, the six-month requirement dragged out much longer because it was just a first step to making many arguments with his insurer:

> I go to Molina and Molina won't cover it unless, you know, for sure this is something that is a definite yes. And in order to find out if it's definite yes, you have to go through intensive counseling, for like six months. Then you get two psychologists to sign off on paper stating, yes, this person is suffering identity dysphoria, they do not belong in the body that they have. It was I'd say two years before I can finally get Molina to agree [to pay for surgery], even though I had those consents.

A medical provider's letter insisting that services were medically necessary was often insufficient for the insurance company, which had an unwritten and opaque internal process for how it determined medical necessity. Phoenix also had endometriosis and their doctor had determined that a hysterectomy was medically necessary on that basis but also wrote to the insurer that "this will help with [Phoenix's] transition." Phoenix was thus presenting two different accounts of medical necessity (both valid), but their multiple diagnoses caused significant challenges with the insurance company. The insurance company initially denied coverage for the hysterectomy with endometriosis because Phoenix was also transitioning. Phoenix's case shows how someone who does not meet the profile of the binary trans person with no other health issues runs into additional obstacles.

Just as researchers cannot systematically study what is in our nation's health insurance plans, beneficiaries themselves often find that their insurance company does not have to disclose how it makes necessity determinations. "I would say the number one thing [that was the hardest in getting care] was, from the get-go, not having a clear definition of what is considered medically necessary by my plan," Adrian said. Adrian, who is white and non-binary, was seeking services for speech therapy, which their speech therapist identified as medically necessary, and their employer agreed would be covered. When they reached out to his insurance company, it told them that it was not legally required to share information about what it deemed medically necessary. "So there was a lot, and I mean a lot, of back and forth between my employer's HR department who were saying this, and my insurance company basically saying, trying to find out what is actually covered by insurance." All Adrian wanted to know was, "What does this new insurance policy consider medically necessary versus not?" Their employer had a self-funded plan run by a third-party administrator (TPA). In practice, that meant each could blame the other for conflicting views of medical necessity. Adrian was caught in the middle. It was "just an awful back-and-forth experience of finger pointing," they recounted, with "the insurance company saying, 'Well, my employer puts this policy together and agents provide the services for it,' whereas from my employer would say, 'Well, we pay the insurance company to do this.'" Adrian ended up spending eight months and six thousand dollars of their own money for services that their HR department had said would be covered in a memo to all employees. Finally, the insurance company provided sufficient documentation to the hospital to stop billing them.

Trans people seeking care read their plan documents very carefully and put in many hours of labor trying to use them for coverage. Adrian still found themself trapped between their employer and the employer's TPA in a cycle of obfuscation. Others found confusion and ignorance on the other end of the phone at the insurance company. Insurance company staff tasked with answering questions often lacked sufficient information to answer questions about coverage for gender-affirming care. For example, after learning from a pharmacist that hormones would be covered with prior authorization, Billy, who is white, looked more closely at his health insurance plan, trying to plan for the full scope of care he hoped to get. "I was interested in pursuing surgeries and I knew that documentation would be needed obviously to try and obtain an authorization," he said. He called his insurance company and spoke to four different people, but no one could help him figure out how to start obtaining those authorizations.

> I said can you please give me some direction as to what I may need? Would I need to go see someone specifically, a special type of doctor? Or would you need a letter from my primary care? Would you need one from my neurologist? And they couldn't direct me, give me any type of guidance. It was useless.

Black trans people with distinctively Black names such as LeVar and Malik encountered microaggressions and dismissals as insurance company staff tasked with helping people understand their benefits and problem-solve instead treated their requests as trivial or funny.

LeVar described how his insurance company repeatedly sent him his insurance card using his former name. This created problems because his insurance card would not match the information submitted for services. Racism compounded barriers for trans people of color. When he called the insurance company, he usually got the "runaround" and felt like "it was a joke" to them. Malik recounted a very similar experience with insurance staff after changing his name:

> It didn't seem at all that they have any sort of policy or training or anything about that, how to go about updating that in the system. So when I went to the offices and gave them the proper documentation to show that I've changed my name, the guy just wrote it down on a piece of paper and said, "Yeah. I'm not sure what we're supposed to do about that, but I'll get back to you." And then nothing ever came of it.

While white trans people described painstaking processes to navigate insurance company mistakes and structural barriers, few conveyed the same sense of invalidation that Black trans people expressed.

DIFFERING PROFESSIONAL PERSPECTIVES ON MEDICAL NECESSITY

Doctors and insurers mobilize the medical necessity framework in different ways. Insurers deem a medical procedure as medically necessary if there is a physical, functional benefit. As one surgeon we'll call Dr. Fischer noted, "We get into this debate about what's medically necessary and what's not. The insurance companies tend to say unless [insurers] are going to see improved physical functioning or reduced cost of medical burden going forward, that is not a medically necessary operation." Other providers noted that insurers consider a procedure medically necessary if the effectiveness of the procedure is grounded in evidence-based research or consistent with international and national consensus.

Surgeons and social workers who work with trans people seeking care take a broader view. They think that medical necessity should be determined by whether a procedure improves the well-being and quality of life for the person, including improving the mental health of a group of people with a very high risk of suicide. Dr. Fischer described how insurers go back and forth over functionality and the required evidence base, where sometimes one factor is present but the other is lacking:

> It's not a hard-and-fast thing. If there's clear functional benefit, it's not difficult. If there is data available to show clear quality of life, mental health, you know, functioning-in-society data, that's not hard. It's in the gray zone where you really can't perceive a definite functional benefit, there's not real data to show a lot of quality-of-life benefit. Then it becomes hard. A good example is body contouring after massive weight loss. So insurance companies, if you've lost one hundred pounds, they will, without a whole lot of argument, pay for your abdominal body contouring. They rarely or

never pay for arms or breasts or thighs, even though the people would clearly benefit sometimes not only in terms of quality of life but in terms of functioning.

Surgeons may see some ordinary, nonsurgical procedures as much more medically necessary than insurance companies do. It is typical for surgeons to require laser hair removal from the genital area before surgery so that the result does not leave hair growing in undesirable places. Electrolysis services are difficult to bring into the insurance context because they are not a medically elite service with billing to insurance already set up (since hair removal is not part of other medical services). Barriers to coverage extend from insurance denial out to the mundane, such as whether the electrologist has the required secure fax machine to transmit patient information.[28] The impacts on trans people who are poor, elderly, or disabled are especially harsh as Dr. Pace, a psychologist, explained: "There's people who have Medicare and Medicaid or are on disability can't get their surgery, and they can't do it because they can't do the hair removal." Jill, a clinical social worker who works with trans people seeking care, highlighted the frustration of a narrow construction of medical necessity:

> Hair removal. This is huge. So genital surgeries are often covered. But what is not covered or treated as medically necessary is hair removal at the surgical site. So that is bonkers, like straight up. It's a part of the medically necessary surgery, but I cannot think of any insurance companies right now that [are] covering it. Our plastic surgeons write a lot of letters saying it's a part of a medically necessary surgery. You guys need to cover this!

Doctors believed the context in which the procedure is performed matters for whether it is medically necessary. They see it as based on the medical condition or diagnosis, not the procedure, even in the case of breast implants, which are nearly always considered cosmetic. "The distinction for me," says Dr. Pielson, "between the cisgender woman and a transgender woman is the medical condition." He continues: "I would argue that there's no particular procedure that's inherently cosmetic or reconstructive, it's the diagnosis for which that procedure is being performed. Insurance companies have simply chosen to view the issue of gender dysphoria as cosmetic." This doctor views medical necessity based on the diagnosis, one that accounts for the quality-of-life needs of the patient seeking such care, while the insurer applies a more uniformly restrictive approach (e.g., breast implants are always cosmetic except for post-mastectomy reconstruction after cancer treatment as required by the Women's Health and Cancer Rights Act).

This disagreement also helps explain disputes over facial procedures. A transwoman may have facial features—hairline, jaw, Adam's apple, brow ridge—that are perfectly functional for breathing and eating but present as masculine. These are among the most difficult to obtain coverage for, perhaps because they are not focused on genital organs or secondary sex characteristics and may involve making a person more conventionally attractive as well as more feminine or masculine. More problematically, these procedures also involve making a person more white-looking.[29] That is, decisions about what surgical procedures are medically necessary for one's proper gender presentation to the world are also decisions about racial presentation, an illustration of the feminist argument that race and gender mutually constitute each other.[30] Providers repeatedly expressed frustration at the lack of coverage for facial-confirmation procedures despite insurers announcing that they cover gender-affirming surgeries.

Interviewees thought that insurance company interpretation of medical necessity ignores that the stakes of personal appearance are much higher for trans people, especially binary-identified transwomen. People seeking gender-affirming surgery often view facial procedures as vital to their life (since after all, we see each other's faces, not our genitals, in everyday life). The suicide attempt rate for transgender and non-binary persons is significantly higher than for cisgender people, reported in the 2015 Transgender Survey to be forty percent of respondents or nine times the rate in the US population.[31] Facial-confirmation procedures or breast reduction or augmentation do not feel "elective" or "cosmetic" for the trans people who seek them but vital to their mental and physical security and to decreasing the chance of discrimination, stigma, and violence against them. Providers argued that even if randomized controlled trials cannot really be done to show the benefit of these procedures across a large population of trans people (as they cannot be done with surgeries generally), medical necessity should be determined by whether a procedure improves the well-being and quality of life for a particular person in their care. That means improving the mental health of someone who is part of a group with a high risk of suicide.

ALLIED PROFESSIONALS PUSH BACK

The doctors who treat trans people bill their insurance companies, and they are part of the process of wrangling the insurer to pay. The surgeons we spoke to employ office staff to schedule surgeries. The first step is to make sure all the steps to secure coverage have been completed. Just as the grievance handlers shape the experience of rights on the ground for people trying to complain about injustices in hospitals, these office staff manage the tumultuous process of insurance coverage and are the ones to deliver the news to patients about whether the insurer will pay or not. They want the person to receive their care, so they push back against hoops and initial denials. In addition to the professionals in the medical offices who work with insurers, other professionals such as social workers and therapists also mobilize to help with coverage because there are additional requirements for trans people to access care.

Medically necessary care is not simply a list of covered procedures but, as Phoenix described, it also includes fulfillment of other criteria to demonstrate worthiness and readiness. Health insurers impose a series of rules that a patient must satisfy to qualify for medically necessary treatment of gender dysphoria.[32] These rules may be laid out in the plan's list of coverages and exclusions or they may be found in the insurer's interpretation of the prevailing professional association guidelines and tucked away in a medical policy document. While many insurers claim that they cover gender-affirming surgeries, the details reveal insurers cover far less because these rules give many more occasions to deny or delay. These requirements may include two referral letters from mental health professionals, reaching the age of eighteen, all other health concerns being reasonably well controlled, twelve months of continuous hormone therapy, and twelve months of "real life experience" or living in the congruent gender identity.

Additional requirements that go beyond the World Professional Association for Transgender Health (WPATH) guidelines and recommendations were the among the most frustrating things insurers did according to health care professionals whom we interviewed. These additional obstacles lead to denials of coverage that providers view as simply excessive and not medically necessary. As Jill, the clinical social worker, explained:

> For example, some insurers require that trans men who want a mastectomy are on hormones for twelve continuous months at least. That is not part of the WPATH standards of care. That is just one insurance company saying, 'This is what we want.' It's silly. It's not medically necessary. It's just the insurance company sort of deciding that this is what they want. It's not based on anything real.

These providers were highly aware that an informed consent model for care would grant trans people the same level of autonomy that other patients receive and that even the WPATH standards are regarded as overly restrictive.[33] Nonetheless, these healthcare providers must use them as an externally valid benchmark to bargain down what insurance companies demand, which is even more restrictive.

The number of mental health letters required to have procedures performed was a particular source of contention. Angela, a surgery scheduler, explains how adding extra requirements works:

> Sometimes the criteria don't necessarily align with the WPATH criteria. The insurance criteria for surgery, they model it by the WPATH, but they don't follow it exactly. I recently had a patient for chest reconstruction. The WPATH criteria is that they need one letter of referral from a mental health specialist. I've had two Blue Crosses now say that we actually need two, two letters. We've tried fighting that that's not medically necessary.

Insurance companies also selectively reject letters if the therapist does not hold a PhD (so excluding MSW-degreed social workers) or the right kind of PhD. The lack of doctors and mental health professionals available to treat transgender and non-binary people in particular geographic areas makes it difficult for people to get the appointments they need to fulfill these requirements. Dr. Pace, a psychologist in a gender services clinic who is trans, noted that some of his trans clients drove six hours each way to attend a therapy appointment with him. Rather than contest the additional hurdle like a second letter, people often "lump" their losses and just do as the insurer requires, as Angela recounts:

> Ultimately it was decided that it would take less time for the patient to go to another therapist and get another referral letter. That was the patient's decision, of course. You meet criteria, but their criteria states that you need another letter. We can fight based on, you know, [the insurer] not meeting WPATH criteria, or you can appease them and sort of dance the dance.

Rather than fight the requirements, people choose the path of least resistance to obtaining coverage, even when the insurer is adding requirements that go against the consensus standard of care. But sometimes it is still not enough. Dr. Barker, an ob-gyn physician, after saying how much the insurance coverage situation had improved in recent years, went on to say moments later that she had just had someone cancel a surgery because they had not been able to get two letters in time.

We saw how allied professionals pointed out the much higher suicide risk for trans people when arguing for facial-confirmation surgery coverage. They also argued in these terms for seventeen year olds to obtain gender-affirming procedures, which are not recommended for minors except in some cases. Doctors and therapists would like to maintain control of this discretion for treatment at the cusp of adulthood when they think their patient's mental health is at stake and they are capable of giving consent. Despite the impression that conservative opponents try to create that young children are eligible for gender-affirming surgeries, the fact is that insurance policies typically do not cover procedures before age eighteen, and some restrict until age twenty-one. Dr. Pace, the psychologist, described a case of a seventeen-year-old trans boy seeking chest surgery who had gone through therapy and secured the necessary letter.

> The surgeon said, "Yep, I'll do your surgery." They went to do the pre-authorization with the insurance company, and the insurance company denied it. And when I talked to the person at the insurance company she said, "There's no research evidence to show that this is helpful." Okay. So just correct me if I'm wrong. We know that the suicide rate, the suicide attempt rate—not suicidal ideation, not completed suicides, but the rate of people who attempted suicide, is forty-one percent of transgender people. This person's seventeen, they're not eighteen. Do we really think they have a lower suicide rate because they're seventeen and not eighteen? I don't think so. Here's the insurance company. They're supposed to be helping their members get the services they need so that they're healthy. I think it's a ruse, I think it's a cover. I think they'll do anything they can not to pay.

Refracting rights through insurance disrupts health care rights expansions for trans people in ways that are hard to see because they scatter through tedious, bureaucratic, and mostly private disputes in the context of ongoing yet interrupted care.[34] Rights blockages may not take the form of outright exclusion of transgender coverage but rather emerge through a rigid construction of medical necessity and a series of barriers put up by insurers. Trans people find the process of trying to use their supposedly nondiscriminatory health insurance exhausting, expensive, and insulting.

Allied professionals contest terms like *medically necessary* with alternative views of what the medical interventions mean for a trans person's life, raising points like heightened suicide risks. As I discuss in chapter 5, sometimes insurance rights are realized and some of these arguments and frameworks secure coverage for care. But any approach to health care civil rights must take seriously the fact that insurance companies still control decision-making about coverage with considerable industry autonomy from regulation. Not only do regulatory civil rights carveouts protect insurance-industry management practices, but the whole private employer-based health insurance system remains fundamentally disconnected from federal health care civil rights regulation. If we thought of the tax breaks companies receive for providing health benefits as federal funding for health care, then all Section 1557 civil rights protections would apply.[35] Instead we maintain a healthcare system in which private employers broker care for the majority of working age adults and their families through insurance that is obscured for research, managed for insurer's profits, and yet quietly subsidized by our government.

Insurance companies are what I have called the mesolevel of health care civil rights governance, removed from the patient interactions in a care setting to a more distant institutional level but not yet as high as the executive level of government or the prevailing legal interpretation of the Supreme Court. All these three levels still shape people's lives, so by "removed" I do not mean less impactful. Moving across these levels has helped me explain and sort all the different ways that health care civil rights are refracted rights and to specify the frameworks and mechanisms that scatter them. In chapter 4, I move to the national level of organized political and legal disputing about health care civil rights. I focus on religious conservative opponents of health care civil rights on the basis of gender identity, arguing that one critical way that antidiscrimination law fails patients is when discrimination against trans people is allowed, defended, and even celebrated.

4

How Conservatives Oppose Health Care Civil Rights

As I waited in the lobby to interview Erica, a patient advocate who was also the Section 1557 coordinator, I watched workers taking down the large hanging logo and name of the hospital system and replacing it with the logo and name of the Catholic hospital system that was taking it over. Later, as we were talking, I asked Erica if she had noticed anything about the changeover to Catholic ownership in her role as the Section 1557 coordinator. She replied that no, she had not been told anything, "but I did bring it up, because the implementation that 1557 holds is kind of against the Catholic religion." Erica wondered if her job enforcing health care civil rights based on gender identity would have to change because of the new Catholic ownership of her hospital.

What Erica noticed is a national debate playing out across our courts, state legislatures, and administrative agencies—will conservative religious opposition to trans health care rights block and deny care? When religious freedom means not providing gender-affirming care or even making its provision a crime, what happens to civil rights based on gender identity? Religious opposition to health care civil rights based on gender identity is a major problem for American healthcare because bishops run entire healthcare systems. Religious entities are also both employers and health insurers in the United States. Their interpretation of trans health care civil rights turns the antidiscrimination model completely on its head. In their version, they are the victims of discrimination when civil rights law protects people on the basis of gender identity. In this chapter, we move up to the higher levels of governance where additional structures—healthcare systems, federal and state laws, and constitutional law—and the highly organized and well-funded law firms of the conservative legal movement refract health care civil rights.

Refracting rights happens through absorption frames, such as patient experience, and deflection frames, such as medical necessity. It also happens through defeat frames, when opposing interpretations of rights meet in court and one side loses. Discrimination law can fail patients because it has been weakened and dismantled by its opponents. Religious opposition to gender-affirming care as a health care civil right—melded almost completely with Republican party politics—has rolled back rights at the national political and legal levels and across many conservative states. There are many reasons that opponents have been able to push back against health care civil rights protections for gender identity in health care. There are long-standing religious rights protections in our laws and Constitution, so the tension here is between different concepts of rights that are incompatible with each other. The United States is a relatively religious nation among similar democracies, and despite our religious pluralism, the religious opposition to trans health care rights is unusually united around conservative evangelical Christianity and conservative Catholicism. The first Trump administration was successful at making the federal judiciary more conservative and thus inviting to opponents of transgender rights, and many features of our political system make it vulnerable to minority rule or at least veto power by well-organized interest groups. Opponents of trans health care civil rights thus have formidable legal and political tools available to fight on religious grounds, and a second Trump term in which to do it.

My focus in this chapter is primarily on the religious opponents of health care civil rights because explicitly religious legal arguments and institutions like the Catholic Church have been critical in challenging and sometimes dismantling trans health care civil rights. But in what Joanna Wuest and Briana Last call a politics of "church against state," religious and business interests have long been aligned in a broad antiregulatory agenda with the goal of dismantling the administrative state.[1] The right-wing industrialists in this coalition oppose the regulation of fossil fuels and dietary supplements just as much as they oppose religious employers covering contraception in their insurance plans. A government too weak to regulate discrimination by employers and the healthcare industry is also too weak to regulate Wall Street, polluters, misleading advertisers, or predatory lenders. Sometimes anti-trans advocates hide their religious views to seem more secular and thus more scientifically credible. Religious opponents of a wide range of LGBTQ+ rights have created professional organizations and publications with an importantly secular gloss and then mobilized them in an alternate story of expertise to use in litigation to create doubt and justify denying gender-affirming care. They also promote scientific and medical uncertainty about gender-affirming care alongside secular opponents such as trans-exclusionary radical feminists, an anti-trans activism that has been stronger in the United Kingdom than in the United States.[2] Religious opposition to trans health care civil rights flourishes in a rich political economy, in other words, as well as draws strength from built-in features of the US healthcare and legal system. This chapter explains how these forces have done their work so that discrimination law cannot really protect patients.

FRAMEWORKS FOR CONTESTING TRANS HEALTH CARE CIVIL RIGHTS

As I have argued throughout this book, when civil rights refract through health care and healthcare systems, they become weakened and diverted in distinct ways. The patient experience framework is an absorption that is not overtly hostile, but it is overwhelming and digestive as it takes in the civil rights obligation and processes it according to alternative organizational priorities. Insurance companies can also absorb civil rights, perhaps changing their policies to cover gender-affirming care but then deflecting the actual provision of care using industry tools such as medical necessity determinations that are untouched by civil rights obligations. In this chapter, I analyze how religious structures within the American healthcare system support denials of care and have come into direct tension with health care civil rights laws. Health care civil rights can fail because they are simply defeated in a head-to-head contest with religion. Religious control of health care has a long institutional history in the development of Catholic clinics and hospitals in the United States.[3] Organized opposition to abortion in the last half century has resulted in many federal legal protections for religiously based objections to providing care and referrals.[4] Constitutional religious freedoms and free speech protections are also powerful foundations for religious groups opposed to trans health care rights. A conservative federal judiciary and an ultraconservative Supreme Court are inviting grounds for conservative impact litigation, which has been well funded and impactful.

Conservatives resist the idea that health and health care are civil rights contexts that should offer legal protection to statuses, acts, and needs they object to, typically on white evangelical Protestant or conservative Catholic religious grounds.[5] The United States is home to many different religious groups and traditions, and in some ways, we display an outward commitment to religious pluralism. Christian groups provide social services, such as refugee resettlement, for religiously diverse groups of people, for example.[6] Yet because of the near-complete overlap between a deeply conservative Republican party and white evangelicals and Catholic traditionalists, opposition to trans health care rights is a unified political project for the religious right wing beyond the influence of religious pluralism. Conservative Catholics and white evangelicals have become more politically unified under this banner over the past few decades, overcoming historical political divisions and prejudices between them. I present religious opposition arguments as I find them in their own words, focusing on the most influential groups and structures even though they represent a small minority of the American public overall.

Religious groups and religious healthcare institutions have strongly resisted a health care frame for issues from contraception and abortion to trans and non-binary people's needs. Instead, they frame providing and accessing abortion care and gender-affirming care as deviant and morally indefensible actions that defy theological mandates. They counter health care civil rights with a religious objection frame. The religious objection frame turns the civil rights question around, placing religious healthcare workers and religious institutions in the victim role. The civil rights violation is the interference with their religious freedom and freedom of conscience if they are required to provide or participate in care that they define as theologically abhorrent.

The religious objection frame has a fully institutionalized version in which large Catholic healthcare systems are the claimants asserting the right not to provide entire categories of health care to certain groups of people because the treatments violate Catholic religious doctrine. It also has a more individualized version that health care providers, many of them evangelical or conservative Christians who are not employed in a Catholic healthcare system, invoke as plaintiffs in impact litigation. Objectors are large healthcare systems, insurance providers, professional groups, and individual providers.

This mobilization also draws on an alternative professional expertise frame, in which spin-off professional organizations participate in litigation for conservative causes, such as the right to practice conversion therapies and support for bans on gender-affirming care for youth and adults. This alternative professional expertise frame is the secular version of their religious arguments, enabling conservative opponents to argue that gender-affirming care is harmful and not evidence based without mentioning the underlying religious basis for opposition. Pushing just a little bit ("Well, *why* is it harmful?") gets to the answer: any challenge to God-given, biologically fixed, and heterosexual gender roles is harmful both to the individual and to society. Conservative religious objection also draws on a free speech frame, in which having to use the right pronouns for a trans patient or calling them by the name they go by is forced speech that violates their rights. Free speech—meaning speech in opposition to LGBTQ rights—can now trump antidiscrimination protections according to our ultraconservative Supreme Court, and there is no reason to think this framework could not expand to eat up nearly all discrimination protections. If a doctor or therapist who accepts federal funds can say, "I think you're deluded and not really trans" while refusing to use a person's correct name and pronouns or provide any gender-affirming care, then health care civil rights do not really exist, which is the goal.

We saw how hospital-level priorities and professional structures refract health care civil rights, downgrading them to patient experience problems. Health insurers refract civil rights by continuing to use coverage-denial justifications to throw up barriers to care even without fully excluding gender-affirming care. Even if we fixed these problems at the first two levels entirely, all the barriers I describe here would still be there. In this chapter, we see health care civil rights refracted through sociopolitical structures at the top governance level in a state or at the federal level. These sociopolitical structures are governmental and legal: state legislatures, state courts, governors, Congress, the Supreme Court, lower federal courts, the presidency, and the administrative state. These structures are shaped by and shape what organized groups and social movements do too. Conservative religious law firms have waged well-planned impact litigation plans, strategically recruiting plaintiffs and bringing lawsuits against health care civil rights in venues where they are likely to win. Features of American politics such as the electoral college, lifetime appointments for Supreme Court justices by the president with confirmation by the Senate, Senate rules such as the filibuster or placing a hold on a confirmation by one senator, and the fact that each state gets two senators regardless of population have driven us into minority rule. These pressures have created a national context in which civil rights opponents have considerable leverage through the judiciary, in red state legislatures, and in the Supreme Court.

THE ORIGINS, CONTENT, AND EFFECTS OF RELIGIOUS OBJECTIONS TO TRANS HEALTH CARE RIGHTS

When religious conservatives object to health care civil rights for trans and nonbinary people, what are their arguments? Why is excluding gender identity from health care civil rights protections important to them? Transgender rights and cultural acceptance of them expanded considerably in the last twenty years. Conservative opponents find this trend alarming and have mobilized their own constituencies around an anti-trans agenda. They have also convinced more of the moderate and right-leaning American public that transgender rights have moved too fast.[7] Religious conservatives have found transgender rights opposition politically convenient, to be sure. Their opposition is not simply manufactured as a political wedge issue, however, nor are they pawns in a broader movement towards authoritarianism or to demolish the regulatory state. My aim is not to construct a clear causal story for the rise in anti-trans sentiment. But there are a few central elements that opponents define for themselves, around which I have wrapped additional interpretation.

Religious opposition reflects understandings of biblical teachings about sex as obviously, biologically binary and gender roles as given by God to match those two male and female options. Only heterosexual sex in marriage is religiously sanctioned. Conservative Catholics and evangelical Protestants share this religious sex-essentialism view even though their religious doctrines differ (and they have a history of distaste between them that has been overcome by their agreement in recent decades on antiabortion, anti-gay, and anti-trans perspectives). In this view, people who experience same-sex attraction or discomfort with their sex assigned at birth are simply confused. They need pastoral counseling and Christian religious salvation to return to being godly men and women, fulfilling complementary roles defined by male dominance and female submission and, for Catholics, continual openness to conceiving children in marital sex.

Conservative opponents of health care civil rights for LGBTQ people understand themselves to be fighting to defend "one of the most foundational realities of what it means to be human: the fact that we are created male and female."[8] "Christian Healthcare cannot prescribe cross-sex hormones to facilitate a gender transition or use pronouns that do not accord with a person's biological sex," opponents of gender-affirming care argue in a complaint, "as that would violate its belief in the immutability of biological sex."[9] Nor should the body be changed through gender-affirming care. "The body is God's creation," the Catholic Health Care Leadership Alliance argues, "and to remove, impede or interrupt functioning body parts that are effectively participating in the biological unity of the body, according to their physiological purposes, would be to blaspheme God as the supreme Artist, Creator and sanctifier of the flesh."[10] Seen through this religious objection frame, homosexuality and transgenderism are recent, corrupt inventions of far-left ideology that are not real or legitimate. Invented by academic feminists and queer theorists, opponents argue "radical gender theory" celebrates pornography and pedophilia and teaches kids to break down the gender binary.[11] Youth and adults who have become confused about their gender or sexuality due to these influences would then be drawn into believing that they are trans, non-binary, or queer by other adults—educators, therapists, doctors, and others outside the family and church.

By deconstructing "any and all boundaries and taboos around sexuality," as conservatives see it, feminist and queer theories celebrate dangerous social change. Conservatives tend to value long-standing traditional arrangements because they fear chaos and disorder. These values are even linked to measurable personality types: more conservative people tend to be more fearful of change, intolerant of ambiguity, and drawn to strong authority, while liberals are more likely to value novel experiences, tolerate ambiguity, and to experience change as interesting rather than scary.[12] Ideas about the fluidity of gender and sexuality are dangerous for religious conservatives because they define them as sinful, but they would also be threatening under this psychological account. As Catholic healthcare ethical and religious directives warn, "[S]ocial change . . . can lead to policies and actions that are contrary to the true dignity and vocation of the human person."[13] People of all ages feeling free to abandon stifling gender roles and to love beyond religiously sanctioned heterosexual marriage seems like liberating progress for liberals, but for religious conservatives, it creates victims. Their victims are female athletes who lose competitions to trans women ("biological males") and confused and mutilated children and adults who wrongly thought gender-affirming care was the answer to their distress.[14]

Fear of trans youth and adults has also been a relentlessly marketed idea in recent years, as powerful fundraising groups and political candidates saturated our media with depictions of gender-affirming care as deviant, spreading, and dangerous, and more mainstream media outlets covered the issue as a "both sides" debate. Conservative politicians and their funders have found trans health care rights to be a highly salient issue that speaks to their constituencies. Republicans are much less likely than Democrats to favor trans rights or to believe that it is possible to have a gender identity that is different from sex assigned at birth. Even though there is overall majority support for antidiscrimination protections for trans people (sixty-four percent in a 2022 Pew Research survey), support is lower for trans athletes to participate on teams that align with their gender identity or to get medical care in transitioning before age eighteen.[15]

The success of these opponents' arguments has had devastating effects on trans and non-binary people, their families, and the professionals who care for them. By 2024, twenty-two states had passed legislation banning provision of gender-affirming care for youth, though not all the laws are in effect due to ongoing litigation.[16] Some of the arguments to exclude trans and non-binary youth and adults from gender-affirming care are presented in secular terms. But when Alabama governor Kay Ivey signed the Alabama bill criminalizing gender-affirming care, she said that she signed it because "if the Good Lord made you a boy, you are a boy, and if he made you a girl, you are a girl."[17] The conservative legal movement has been gaining strength for decades, but as I explain below, they have been particularly successful recently in winning lawsuits and in helping to produce and then making the most of the rightward turn in the federal judiciary.

RELIGIOUS CONSERVATIVE IMPACT LITIGATION: WHAT ARE THE ARGUMENTS?

Mobilized religious conservatives are a well-funded and well-organized political and legal movement.[18] Alliance Defending Freedom touts fifteen recent wins at the Supreme Court in pro-religious rights, antiabortion, and anti-LGBTQ cases, including *Dobbs*, *303 Creative*, and *Masterpiece Cakeshop*.[19] The Becket Fund for Religious Liberty, a smaller organization, has notched wins against the Affordable Care Act. They play to win in everything from injunctions to full-scale shifts in the Supreme Court's fundamental jurisprudence on the balance of power in our government. The first line of argument in the religious objection frame is that it is a constitutional violation of religious exercise to require religious physicians and hospitals to provide gender-affirming care. This argument also extends to religious employers who provide health insurance coverage, so that no coverage would be available for any treatments objectionable to the religion. A second constitutional objection is that it is a violation of their free speech for the government to ban conversion therapies meant to turn people from gay to straight or trans to cis or to direct healthcare workers to address trans people according to the trans person's gender identity rather than their sex assigned at birth (that is, with the pronouns the person uses).

The statutory arguments against gender identity protections in civil rights law are that Section 1557 is limited to its reading through Title IX, where conservatives find multiple instances of judges endorsing binary gender essentialism and plenty of accommodations for single-sex dormitories and sports teams, father-son and mother-daughter school dances, and beauty pageant scholarships.[20] Conceding that under *Bostock*, "sex is irrelevant to hiring or firing decisions," Alliance Defending Freedom attorneys argue that "sex *is* relevant in contexts like sports."[21] Hospitals, they argue, also "naturally provide medical care 'according to the biological differences between men and women.'"[22] Just as educational institutions can have separate dorms and sports teams for men and women based on biological sex, states, hospitals, and employers should be able to "tailor their health care or insurance coverage according to biological sex."[23] In this view, there is not really a new health care civil right in Section 1557 that affirms trans and non-binary people in equal access to health care as they are but rather only narrow protections for biological men and biological women that are static and fixed from birth to death.

Moreover, religious opponents of health care civil rights typically invoke the statutory law that protects religious rights, the Religious Freedom Restoration Act or RFRA. RFRA (pronounced "rif-ra") was passed in 1993 by an enthusiastically bipartisan Congress to turn back a Supreme Court that would have allowed neutral laws of general applicability to apply to religious practices (in the case in question, it was use of peyote in the Native American Church that violated drug laws). In other words, it was a different world back then. RFRA defends religious exercise by banning substantial burdens on it and requiring that any federal law that burdens it must further a compelling governmental interest in the least burdensome way. The Department of Health and Human Services Office for Civil Rights (OCR) has always acknowledged that RFRA applies to its interpretations of Section 1557 to include gender-identity protections.

These are strong protections for religious exercise indeed, but a big question has been how exactly religion is burdened in the case of gender-affirming-care provision. Religious healthcare objectors have sometimes lost their cases because they could not describe anything more than a hypothetical future injury.[24] No one had asked them to perform any gender-affirming procedure and it was not clear there would be any enforcement action against them. Their claims and some judicial decisions in their favor are replete with dramatic hypotheticals, including the abjectly farcical claim that doctors will be forced to perform sex change surgeries on infants.[25]

OCR has pursued a strategy of specification, that is, insisting that whether a religious exercise is substantially burdened and if that burden can be justified is a fact-specific inquiry that can only be resolved in a case-by-case approach.

Religious opponents of gender-affirming care have always wanted a blanket religious exemption that excuses them from any civil rights obligations in a way that they can control and do not have to explain. Republican administrations will give them that, but Democratic administrations prefer to resolve conflicts between religion and health care in the tightest, most specific factual instances. This strategy makes sense if one assumes that these very strong religious protections are not going anywhere, so the best way to try to carve out some continued health care access is to dispute on the specifics. For example, a University of Maryland health system that is public and nonreligious was not able to deny a trans man his hysterectomy even though the Catholic hospital they had merged with did not want to provide it.[26] The specific facts about public versus religious status were determinative, suggesting that details of merger agreements with Catholic hospital systems and secular ones really matter. It could also matter if there were other nearby facilities that would provide the care and whether those providers are in the same health insurance network, for example.

If courts and OCR are inclined to push for specific-fact situations, they will eliminate many far-fetched hypotheticals that play well in right-wing media and campaigns. This strategy forces some separation between politics and law, moving the conflict into legal terrain on which specific types of reasons must be offered in detail with the grounds for those reasons defended in certain ways. As I have argued in my previous work on vaccine injury conspiracy theorizing, the law and legal process can do a very nice job at narrowing what counts as an argument and a reason and dismantling those that fail to qualify.[27] Here, the OCR under Democratic administrations—if it is allowed to enforce the regulations at all—will require religious opponents to defend specific denials of care for specific patients who are supported by medical professionals (and their families in the case of minors) to obtain that care. Specification is a route to permit greater power for expertise and sympathy to play a role in humanizing and elevating gender-affirming care and those who seek it and to lay bare the unequal treatment that someone who is trans will experience in religious settings.

Religious conservatives are also "playing for rules," that is, using impact litigation to reshape the power balances between the executive and the administrative state.[28] They see civil rights bureaucrats in departments like Health and Human Services as hostile to their religious exercise because of rulemaking under Section 1557 to advance trans rights as part of sex discrimination, for example. Religious conservatives argued against the power of the administrative state to regulate more generally, and now they have won.[29] The Supreme Court ruling in *Loper Bright Enterprises* that courts need not defer to agency fact-finding and expertise in implementing laws like Section 1557 (and many others) makes it much more difficult for Democratic administrations who support trans health rights to implement regulations that accomplish anything. The win in *Loper Bright* is part of a conservative legal mobilization against the administrative state and its powers generally to regulate and enforce its regulations for the environment, the economy and business markets, healthcare, and more.[30]

In *Texas v. EEOC*, Judge Matthew Kacsmaryk (a federal district court judge well known for delivering far-right-wing judicial pronouncements) attempted to offer a way around the *Bostock* ruling for trans health care civil rights by arguing that the *Bostock* ruling may protect trans people "for being" transgender in the Title VII context, but that does not bar discrimination against them for "conduct" in health care. Judge Kacsmaryk's stark arguments are useful for exposing the ways that the religious objection frame simultaneously builds itself up while undercutting forms of rights expression for a wide range of LBGTQ+ people's being in the world as well as their health care needs. Going beyond "being" trans in health care would involve "conduct" such as seeking and receiving health care. Much like the Catholic healthcare systems' insistence that they treat everyone with dignity and respect while not providing the health care that many trans people need, this distinction offers a way to claim nondiscrimination while excluding, misgendering, and refusing care to anyone who is not cisgender.[31]

I have argued that health care civil rights require provision and recognition, and this form of anti-trans argument is precisely the opposite formulation that shows why both are so important. Imagine, for example, the claim that one is not discriminating against a pregnant person for "being" pregnant but for the "conduct" of demanding prenatal care, care during delivery, and health insurance for it. Of course, religious arguments for their own protection to discriminate could not possibly rely on such a distinction. For the religious conservative, there is no merely "being" religious, either. The religious entity is a person but also a sprawling healthcare system, an employer, and a health insurer, all with a set of practices that impact other people. All these entities, in their view, are entitled both to be and to do (meaning to believe, to proclaim, to draw and enforce boundaries, and to give and to withhold goods and services). In "being" a religious rights-holder, all these entities claim the right to enact discrimination in "conduct," such as deadnaming, misgendering, declining care, issuing denials, turning away patients, informing people that they are confused and that their condition does not really exist and that they are not who they understand themselves to be, and enforcing Catholic directives for all employees and patients, including hiring and firing to ensure religious actions are taken and sinful ones are not. In other words, the argument is that their religious freedom requires being able to discriminate and to enact that discrimination in speech, business, and health care.

Health care civil rights protecting religious conservatives offer both provision and recognition in many forms, in other words, singling out their beliefs for protection in federal legislation and constitutional interpretation, providing federal funding directly in healthcare and indirectly through tax policy, and creating exemptions from civil rights and employment laws that apply to everyone else so that they may undertake conduct that is otherwise illegal.

Distinguishing between status and conduct is unhelpful for understanding what everyone needs rights for. Rather, the challenge is to manage these conflicts and tensions better and more equitably so that everyone has a chance to enact an authentic vision of themselves—people living their genders in all variations and people of all faiths (overlapping categories, let's not forget)—within systems that still protect the more vulnerable and restrain those who would harm people who are different.

SECULAR AND RELIGIOUS TENSIONS FOR CATHOLIC HEALTHCARE SYSTEMS

Catholic healthcare systems fit uneasily into the American healthcare landscape in many ways and have evolved significantly over time. Religious sisters started hospitals for the poor in the early years of the United States and its westward expansion, establishing Catholic hospitals widely at a time of no national regulation or economic organization.[32] Catholic hospitals were well organized and poised to take advantage of Hill-Burton funding at mid-century, quadrupling their patient load and expanding their facilities.[33] Now, one in seven patients in the United States is treated in a Catholic facility, and in twelve states more than thirty percent of hospital beds are in Catholic facilities.[34] There are more than 600 Catholic hospitals and 1,600 other facilities, such as nursing homes, run by the Catholic Church in the United States.[35] They receive the same types of federal funding as other entities, such as billing to Medicare and Medicaid. Catholic hospitals and systems face the same challenges to remain profitable as other hospitals do, balancing caring for the poor and uninsured with trying to attract patients with better-paying private insurance and merging and consolidating to achieve a larger scale of operations. Despite claims of extra concern for the poor, Catholic healthcare systems provide less care to the poor than average.[36]

Some challenges for Catholic healthcare systems operating in the US marketplace are specific to their Catholic roots, such as the quickly dwindling supply of women willing to work as sisters in these facilities. The biggest challenge internally for the bishops who run these systems has been how to maintain Catholic values, which operate in practice as restrictions on forms of care that are popular with patients or seen as medically necessary in the contemporary healthcare marketplace.[37] The no doubt carefully selected plaintiffs in impact litigation are groups like Little Sisters of the Poor, a group of nuns providing mostly eldercare in small facilities, who can put forth a sympathetic face that hearkens back to the feminized, consecrated, impoverished roots of Catholic care provision. Critics point out, however, that the Catholic Church and its expansive healthcare businesses that the sisters represent are "neither little, nor poor,"[38] nor do women hold positions of power in the hierarchy.

That is, there are multiple ways of understanding and depicting what Catholic healthcare is in the contemporary United States, and the more it looks like a big, consolidated business that operates like its secular counterparts and relies on federal funding, the harder it is to justify its refusals to provide care to whole categories of people. But if it is more like a small order of devout nuns caring for the elderly, then allowing religious diversity to flourish even if it impacts care in some ways looks more acceptable in a pluralistic society. When the Becket Fund for Religious Liberty makes Little Sisters of the Poor their plaintiffs, they are perfectly aware of the need to emphasize that role to the public. My view is that religious rights in health care have expanded too much, and the balance is off. The realities of healthcare operation mean that allowing one religious view to dominate so much of our health care delivery is unfair to everyone else and especially cruel to vulnerable people such as trans and non-binary people and people who need abortion, fertility, and contraceptive care. The Supreme Court has been going the opposite way, however, so it looks like our healthcare system will continue to pull apart, with large swaths of it offering religiously restricted care to ever-larger networks and geographic areas. The main way this dual system could break down would then not be through law and policy but through economic pressures as providers—most of whom do not share the religious views of their employers—choose to work elsewhere.

What the US Conference of Catholic Bishops calls "an effective Catholic presence in health care" exemplifying "authentic neighborliness to those in need" is from another perspective a large healthcare system that receives federal funding and operates in many ways indistinguishably from other nonprofit healthcare systems but with a list of services it will not provide, most of which are popular reproductive health services.[39] The bishops publish the ethical and religious directives that Catholic healthcare entities must follow. They prioritize promoting and defending human dignity. The Catholic view of the right to life from the moment of conception to death "entails a right to the means for the proper development of life, such as adequate health care."[40] Catholic institutions must adopt the directives and require adherence to them for employment and medical privileges. Medical expertise and innovation are subject to religious control. "In consultation with medical professionals," the directives explain, "church leaders review these developments [new medical discoveries and technologies and the social change they bring], judge them according to the principles of right reason and the ultimate standard of revealed truth, and offer authoritative teaching and guidance about the moral and pastoral responsibilities entailed by the Christian faith."[41]

More specifically, the directives ban contraception, abortion, advance directives that are contrary to teachings (because they would hasten natural death, for example), creation of embryos in fertility treatments such as in vitro fertilization if they will not be used, use of donor gametes by a married couple, fertilizing gametes from a married couple outside of their bodies and distinct from "the marital act," surrogate motherhood, prenatal testing or diagnosis when abortion would be an outcome if there is an unwelcome diagnosis, and sterilization (except when such a procedure would cure or alleviate a present and serious pathology for which a simpler treatment is not available). The directives also envision healthcare collaborations with non-Catholics in detail, requiring that the local bishop assess whether those relationships could be immoral, scandalous, or "undermine the Church's witness."[42] Collaborations "must be operated in full accord with the moral teaching of the Catholic Church," and it is not permissible to create another entity to perform "immoral procedures."[43]

The directives do not mention gender-affirming care by name or specifically prohibit it. However, the Catholic Health Care Leadership Alliance explains that "[t]he body is God's creation, and to remove, impede or interrupt functioning body parts that are effectively participating in the biological unity of the body, according to their physiological purposes, would be to blaspheme God as the supreme Artist, Creator and sanctifier of the flesh."[44] They oppose all the standard treatments for gender dysphoria for people of all ages, from social transition to hormones to surgery.[45] Religious hospitals do not offer highly specialized genital surgeries, which are typically only offered by providers in gender-identity clinics or by well-known private surgeons whose primary practice is focused on these procedures. These specialized providers do not work in systems that restrict their care.

Instead, religious institutions object to providing care that their employees widely and commonly provide to cisgender people and that is not specific to gender-affirming care for trans people. Examples of the overlapping categories of care that religious hospitals want to deny only to trans people as gender-affirming care are hysterectomy, mastectomy, and hormone therapies. Removal of the uterus and removal of breast tissue is indicated for transgender men as treatment for the distress of gender dysphoria that these body parts can bring. In cisgender women, breast tissue removal is most often a cancer treatment or preventative. Hysterectomies for cisgender women are a very common procedure, with six hundred thousand performed each year as treatment for fibroids, excessive bleeding, endometriosis, and cancer.[46] While Catholic hospitals do not perform hysterectomies for sterilization, these institutions provide hysterectomies for other medically indicated reasons. Nothing in civil rights law requires doctors to perform procedures that are outside their expertise, but hysterectomies are so common that it is well within the practice competency of many gynecologists. Hormone therapies for cisgender youth with conditions like gynecomastia (breast development in boys) that are gender-affirming care for cisgender youth are part of standard care across all types of institutions. Hormone therapies are not controversial as treatments for menopausal symptoms or as growth treatments in children with very small stature. When lawyers for religious healthcare institutions argue that their hospitals and doctors will be forced to provide care they object to, they are talking about these forms of care that are well within their practice areas and regularly provided to cisgender people. Under Section 1557's principle of parity, care that would be provided to a cisgender person cannot be denied on the basis of gender identity to a trans or non-binary person. A religious exemption would be needed to allow them to discriminate in ways that would otherwise be illegal under Section 1557.

As Catholic hospital systems have downplayed the restrictions that the Church places on their care and moved to resemble other hospitals in many outward ways, their strong market position and even dominance in some areas has become controversial. Simply put, some patients must give over their care to the dictates of the Catholic Church whether they want to or not. Some Catholic hospitals operate as the sole community hospital in rural areas, with more than two hundred thousand patient discharges and one million emergency room visits annually.[47] Employer-sponsored health insurance provider networks can be narrow, and in some areas the only places where one's insurance is accepted is at a Catholic facility. Recall that Joshua in the previous chapter had to change jobs to get different insurance coverage so his mastectomy would be covered because the Catholic provider would not cover it. There is no legal requirement of access to a nonreligious hospital, and religious providers are not required to make referrals for the care that they will not provide. Patients frequently are unaware of the differences in care offered at Catholic facilities and may not even know they are using a Catholic hospital. Many do not realize that the care they expect and is widely provided elsewhere is not available. Most facilities do not post any details about the religious restrictions they follow, and only the state of Washington requires posting about reproductive care restrictions.[48] Section 1557 requires posting a nondiscrimination notice, for example, but it does not require that a religious healthcare institution that has opted out of providing gender-affirming care add an asterisk to that policy, explaining how some patients will be treated differently (because of course, as I explained above, the goal of the religious exemption is to engage in discrimination that is otherwise prohibited under Section 1557). No laws require explaining any of this to the public or to patients and their families.

When hospitals merge to form larger and more profitable systems, a secular system may acquire a Catholic facility or the other way around. Which collaborator will adapt its values and medical care for the other? One option would be for the system to disengage from the Catholic Church. Another option is for the new system to govern itself by the directives as a Catholic facility. In some recent merger cases, it has been too controversial to expand Catholic restrictions through hospital-system growth. Catholic Healthcare West was a large Catholic hospital system operating in northern California in competition with Sutter Health, a secular system there. To grow, it ended its governing relationship with the Catholic Church and became Dignity Health. Some parts of the system continue to operate as Catholic hospitals, but others, including a major center for gender-affirming care in San Francisco, do not. Overall, however, the growth has been in the more religious direction, with the Catholic systems in the more favorable position to absorb secular hospitals and require them to follow the directives.[49] Some arrangements involve public systems, often university teaching hospitals, consolidating with Catholic hospitals so that some part of the public hospital system is governed by Catholic bishops.[50] My own employer, the University of Michigan, has adopted an agreement like this to absorb the once-secular community hospital in the nearby town of Chelsea in a collaboration with a Catholic healthcare system. It is now run by Trinity Health, a Catholic hospital system.

We saw in chapter 2 that the threat of not being able to participate in the new Medicare program was a major force behind hospital desegregation across the South. The stick for civil rights compliance has long been federal funding in healthcare and education. The Supreme Court's objections to the Affordable Care Act, however, have presumptively removed or at least severely curtailed that mechanism for enforcing the antidiscrimination provisions of Section 1557. In *National Federation of Independent Business v. Sebelius*, the 2012 case challenging the Affordable Care Act's requirement to expand Medicaid eligibility in all states to adults earning less than 133 percent of the federal poverty rate, the Supreme Court held that the threat of removing all of a state's Medicaid funding if they did not expand their program was unduly coercive.[51] The Catholic Health Care Leadership Alliance, expanding on the coercion language from *National Federation of Independent Business v. Sebelius* beyond the federalism issue of coercing states, argues that "[t]he penalties that will be levied against hospitals for not complying with the [Biden administration's] proposed rule's gender-identity affirmance policy will be so substantial and financially threatening as to amount to an overtly coercive condition upon religious health care professionals."[52] States were allowed to decide without compulsion if they wanted to expand their Medicaid programs or not, and many more conservative states did not.

The question of how coercive it is for the Department of Health and Human Services to threaten to remove the ability of a hospital to bill Medicare, for example, is up for debate in a way that it was not when President Johnson moved forcefully to enforce racial nondiscrimination in access to facilities in the summer of 1966 as the Medicare program began. Even then, officials had worried that "the sanction may be deemed so extreme as to suggest it will never be employed."[53] Not only are there multiple layers of statutory and constitutional protections for religious exercise that arose since then—including the right to withhold many categories of care around reproduction but likely also gender-affirming care—but the threat of enforcement is significantly weakened even if those protections did not apply. The threat is weakened because the sanction of cutting off federal healthcare dollars is indeed dramatic, has not been used, would meet with furious opposition, and would harm patients. Just as we saw that physicians are out of reach of the hospital grievance handlers because only physicians can discipline other physicians, health care civil rights can fail at the national level of enforcement because the primary mechanism of enforcement has been significantly undercut.

REBRANDING RELIGION, PROMOTING UNCERTAINTY, AND CONTESTING EXPERTISE

Most of this chapter focuses on the explicitly religious arguments against health care civil rights under the religious objection frame. I have argued that there is, in practical terms and in our courtrooms, a head-to-head matchup of rights in which they are substantively incompatible: religious freedom as conservatives claim it means denying gender-affirming recognition and care provision.[54] The case of Catholic healthcare systems trying to maintain religious rules while competing in the healthcare systems marketplace reveals some tensions that this contest exposes, even under favorable legal conditions now. There are additional tensions, though, rooted in the fact that the dominance of the brand of religious conservativism that has notched so many wins against trans health care civil rights is more politically achieved than broadly popular. That is, these religious conservatives represent at best about fifteen percent of the US population and dominate in groups like Republican primary voters, but overall, their views are not widely shared, especially not among younger people. Some rebranding is required. Making claims about gender-affirming care in religious terms is not enough when the broader context for evaluating health care is evidence-based medicine.

A brief detour into another closely related issue gives us an example of rebranding of religious claims into secular language. Because religious conservatives believe that only a married father and mother can rear children into proper roles and self-understandings of themselves as boys and girls, same-sex marriages are also illegitimate. The Supreme Court upheld marriage equality for same-sex couples in the 2015 *Obergefell v. Hodges* decision and surveys show it is widely accepted (seventy-one percent support overall and even among weekly churchgoers it's forty-one percent).[55] Alliance Defending Freedom, staunchly opposed to marriage equality, has been hard at work on this needed rebranding. "Marriage is about equality and diversity," they claim, because it joins "the two equally important and diverse halves of humanity represented in men and women."[56] Legalizing same-sex marriage hurts children and "the underprivileged."[57] Even though their reasoning is based on biblical foundations, Alliance Defending Freedom borrows progressive terms in equality, diversity, and concern for the marginalized and repackages them to justify excluding same-sex couples from marriage.

The organizations bringing impact litigation from the right wing clearly have their sights set on overturning *Obergefell*. They are in a tricky position, however, because even though the lower federal courts are easy picking grounds for wins in certain district courts and the more conservative appeals courts, there are risks of pushing too fast. The electoral popularity of abortion in statewide elections and ballot measure votes after the *Dobbs* decision overturned *Roe* has shown that the public generally does not like rights being taken away. Trans youth and adults are a much smaller group than people who have had abortions and an even smaller group than people who are in a same-sex marriage or know someone who is. Winning cases opposing trans health care civil rights is much easier for groups like Alliance Defending Freedom than eradicating same-sex marriage because they do not have to argue for overturning a recent Supreme Court precedent. Rolling back marriage equality using frameworks of equality and diversity may seem far-fetched. The point is to supply cover post-*Dobbs*, recognizing that rolling back rights that are broadly popular will work best if shaped within progressive terms. Opposition to gender-affirming care has been an easier rebranding, however, because evidence-based medicine itself supplies alternate terms of contestation, and opponents have been able to produce professional organizations, experts, and research to argue on those terms.[58]

The religious objection frame directly contradicts a mainstream medical expertise frame. The mainstream medical expertise frame explains being trans as having a diagnosable condition that is treatable with therapy, hormones, and surgery to align the person's gender identity with their body. It takes a firmly realist view of trans identity in which gender dysphoria is a real phenomenon that presents with certain characteristics, persistence, and duration that are clear enough to meet medical definitions. Major medical societies in the United States support gender-affirming care and insurance coverage for it, including the American Medical Association, the American Academy of Pediatrics, the Endocrine Society, and the American Society of Plastic Surgeons.[59]

The mainstream medical expertise framework is contested from within the trans community and within the broader coalition of those supportive of trans health care needs, as trans activists within medicine and on its outskirts argue that there is still too much gatekeeping and pathologizing from cisgender medical experts and that they ought to be able to give consent to treatments without having to claim a diagnosis, for example.[60] Non-binary people have struggled under the medical expertise frame because of its presumption that what trans people want is to move cleanly from one side of the gender binary to the other rather than to live in between or beyond it.[61] The medical expertise frame has shifted in response from being more paternalistic and gatekeeping toward greater acceptance of trans and non-binary people as experts themselves and as capable of consenting to and directing their own care without pathologization. This trend has meant expanding treatment options over the last quarter century, including for youth, and shifting power away from gatekeeping and toward expanding access.

Religious opponents of gender-affirming care as a health care civil right have mobilized alternative frameworks of expertise to argue that gender-affirming care is ideological rather than scientific, capriciously handed out by advocates rather than carefully extended by detached professionals, damaging to youth, and not well supported by long-term studies that meet the gold standard of evidence in medicine.[62] They see increases in people identifying as trans or non-binary and expansions in gender-affirming care as sudden and faddish, spreading like a disease in the culture. Lawyers and activists have worked very hard to generate controversy and then characterize gender-affirming care as "controversial and dangerous."[63] As I discuss in the next chapter, partisans on the religious side have run into trouble presenting themselves in court as the scientific and medical experts that groups like Alliance Defending Freedom need to fully mobilize an alternative account of expertise, however.

The American College of Pediatricians (ACPeds) has been a leader in the conservative effort to push gender-affirming care outside the mainstream medical expertise frame. It describes itself as a reputable medical organization and not a religious or political organization.[64] In amicus briefs on behalf of their approximately six hundred members, they oppose provision of gender-affirming care for youth on the grounds that it is not evidence based, is insufficiently studied, and is harmful. ACPeds assiduously presents itself using all the cues of neutrality and expertise rather than religion or politics, with the aim of destabilizing the mainstream consensus that gender-affirming care, including hormones and puberty blockers for youth, is the recommended course of treatment for gender dysphoria. Its founding tells a different story, however. ACPeds was founded in 2002 by a small breakaway group of conservative doctors who objected to the American Academy of Pediatrics' endorsement of second-parent adoption by gay and lesbian couples. The Southern Poverty Law Center designates ACPeds an anti-LGBTQ hate group because of their leadership's statements opposing family formation, marriage, and parenting by LGBTQ people, that the LGBTQ movement is intrinsically in support of pedophilia, that trans people are mentally ill, that gender-affirming care is child abuse, and in support of conversion therapies for LGBTQ people.[65] The group's entire existence has been devoted to anti-LGBT politics.

Opponents of gender-affirming care have put forth experts with sufficient credibility to clear the bar of creating uncertainty, at least for conservative judges and legislators. At least twenty-two state legislatures have agreed with ACPeds' view, enacting legislation prohibiting gender-affirming care for minors.[66] Judges hearing cases challenging these bans have ruled both for and against them with starkly different levels of deference to and framing of the mainstream medical consensus in support of care. There have been some full-scale bench trials with expert witnesses.[67] Findings in favor of the bans on care concede that the medical organizations support care but refuse to import that consensus into constitutional law. "What is it in the Constitution, moreover," asked the Sixth Circuit panel upholding bans in Tennessee and Kentucky, "that entitles experts in a given field to overrule the wishes of elected representatives and their constituents?"[68] One option to defend these bans on care is to simply disregard what mainstream medical and scientific professionals think. Judges note that the Food and Drug Administration has not approved hormone therapy specifically for gender dysphoria so that doctors are prescribing it "off label," which they interpret as uncertainty among experts.[69]

Producing just enough uncertainty ("dueling affidavits," as the Sixth Circuit put it) to justify dismissing mainstream consensus is helpful for opponents. Conservative movement litigation has already spelled out the constitutional arguments the Supreme Court will need to find against the parents and youth who need gender-affirming care. Lower federal courts have found that there is no protected class status under the equal protection clause for trans youth or adults, so these restrictions clearly pass the low standard of rational basis review given some level of medical concern or uncertainty. Nor are these bans a burden on one sex or the other because they apply to both sexes, in this argument, so there is no access to heightened scrutiny as a sex classification. Restricting medical treatments that only one sex would need does not even trigger heightened scrutiny under the equal protection clause anyway, a conclusion nicely laid out for the conservative canon in *Dobbs* (removing the right to an abortion despite its impact on cisgender women). Substantive due process could offer grounds for affirming parents' rights to direct care for their children. But it is always possible to select a preferred level of generality to describe a right in a substantive due process analysis that makes it seem new and weird and therefore not rooted in our nation's history and tradition. Parental rights over children are certainly long-standing, but the right to puberty blockers is not. A court that upheld a ban pointed to "regulatory debate" and preferred to leave such matters in the hands of the state legislatures.[70]

Alliance Defending Freedom promptly sued the Biden administration over its most recent Section 1557 regulations with a Mississippi pediatrics practice as the plaintiff. Their publicity photos feature Black babies prominently. Complying with Section 1557's civil rights protections for trans people, their complaint argues, would "effectively prevent [the pediatricians] from treating the most vulnerable children in Mississippi unless they ascribe to the radical gender ideology imposed by the president and his bureaucrats in Washington, D.C."[71] Promoting their cause through Black children on Medicaid and the Children's Health Insurance Program is useful because it counterposes the interests of low income (Black) children against (white) trans people while erasing the long history of anti-Black racism in white evangelicalism justified by the Bible.[72] It also hides the fact that the arguments dismantling the ability of the federal government to legislate and regulate against gender-identity discrimination undermine civil rights based on any other trait including race too. Open arguments that interracial dating violates God's commands are out of fashion now, but Bob Jones University defended its ban all the way to the Supreme Court in 1982 and only lifted its ban in 2000 when it received bad publicity after George W. Bush's campaign visit there.[73] Separating racialization from transness is a rhetorical, political, and legal strategy of white cisgender supremacy to disguise itself and its broader implications.

In the next chapter, I turn to the arguments at the governmental level that have prevailed in defense of trans health care civil rights. But it should be clear that religious opponents have multiple sources of powerful arguments that are more than capable of defeating the foundational underpinnings as well as practices of health care civil rights for anyone who deviates from cisgender heterosexuality and binary, acceptable gender presentation. If groups like Alliance Defending Freedom have their way, there will be no gender-affirming care, no name changes, and no changes to pronouns at all. They are well on their way to securing expanded exemptions for religious individuals and healthcare systems to discriminate on the basis of gender identity (and sexual orientation, gender expression, and gender stereotypes too), exemptions that restrict statutory and constitutional protections based on "sex" only to binary male and female categories assigned at birth. A Supreme Court majority likely shares their policy preferences against gender-identity protections in civil rights. The Court has already given itself the power to ignore the regulations of the administrative state, developed through years of information seeking and tens of thousands of public comments from experts and ordinary people. The religious protection arguments are sufficiently strong in their favor that the efforts to destabilize the medical consensus behind gender-affirming care function more as backup and facade but are likely enough for a judicial nod of approval. The core argument is that health care civil rights for trans people cannot exist because trans people do not legitimately exist.

Realizing Health Care Civil Rights

Jason had been newly hired to be the Section 1557 coordinator for a large hospital. He was an attorney, and his previous position was working as a state-level civil rights investigator. In one case Jason described to me, he confronted a doctor in clinical affairs about staff canceling appointments for deaf and blind patients if proper interpreters were not available at the scheduled time, which he thought was discriminatory denial of care. The doctor deflected the issue, which seemed to Jason to be "more of a response of a doctor protecting other doctors than it was actually of a concern for the patients and for being compliant, which is interesting to me." Compared to the other grievance handlers we interviewed, Jason was unique in his willingness to label patient problems as discrimination, to confront doctors, and to express frustration that doctors protected each other in what he saw as a clear example of denial of care based on disability. Because he was previously an attorney, his professional tool kit included adversarial confrontation without regard to hierarchy. He confronted a doctor even though doctors are beyond the disciplinary reach of nonmedical professionals like the civil rights grievance handlers in patient experience. Critically, he did not receive the patient experience professional socialization described in chapter 2. Jason eschewed the techniques of disbelief, reinterpretation, and soothing that we saw were so important in that professionalized patient experience framework.

My argument has been that there are many ways for discrimination laws to fail patients and that generally they do. Refracting civil rights through health and healthcare happens through absorption, deflection, and defeat. All these outcomes fail patients because they diminish or demobilize what we hoped civil rights could do for health inequality. But my theoretical framework allows for on the ground variations as well as legal and political mobilization to transform what rights are in practice, so of course it is possible for rights to be refracted in ways that amplify them or at least scatter and change them in ways that still advance the goals of trans health care civil rights. At each level of analysis in this book, people still found ways to realize rights. If conservative opponents succeed in dismantling trans health care civil rights in the formal law, they could still live on in these everyday voluntary practices.

In this chapter, I revisit all the frameworks and sites of the previous chapters, showing how rights are sometimes realized at each of our three levels. Different approaches to management and conflict over patient rights in healthcare settings allow alternate accounts to emerge. Intermediaries and trans self-advocacy in health insurance coverage disputes sometimes succeed in navigating insurance complexity to secure coverage for gender-affirming care. And despite the very conservative turn against trans health care rights at the Supreme Court and across nearly half our state legislatures, advocates for health care civil rights based on gender identity have won in litigation across the country.

SCATTERED EXCEPTIONS IN HEALTH CARE CIVIL RIGHTS ON THE GROUND

When civil rights are refracted through healthcare, that means that they move through the professional structures, training and attitudes, and material and digital tools that people use to do rights work in those settings. I argued in chapter 2 that the patient experience framework and tools explain much of the absorption and then demobilization of rights that I saw in hospitals. Rights broke through occasionally and inconsistently. Indeed, the lack of consistency in when and how health care civil rights were able to be realized shows that there is not a coherent alternative framework. The exceptions prove the point, that is.

Most grievance handlers drew on that patient experience framework, but a few—like Jason, the lawyer and former civil rights investigator—more clearly articulated discrimination as a problem and handled situations differently. Jason looked within his organization for discriminatory people and practices and did not sit within a patient experience department. Rooting out discrimination was even easier in other healthcare business models. Although my final sample was admittedly lopsided towards hospitals, where access to interview subjects was easier, I was able to see how a freestanding surgical center is a different organizational model that matters. Over half of surgeries in the United States every year are performed in these outpatient settings, which are often physician owned and quite profitable. They are covered by Section 1557, but they lack the bureaucratic problem management structures that hospitals have, such as patient experience departments and labor unions. They are more like standard businesses, with heightened profit motives, competition for customers, and the ability to fire at will.

Larry, the CEO of an ambulatory surgical center in New York City, simply fired staff whose actions upset or offended patients. In one instance, a patient waited alone in a cold preoperative waiting room in a gown for two and half hours because the surgeon was late. When the surgery ended, a porter escorted the patient in an elevator with garbage bags. "We literally took the patient out with the trash," he said. Larry uses the common formulation of failed communication ("[T]here was a total lack of communication"), but in contrast to the nonconsequences we frequently heard about from other interviewees, he fired the porter (but not the surgeon). Larry also fired a doctor in another example for what he understood to be explicit sex discrimination (asking a cisgender man with long hair to take a pregnancy test).

There is no fellow doctor as chief medical officer to shield doctors from consequences in Larry's business model. Ambulatory surgical centers are in competition for patients, and Larry believed their complaints. "There's some validity in every single complaint," he said. "You have to realize that to some level." He was also highly aware that most patients complain because they do not want the same thing to happen to someone else and that a real apology can be effective. "Though we do live in a litigious society, you've just got to be very honest about exactly what occurred. 'I truly am sorry this happened to you. I've actually made [sure] that this won't happen to you again.'" Here, Larry distinguishes his approach from the "blameless apology" by expressing a belief in the importance of sincere apology, acknowledgement, and accountability. There is a version of the patient satisfaction survey for outpatient surgery centers, though the existence and pressure of the surveys are not organizationally instantiated through a cadre of professionals as in hospitals. Larry led a boiled-down, customer-focused small-business model that does not have those layers of organizational culture to absorb, diffuse, and ignore complaints. This model is dependent on the whims of the leader and thus only weakly capable of rights enforcement overall.

Others I spoke with drew on identity and understandings of discrimination to see rights differently. Some hospital grievance handlers openly wrangled with the implications of conflating customer service issues with rights violations, though this was rare. Dan, a nurse and patient safety officer in rural Michigan, identified himself as gay and felt that his sexual orientation gave him a different perspective on patient conflicts. Dan mused that his hospital could do more to distinguish discrimination complaints from other kinds of complaints, noting, "I think there's a delineation between addressing the customer service aspect for the complaint versus 'This is a really bad violation where we violated a human being's rights.'" He clearly saw that failures of recognition (say, deadnaming a trans person seeking care) would violate their health care civil rights but also that such a case would seem like staff rudeness as a customer service issue instead. Dan's reflectiveness shows how heightened awareness about discrimination could break through the patient experience framework. Dan and Jason did not work in the same hospital, but combining Jason's explicit civil rights investigatory perspective with Dan's more nuanced sense of what discrimination looks like would be a helpful correction to the patient experience framework.

Finally, some providers wrestled with the fact that there was simply a gap in healthcare for a vulnerable person who called it discrimination. They did not rationalize the harm away but saw that it was bigger than what Section 1557 can fix. Like Dan's thoughts, this reflection was not fully formed but nonetheless shows how care providers confronted the challenges of rights with little provisioning to support them, what Michael McCann calls the "unbearable lightness of rights."[1] Jan, director of a Federally Qualified Health Center (FQHC) serving low-income people, explained their denial of a root canal for a dental patient who was angry about it and claimed discrimination. "He needed a root canal," she explained, "which is unfortunately a thousand-dollar procedure, and we don't offer that level of care." The director saw that her facility could "barely scratch the surface of what the community needs" because of the structural inadequacy of FQHC resources for the poor. "I think he was just angry," Jan said. "It really didn't get resolved and he's probably still mad." There is no minimum dental care that must be provided to low-income adults under Medicaid, and most states provide only emergency dental care under their programs. Unlike many hospital grievance handlers who worked hard to soothe patient annoyances, Jan acknowledges that ongoing anger is a reasonable response to poverty and pain. Her formulation of "just angry" minimizes what could be a structural critique into individual feeling. Treating dental care as something outside regular health care and insurance is a political choice we've made that causes suffering as oral health needs go unmet. "It didn't get resolved" because there was simply nowhere for a poor person to get a root canal.

BEYOND COMPLIANCE: HOSPITAL-WIDE MOBILIZATION FOR GENDER-IDENTITY PROTECTIONS

Some hospitals approached 1557 compliance very broadly, almost always focused on trans patient rights rather than other gender-related issues, such as sexual harassment, which no one named as a civil rights obligation under 1557. I borrow the term *beyond compliance* to describe an organization that does more than is legally required.[2] Beyond compliance happens when the organization and its leaders begin to think through exactly what it would look like on the ground to avoid misgendering trans patients, to treat them with respect in every interaction, and to provide the best care. The Section 1557 committees I observed had a handful of core members and about a dozen participating members from throughout the hospital system and met approximately monthly. They pulled in allies from all around the organization, such as within the medical records management system, where one hospital created their own add-in to the medical records system to record a patient's sex at birth, gender identity, preferred name, and sexual orientation. In a few instances, leaders analyzed patient experience surveys to see if patient experience varied systematically by demographic traits including gender identity.

The defining feature of a beyond-compliant organization was the presence of entrepreneurial professionals beyond the grievance process, often doctors and nearly always cisgender women, who took up the cause of improving trans care and promoted wide-ranging reforms. They formed committees, sometimes meeting on their own time and sometimes supported by staff assigned for the purpose. The same people who already worked on diversity committees, in the staff LGBT group, or on related areas such as HIV care would join the committee along with medical providers interested in transgender health (therapists, social workers, gynecologists, pediatricians, endocrinologists, and surgeons). They found and used trans health resources and best practices from sources such as the Fenway Institute and the World Professional Association for Transgender Health. Evaluations of hospitals by the Human Rights Campaign through their Healthcare Equality Index provided a way for internal advocates to convince higher-ups that attention to LGBT rights would have a reputation-enhancing effect. Once the organization asked what it would really mean to treat trans people seeking care respectfully and equally, it became clear that the task of change implicated professional culture, information systems, staff training, building layout and signage, and beyond, all in interconnected and messy ways. Each suggested change—let's modify our electronic medical records (EMR) system, let's add to the chart sticker or the inpatient wristband, let's have a new mandatory training—competed with other priorities, demanded staff attention and resources, and had to climb the agenda in multiple departments.

Take the example of using the correct name for a patient. There are physical and digital points of naming: the entry in the electronic medical record, the sticker that goes on paper charts, forms, and specimen containers, the wristband for those admitted to the hospital (often the only thing on the person's body besides a gown and which is checked by every employee from the food deliverer to each nurse on every shift), the white board in an inpatient room, and the electronic board projected in the operating room. A name is attached to a body, and what body parts someone has are critical to know and track, so advocates also developed organ inventories in EMRs to know when to do a prostate exam, for example. Each item a name is attached to belongs somewhere in the institutional landscape and hierarchy and often has very limited real estate on it (for a physical thing like a wristband) or has demands on its use from many constituencies in a health system. The billing department will insist on legal names for payment even if another name a patient uses has been added in all these other places, for example.

While some committee-led reforms had to grind through significant barriers like this example of billing system incompatibility, we observed other moments when the energy of one person had a significant impact. For example, a pediatrician at one beyond-compliant hospital who works with gender-nonconforming youth in poverty secured free hormones for her patients throughout her city. She simply asked the pharmacist in their health system if such provision could be part of their community benefit program. Describing the pharmacist's response, the doctor said, "And she's like, all about it [snaps fingers], you know. She is totally supportive and didn't blink an eye in terms of like using the community benefit dollars for that." Free delivery to the LGBT community health center is included. This doctor emphasized that her hospital system's broad support for LGBT issues was deeply rooted in the culture because a prominent leader was a lesbian and had made it a priority.

CONSTRUCTING RECOGNITION IN ELECTRONIC MEDICAL RECORDS AND ORGAN INVENTORIES

The original Department of Health and Human Services regulation that enacted a trans-inclusive Section 1557 required "treating individuals in a manner consistent with their gender identity" in health care.[3] This requirement is the foundation of trans health care civil rights in its strongest iteration. But what does that mean? I have argued that health care civil rights must involve both proper recognition and sufficient provisioning. Recognition turned out to be a major challenge in health care settings. To treat someone in a manner consistent with their gender identity in a health care setting, one must first know what that patient's gender identity is. One must have a way of seeing and tracking when transgender patients experience discrimination. As I argued in chapter 2, when that organizational task becomes more about tamping down problems and "moving those scores," the seeing and knowing cannot become part of rights enforcement. Knowing people's gender identity is the route to successful rights implementation prior to managing problems, though. Done well, it means that baseline conditions for rights protections exist in the organization. Enacting civil rights in healthcare means adapting systems to gather knowledge that can comprise proper recognition: managing complaints, determining gender in common interactions with frontline staff (such as signing in at the registration desk), and delivering clinical care focused on the body and its organs (such as determining who needs a cervical cancer screening). These technology systems powerfully shape health equity for trans people.[4]

The idea that health care records should include a patient's gender identity and sexual orientation gained prominence in a 2011 Institute of Medicine report on LGBT health. It recommended that SOGI (sexual orientation and gender identity, pronounced so-gee) data collection be part of "meaningful use" of electronic medical records.[5] Federal regulations subsequently required that demographics in EMR include SOGI by 2018.[6] The earliest implementers were federally funded health centers, required to report SOGI data in 2016 by the Health Resources and Services Administration.[7] I found that the concreteness of being required to find out patients' gender identities and sexual orientations could anchor rights practices as both early adopters and more robustly compliant healthcare providers wrestled with how their information systems documented this information and what needed to change, how to go about asking patients, whom to ask and when, and how to prepare their staff to gather this information. Talking about one's sexual orientation and gender identity was supposed to become a normal part of medical registration for everyone. For the cisgender people working in patient registration and records and for the cisgender patients who encountered it for the first time, it was a learning experience. The SOGI requirement pushed tensions into view. Jean Marie, who runs a small rural FQHC that was required to implement SOGI documentation as a condition of their funding from the Health Resources and Services Administration, explains how that data collection requirement touched off an education process throughout her organization:

> Once you start [documenting SOGI], then it opens up the door to other things, the discrimination, the healthcare aspects of it, that kind of thing. Our front office supervisor has been to some conferences and seminars on how to collect that data. Our providers have been involved in some education as far as treatment and you know, transgender and that kind of thing, stuff that was put on by the LGBT community.

In other words, creating a legal obligation to "treat individuals in a manner consistent with their gender identity" in health care settings as a matter of civil rights started a cascade of information technology shifts and office-level practices that were visible, concrete, and radiated throughout a healthcare organization.

Working with technologies to achieve proper transgender patient recognition was both a result and a driver of mobilization. Frontline staff had to be trained to gather someone's name and to handle it smoothly if legal name, name being used, and gender presentation did not seem to match. Some of the named Section 1557 coordinators we spoke with understood this moment as critical and possibly embarrassing for all. They explained that transgender issues were new and strange to the frontline staff. Many settings that had achieved midrange compliance had not done much reception staff training. Others simply asserted that they were sure everyone would be treated with respect, although without any training, this confidence seems misplaced given the clear patterns of disrespect trans patients describe.

As hospitals began grappling with implementing Section 1557, they confronted myriad ways that a patient's sex classification could be recorded and be misaligned with their gender identity. A patient could be greeted with the wrong name checking in for an appointment. Insurance billing could fail to match recorded sex to sex-specific procedure codes (if, say, a transgender man had changed his legal sex to male but then sought a hysterectomy). Many different people would need to know the correct information to treat the patient the right way, from the nurse checking a bracelet to make sure the right medication is delivered to the right patient to the food delivery to the automated voice sending the patient an appointment reminder call. Actualizing transgender patient rights took the form of organizational advocacy to change the objects that materialize gender identity. In a complex organization, that meant making SOGI designations important to a lot of different stakeholders. Dr. Byrd, a medical resident who joined her large hospital's 1557 implementation committee, related how hard it was to change the name on the precious real estate of the lab-specimen stickers:

> We have these stickers that print out that get pasted on specimens, on people's labs. Some medical assistants used to call people from the waiting room, and until about a month ago, those only had legal name on them. And it was a whole long bureaucracy. It's a tiny space on a sticker and various groups want to claim that space to put certain markers on there that help their particular group. But [the 1557 committee] advocated and finally got "preferred name" on those stickers.

Dr. Byrd described going around to different groups in the hospital, bringing problems about gender misrecognition to their attention. "Security is a really good example where I was like, I don't know who I'm going to run into in security," she recalled.

> And we identified some major problems, like currently if a visitor checks in, they have to provide a government-issued ID and that ID gets scanned. And then whatever name is on that ID populated onto a badge that that person has to wear. And there's no way for the security personnel to change the name that appears on the badge. So if a trans person, for example, has an ID that does not match the name that they use, and maybe their appearance, they could potentially be outed by this badge that they're supposed to wear. When I pointed [this] out to security, they identified it as a huge problem that needed to be fixed immediately and called the software company and are in the process of making a change so that last name only will appear, because we had this conversation.

Getting transgender recognition right in electronic medical records (EMR) was the biggest problem for organizations. Some hospitals had the resources to create their own gender-identity forms in EMR as the early requirements were enacted, but many relied on the corporate providers to update their software. Dave is a trans man who works on SOGI implementation at a major national EMR company. He has been the go-to person for clients to call when either "the organization just had their first out trans patient" and "something goes wrong" or when "there is a trans employee or some employee that, you know, kind of is an ally of the trans community and they are pushing their organization to do something." He described how people in hospitals pushed for SOGI recognition in their EMR:

> It's an analyst who works with the software or, you know, not someone very high up on the food chain kind of pushing [better SOGI documentation], telling their organization, "You know, this is patient safety. We're not treating these patients correctly and we need to do so." Or they might be nurses. Some of the organizations, they

have like an LGBT employee group, and that group will get together and discuss, "Hey, our software isn't really that great for LGBT patients," and they'll approach their executives and say, "We've been talking about this. We know we can do more. Can we get started on that process?"

Before 2018, he explained, all their institutional customers had access to a smart form that would collect SOGI information and an organ inventory. But in the 2018 product release, SOGI and the organ inventory became opt-out, that is, baked into the default program that every client gets. "We did that deliberately," Dave says, "because this is a patient safety issue."

Susan is part of the gender-identity working group at her large hospital, working in the IT department on adaptations to their electronic medical records system for SOGI. Before the new build that Dave worked to develop was available, she helped design her hospital's own form. She explained how she developed the gender-identity options in their system:

> [So on the gender-identity form, is that a write-in or is it a drop-down?] I could show you. It is a drop-down. See, we got the list of gender identities. If you're not one of these gender identities, you choose "other," then you need to document what did the patient say their gender identity is. And same thing with pronouns. We've got some people, their pronouns are zi, like Z-I. Gosh, I don't know what that is. We don't have that on ours because it's not very common. Non-binary was one that we added after a while, because we did have more than a handful of patients that indicated that's what they were. Like every six months, I'll run the report and see is there's something that's showing up in "other" that shows up frequently, then maybe we should add it as to one of our choices.

Tellingly, Susan's IT work on the gender-identity-recognition interpretation of Section 1557 does not interact with the patient-driven complaint side or the satisfaction surveys. "[When you guys do HCAHPS surveys or if they're in your event reporting system, like if there are complaints and grievance filed, do those interface with the medical records?] I don't really know what HCAHPS is. [The patient experience surveys.] They're not in here at all. This is just really medical information. Those have their own separate databases."

Accurate SOGI recognition is part of determining gender that everyone who uses EMR to interact with and name a patient would need. Clinicians wanted more, though, because for them proper care involves both the story of proper interpersonal gender-identity recognition and also caring for the body parts one has regardless of their role in lived gender identity. I opened this book with Sam's tragic situation, in which he was properly recognized as a man but was also pregnant and experiencing an emergency complication that went undetected until it was too late. Conservative opponents of recognizing trans people as they are claimed that the problem was that Sam received gender-identity recognition as a man but was really a woman, thereby blaming him and trans existence itself for causing confusion. But the doctors I spoke with all saw gender-identity recognition and proper care of the body, no matter what parts it has or doesn't have, as perfectly compatible.

The trans-affirming doctors and other clinicians who were active in their hospital's 1557 committees explained how EMR and organ inventories bolster trans rights and provide the best care. Lisa, a doctor at a beyond-compliant urban hospital, explains: "At the end of the day who you are or your gender identity is not always going to line up with your anatomy. What I really care about is what is the anatomy that you have. If you're a guy but you still have a cervix, we need to do a Pap smear." The solution is the organ inventory within the EMR that lists what organs a person has or does not have. Many people have an organ removed at some point in their lives—their uterus, gall bladder, or appendix—and that fact is medically relevant. An organ inventory lets a clinician know about a person's body at the same time as they recognize their gender identity. Religious opponents of trans health recognition do not want to use correct names or pronouns or be compelled to collect this health information, which would endanger trans people's health and make experiences like Sam's more likely to happen again.

Grievance records and satisfaction surveys did not track trans experiences well at all, while EMR entries recognize both the current gender identity and the organs that may not match it. These records are a helpful technology that is consistent with the organization's needs rather than transformative or challenging.[8] They offer the hope of resolving several possible conflicts. The first is the interpersonal awkwardness between frontline staff and someone whose gender presentation is unexpected, say when the registration desk calls out the wrong name. But the second is quite different: it is when a provider whose job involves probing someone's body parts must properly acknowledge the body as it is while also recognizing the person's gender identity. No one who thought this was important thought it was hard. The frontline staff person needs to determine gender socially and affirm the patient's "preferred name," as the EMR then described it, while the care provider needs to do that, too, but also to integrate the person's gender identity with whatever organs they have.

These systems are used and controlled by medical professionals and designed by private companies, not by the trans people seeking care whose bodies and identities are represented within them. Dave, a trans man, played an important role in shaping the dominant EMR software to better recognize trans people as the first set of Section 1557 regulations rolled out. Current EMR structures build in possibilities for gender change and recognize that it has happened, but they are still far from being what Oliver Haimson calls trans technologies.[9] They would need to be much more open to control by those they describe and capable of representing more realness and diversity of trans experiences with the medical world, for example. These are, of course, not what companies build EMR to do. Records are mostly for billing insurance companies. All the same, they are technological systems that permeate every health care interaction, and civil rights law requires that they recognize trans people properly and respectfully. A government specifying that some data about its population must be collected is one of the hallmarks of modernity and a foundational practice of governance. It's easy to tell if an EMR system is collecting SOGI data or not. Outcomes are clearer than knowing, for example, if care has become more respectful.

The organ inventory is an example of how taking a person apart and seeing them as dissembled or out of alignment with their lived gender is not necessarily an undignified view of personhood (though it often is).[10] By contrast, grievance handlers often spoke of treating "the whole person," which they meant to be dignifying but also hewed closely to denying that minority identity might explain poor treatment. Which is better as a basis for rights, a technology controlled by medical professionals that encodes bits of information about trans identity and change over time accurately or a set of organizational practices that gushes about patient centeredness and respect for everyone in generalized terms? I pose the question to illustrate the options, but there is no need to choose. These practices coexist in the refraction of health care civil rights at the patient level and thus mutually constitute what rights can be.

RECIPIENT RIGHTS IN BEHAVIORAL HEALTH

One particularly detailed, vivid, and highly rights-oriented account was able to stand out. It came from what grievance handlers called "recipient rights" in "behavioral health." The complaint bucket generally is a jumble, but the rights of people getting mental health care have broken through as unique and specifically legally protected rather than watered down into complaints and miscommunication. Dave, a middle-aged white man who is the 1557 coordinator at his small critical access hospital, knows the law well: "Recipient rights is specific to patients receiving mental health services . . . mandated by the Michigan Mental Health Code, which is a law here in Michigan." June, a white woman in her sixties handling HR and compliance in an FQHC, explains how being trained in mental health recipient rights frames her general approach: "Once you get the understanding of why we have recipient rights and what purpose they serve, it's fairly easy to transfer that base of knowledge to working with patients in other areas too."

Jordan worked as a McDonald's manager for fifteen years before becoming a mental health technician. He was then promoted to patient advocate and recipient rights supervisor in a large hospital system. Jordan first describes his main job as "dealing with patient complaints," then adds that he handles "recipient rights complaints from our mental health unit." Jordan launches into a long description of the steps he takes for anyone in community mental health services or a psychiatric unit. When we asked why the language of rights get used for mental health patients but not for other patients, Jordan struggled to account for it. "They still have patient rights, general patient rights," he replied. "It's just that the Mental

Health Code, or all patients do. Just that the Mental Health Code happens to have . . . that's what they called it [laughs, trails off]." Rights for people receiving mental health care have an unusually robust elaboration in Michigan that breaks through the mishmash of bureaucratically managed rights encrusted in policies and captures grievance handlers' attention.

How did mental health services come to be called "behavioral health" and become so much more clearly tied to rights? (Every patient is a "recipient," right? How are they so well specified as rights holders when other patients are not?) What institutional structures shape rights recognition here, and what does it mean for healthcare civil rights more generally? The idea of behavioral health dates to the 1970s as health psychology was gaining a foothold in the discipline and psychologists pushed for understandings of health and illness to take individual responsibility for health behaviors seriously.[11] It was a moralistic push by psychologists for professional ownership with physicians.

But by the mid-1990s, mental health facilities were renaming themselves "behavioral health" facilities, behavioral health managed care plans were highly profitable, and the term had migrated from its more obvious meaning (behaviors, presumably personal choices, that affect health) to functioning as a more palatable overarching term for mental health services that included a wider range of outpatient services for substance use disorders, smoking cessation, and more. They are part of the institutional structures that insure employee retention and performance in our employer-based health insurance system, including wellness programs, employee assistance programs, adoption assistance, marital counseling, eldercare advice, and managing the aftermath of workplace violence. Psychology never secured professional dominance over individual responsibility for health behaviors likely because the idea was central to other health paradigms that arose around the same time, particularly wellness and preventative health. But while the term *behavioral health* was a successful new buzzword because it was broad, flexible, and more appealing than "psychiatric" or "mental health," the conception of rights in behavioral health would remain tied to the most medically intervention-ist treatments for severe mental health issues, such as electroconvulsive therapy and involuntary commitment (even though the illnesses being treated are understood as genetic or brain-based diseases, not behaviors).

There is good reason why Dave, June, Karen, and Jordan, all working in Michigan, focused their energy on recipient rights and channeled their understandings of health care rights through this prism. In 1995, the Michigan legislature substantially rewrote its Mental Health Code and created an extensive rights regime for people undergoing psychiatric treatment. Chapter 7, "Rights of Recipients of Mental Health Services," lays out explicit rights ("a safe, sanitary, and humane treatment environment;" "least restrictive setting;" "right to be treated with dignity and respect;" rights of family members; consent procedures for surgery, electroconvulsive therapy, and administration of psychotropic drugs; minors' rights to treatment without parental consent; and protection from abuse and neglect). Mental health services providers (meaning community mental health facilities, licensed hospitals, and anyone contracting with the state) must have written policies that cover twenty-three specified rights from the statute, governing everything from the use of one-way glass for observation to resident labor, property, and funds.

The recipient rights booklet that each patient must receive is twenty pages long, including plain-language descriptions of all specified rights, "questions you may want to ask about your medication" with an extended list, a list of seven advocacy organizations that can help with rights claiming, and a civil rights section. The booklet goes on to list eight additional laws that may offer protections to a person with a mental disability, complete with instructions for making a rights claim. Page nineteen features a quote attributed to Nelson Mandela: "To deny people their rights is to challenge their very humanity." There is a state Office of Recipient Rights with review and investigatory powers including annual site visits and "appropriate remedial action," mandated trainings (three full days of in-person training), and the duty to make referrals to advocacy organizations to support claims-making. The Office of Recipient Rights website declares, "Rights is everybody's business!" and includes the hotline reporting number, maps to find the rights office nearest you, the rights complaint form for easy download, copies of the patient booklet, links to training resources, and many other documents. The Office of Recipient Rights sponsors continuing education, hosts an annual conference, and bestows annual awards for Innovation in Rights Protection, Advocacy on Behalf of Mental Health Recipients, Consumer Empowerment, and the Cookie Gant Spirit Award, named for a mental health disability activist.

The Michigan policy for patient rights in mental health care catches the attention of those it regulates with its specificity, its enforcement, and its bureaucratic investments in the tools that people would need to understand and use these rights. Michigan policymakers rightly saw that people in mental health care facilities were uniquely vulnerable to abuse in specific ways—having their belongings stolen, being administered electroconvulsive therapy without their consent—and that a high level of formal vigilance would be needed. I call this formal vigilance because I have not evaluated the on-the-ground workings of this system and therefore I cannot say under my theoretical framework whether rights refracted through this recipient rights framework are indeed more robust. But it was clear that the same grievance handlers who failed to see discrimination problems as health care civil rights overall saw recipient rights in behavioral health very differently.

In contrast, recall that Section 1557 passed in the Affordable Care Act (ACA) with no elaboration about what it would mean at all. When regulations finally came out six years later, they offered some specifics (room assignments by gender identity not sex at birth, for example, echoing the desegregation fight about putting patients of different races in the same inpatient rooms) but left critical areas like medical necessity determinations to insurance companies. Updated regulations leave that deference to medical necessity determinations in place. Announcing in detail how Section 1557 protected trans people threatened powerful social and religious identities but could only mobilize a smaller group as its direct beneficiaries. So while recipient rights in behavioral health are highly specified, people in mental health care are not a target group for right-wing mobilization to deny their existence and remove their rights. If they were, these specifications and robust bureaucratic investment in promoting rights would be much more politically costly and would likely become partisan and contested. Nonetheless, recipient rights in behavioral health care is a useful alternative reality that shows us that rights consciousness is compatible with healthcare bureaucracy.

PATHWAYS TO MEDICAL NECESSITY

I argued that expansions in insurance coverage and access for gender-affirming care, which were driven by the Obama administration's 2016 regulations that prohibited categorical exclusions in qualified plans, are the most significant achievement of Section 1557. Nearly all plans offered for sale on the ACA marketplace exchanges removed their exclusions for gender-affirming care soon after. Total exclusions for gender-affirming care, particularly surgeries, were common into this century before the ACA. At the time of the 2016 regulations, those plans only covered about ten million Americans (a relatively small share since most people are either old enough to be on Medicare or are covered by an employer-sponsored plan), but the share of people relying on these quasi-public plans and their subsidies has doubled since then. I call them quasi-public to make it clear that they are a shrunken-down version of what national health insurance might look like: plans with highly specified government requirements for generosity that private insurers would not otherwise sell that are heavily subsidized with public funds so that they are accessible for those who do not have another way to obtain health coverage. Most trans people report having employer-sponsored health insurance and another large share are on Medicaid due to lower incomes, but these ACA plans have been a critical source of coverage too. The marketplace plans are also policy drivers, normalizing removing exclusions and providing templates for companies not covered by 1557's requirements to mimic them anyway.

Insurance is the mesolevel of health care civil rights, between the hospital- or clinic-level interactions that people have when they seek health care and the government and legal level of legislatures and courtrooms. People wrangle over their rights with their health insurance company on the way to securing the health care interactions that they need in the hospitals or clinics. In chapter 3, I detailed how refracting rights through insurance diminishes and even extinguishes them through the interpretive ambiguity and procedural hurdles of medical necessity. Under health care civil rights law, insurers retain the power to construct medical necessity because Section 1557's rules let them keep that power.

Medical necessity is also constituted through achieved understandings of what the proper standard of care for a condition ought to be and to include. Allies act as intermediaries on an exclusive professional plane, such as when a surgeon gets on the phone with the doctor at the health insurance company to argue for coverage for a patient. Some gender-affirming procedures, such as facial surgeries, remain in a contested zone where they shift between being framed as merely cosmetic or as medically necessary. The World Professional Association for Transgender Health, or WPATH, publishes guidelines for health insurance coverage that are comprehensive and generous. Most actual policies do not cover the full range of WPATH-recommended procedures. Trans people and their allies can sometimes achieve an understanding of medical necessity that results in coverage, though, and there are specific ways to get there.

In this section, I delve into the success stories for rights mobilization through insurance. Trans people deploy strategies to qualify for medically-necessary care and fight for their rights against health insurance companies, typically outside any formal legal process. There are possibilities for eventual lawsuits or administrative proceedings against an insurer for coverage, but I focus here on the internal disputing processes within this mesolevel. These internal processes range from the more informal, such as repeated phone calls, to the formal internal layers of appeals and review that look like doctors being lawyers inside insurance companies. Health care intermediaries such as doctors, therapists, and administrators act as advocates for trans people seeking care by coding recommended procedures, drafting referral letters, and appealing insurance denials with an eye toward triggering medical necessity.

Most people do not insist on their rights in any context, especially when it is threatening to do so. Most people do not contest an insurance coverage denial and make an appeal.[12] Trans employees are no different and also have good reason to fear discrimination when their health insurance depends on their job. Even people aware of their rights hesitated to ask questions of their employer about health insurance coverage for fear of retaliation. Jill, a clinical social worker in a gender-services clinic, explains what she sees when people consider asking about their insurance benefits for transition care:

> Anxiety among the trans population is very high. So of course that trans person could want a copy of their insurance plan for any reason at all. But sometimes people think like, 'Oh, HR is going to know that I'm trans and then they're going to fire me.' This is the kind of stuff I hear from my people. Of course, people can go online and log in. But some people are daunted to do that.

A critical point here is that ambiguous or silent terms in one's health insurance plan can be particularly confusing. An explicit exclusion is hard to contest, but I have found that many plans do not describe coverage and exclusions clearly or at all.[13] There is no legal requirement to state coverage terms about gender-affirming care clearly or in any standardized way. (The ACA's requirement that group health plans publish standardized benefit information in a statement of benefits and coverage goes a long way towards transparency but does not include enough specifics to determine details about gender-affirming care.) So naturally many trans people would have questions about their benefits when they read their plans but then confront the problem of safety in raising the issue.

Despite the reality that even asking questions about insurance benefits that they are entitled to can be disconcerting, my team found that trans people often worked hard to mobilize their health care rights and that these efforts sometimes worked to secure care. As described in chapter 3, Phoenix engaged in "continuous letter writing after letter writing after letter writing" for two years before his insurance company would cover his surgery. Our interviewees spent hours on the phone to haggle with their insurance companies. These hours were unpaid labor—on top of extra jobs, loans, and consequences of delays in care that trans people already bore. Their cisgender coworkers did not have to spend these hours to use their benefits, meaning that in real terms, trans employees received less compensation at the same jobs. Even in the context of large expansions of formal insurance rights, rights mobilization is a costly undertaking that is privatized to trans employees' "spare" time.

Some people navigated the additional cost burdens of coverage denials by getting additional jobs. At one point, Quinn, a Black trans woman, had three jobs simultaneously to pay for out-of-pocket expenses while negotiating with her insurance. Riley, who is white and non-binary, paid for their electrolysis services by working part time at their electrologist's clinic. Other people relied on credit cards to fill this financial gap. People sometimes simply switched insurance plans. After Joshua, a white trans man, learned that his Catholic insurance plan would never cover his mastectomy, he switched jobs. Another person relocated to a job out of state to obtain insurance that explicitly covered the services he sought. Other interviewees began saving hormones after encountering challenges with coverage. Quinn explains:

> I've had two enrollment periods with the marketplace under the Trump administration. And each time there's been less and less that they've covered, and things are more and more expensive. And every time I can get it [the oral and injected estrogen] filled, I get both filled. And I've got a stockpile about a year's worth of oral estrogen on the chance that it won't be covered fully.

Saving medications is a common behavior for many people that is well studied in the medical literature and sympathetically understood as driven by fears of loss, exacerbated for Quinn by the Trump administration's anti-trans policies.[14]

Some trans people also recognized the importance of structural change and saw fighting with their insurance company as activism. For example, Joshua wished he "could have been a trailblazer" to create change with his insurance company. He took pride when insurance company staff noted that he was "certainly not the first person with this company to fight for transgender services but was certainly the most persistent," even though he eventually got a new job to get his care without any policy change at his previous employer. (It is unlikely that he would have been successful with a Catholic facility.) Others continued to push for structural change within their insurance company despite significant cost in labor and time. For example, Adrian spent eight months demanding his insurance company produce a written document to clarify coverage after his employer (with a self-funded plan) assured that him that it had negotiated coverage for these services, but the third-party administrator would not present the details. At the time of the interview, the document had not yet materialized; however, Adrian was committed to persisting. Jayla, a Black trans woman, advocated for structural change by working with nonprofits seeking expanded coverage both in policy language and in practice for trans people. Other trans people identified the importance of sharing information about their experiences in online communities and networks to help others avoid the time and labor they expended navigating insurance barriers. This information exchange created a type of interpersonal mobilization in response to the complex barriers they navigated.

Trans people seeking care could sometimes count on professional allies to work with them to mobilize for coverage from their insurance companies. It is after all in the interest of the provider that the insurance company pay. These health care intermediaries strategically reframe medical necessity to include the care they want to provide. Their reframing happens in three distinct ways: letters by mental health providers defining care as medically necessary, letters and phone calls from physicians appealing coverage denials by insurers, and careful, negotiated, and sometimes creative coding of procedures by physicians to trigger their own reimbursement.

Trans people are often required to obtain two letters from mental health providers indicating particular procedures are appropriate. The first concrete step to convincing an insurer about medical necessity comes through careful letter writing and framing concerning the importance of the care. Documentation of gender dysphoria, for example, is a key hurdle to establishing medical necessity. As discussed earlier, these are burdensome gatekeeping mechanisms that may require a trans or non-binary person to describe themselves as afflicted in ways they do not really feel just in order to jump through hoops. Their allies understand their gatekeeping role and often feel uncomfortable with it too. They focus on "keeping it moving," that is, doing what needs to be done to check the insurer's requirements off so the person can advance to the next level for their care. Health care professionals are particularly careful in how they frame their letters to insurance companies to support a finding that the requested coverage is medically necessary. Jill describes how she approaches letter writing:

> I know what the insurance companies want to hear and need to hear, and I write what they want and need to hear. [So what do they need to hear?] That the patient

checks those boxes, if you will. And I give as little information as possible. Because I don't want them to sort of glom onto anything that I said to use it to deny care. And this is how I teach other people to write letters as well. Like, let's keep it short and simple, basic, just outline that they meet the criteria, and keep it moving.

Referral letters convey a particular kind of clinically recognizable qualification for treatment and are written to satisfy that requirement. Professional allies often provide training and guidance in an informal network to other social workers and therapists writing evaluations on how to properly draft letters.

Once a person has passed through these points of diagnosis and gotten their letters, their doctor needs to help them secure prior authorization for surgery to go forward, and then the office needs to bill the procedure in a way that will result in payment. Gender surgery specialists have staff who are well versed in the steps and act as intermediaries and interpreters of the insurer's requirements. One major center employed a "health insurance navigator" whose job was to help trans people manage their insurance issues once they became prospective patients at the clinic. Other staff, such as surgery schedulers and office managers, were performing much of the same work.

Angela is the surgery scheduler in the surgery department at a large hospital where gender-affirming procedures are commonly performed. She can "look at this policy and say, okay, I have one referral letter. I have well-documented dysphoria. The patient is over the age of eighteen. I can check these marks, and I can tell a patient if it's going to be covered or not." But then there is still unpredictable behavior from the insurance company's own doctors. "If [the claim] gets there, it depends on the doctor whose desk it's sitting on," she explained. "Like, 'Oh, maybe they meet that criteria, but maybe they don't. So I'm going to deny it for that reason,' you know." The office staff and the surgeons need to stay engaged all the way through the process, managing problems that they cannot entirely predict.

Doctors negotiate with insurance companies directly, writing appeal letters when insurers deny coverage for certain services. There is an internal appeal process after an insurance company denies pre-authorization for coverage. Doctors assume the role of a quasi lawyer, blending their medical knowledge with their knowledge of WPATH guidelines for gender-affirming care and the insurance policy in question to advocate for coverage up through the layers of authority at the insurance company. When doctors join in appealing insurance company pre-authorization denials, for example, they must present the case to a medical director at the insurance company. The medical director is an MD who does not practice medicine and, in their view, is not aware of the needs of trans people. As Dr. Pielson, a surgeon, put it: "You can be speaking with a physician who's a medical director of an insurance company with absolutely no medical knowledge related to the procedure. They're just interpreting it in regard to their contract." If the surgeon can mobilize their expertise convincingly enough in this peer-to-peer conversation, that can successfully turn around a denial.

Allied professionals were exasperated because they thought these work-arounds would not be necessary if insurers followed the WPATH guidelines in their insurance policies and did not add additional requirements and hurdles. Although doctors conceded that the WPATH guidelines are not perfect, they considered them to be the best set of comprehensive recommendations with a stamp of consensus-driven expertise. "WPATH is full of experts in the field with a lot of experience, whereas insurance companies are not," Dr. Barker argued. In other words, they thought that insurance company practices undermined their expert judgment. In stef shuster's study of twenty-three trans medicine providers, the doctors and other clinicians moved between invoking the firmness of WPATH guidelines and interpreting them more flexibly, trying to manage the lack of a body of evidence that would normally undergird their gatekeeping role while managing to secure the services their people wanted.[15] We found more affirmation of the WPATH guidelines in the insurance context, perhaps because invoking it to an outside entity (the insurance company) is straightforward. Physicians note that they often reference WPATH guidelines in appeal letters and peer-to-peer conversations with the insurance medical director. Intermediaries counter the contested meanings of medical necessity and the barriers by countermobilizing with careful coding of procedures, thoughtful but equally strategic letter writing, and at times taking on a role of a quasi lawyer. These tactics and strategic narratives appear to at least partially assist trans people in establishing that the requested procedures are medically necessary.

Once the surgery has been approved, the surgeons remain concerned about how to bill the insurer and get paid adequately for their work. Insurers use detailed medical policies to tell doctors what they will cover. These documents are also not publicly available and are written in medical language. Doctors communicate what they are billing for through coding, which is the practice of breaking down and listing out everything that can be billed to the payer with a code (Current Procedural Terminology) from the International Classification of Diseases (ICD-10 to indicate current version 10). Doctors told us that insurers' approval for gender-affirming procedures has improved since the ACA's passage. They noted there are fewer appeals and battles with insurance companies over coverage, and the process of applying codes to describe gender-affirming procedures, especially surgeries, has become clearer and easier.

Although the situation has improved, doctors were also quick to point out that things are not perfect. There remains significant variation in coverage by insurers. This variation forces doctors to be mindful of how they code to achieve coverage. "If you look at trans surgery coding, it's a total mess," Dr. Fischer explained. "And different insurance companies have different rules." Here is a delicate balance for doctors between framing medical evaluations in ways that trigger medical necessity when they believe such care is warranted but do not go so far as to mislead insurance companies. Dr. Fischer elaborated:

> So it becomes one of those things where there's a lot of gray zone. On one hand, you
> want to advocate for your patient and you want to try to help them to the maximal

extent to achieve coverage for the surgery that is appropriate for them. On the other hand, you can't lie or defraud insurance companies. And so, like I said, our team is pretty good. Our team may err on the sort of overly strict kind of, you know, totalitarian side of things. But it is an issue. The coding is very imprecise.

Coding is imprecise. A whole operation could plausibly involve a range of procedures that could be defined and thus coded in ways that are somewhat open to interpretation. Coding is also how to get paid. One surgeon explained that "the way we get paid as physicians is by a system called the relative value unit [RVU]. And that's how insurance companies reimburse for procedures." All involved are aware of the importance of coding procedures in terms of coverage and reimbursement for services. "There are codes that are, you know, male to female and female to male, genital. I think it's actually called genital sex reassignment," he continued. But procedures common for transgender and non-binary people are often devalued or given low monetary amounts for reimbursement. "Those codes are associated with a very low RVU value. Not even remotely close." His office negotiated both for meaningful coverage for their patients and fair compensation for themselves:

> So we have to negotiate with insurance companies on how they're going to reimburse for these things. We went through a long negotiation with [insurers] about vaginoplasty, about which codes would be included and what RVU values would ultimately be reasonable. The coding, the whole coding thing and how to code ethically becomes a complicated thing.

Low RVU values are an obscure detail only visible to those within the medical system, but they are an example of problem navigation that complicates trans people's access to care because of the way insurance payments to surgeons work. Here, however, this team at a large hospital with a gender-services center was able to push insurers to achieve coverage and to pay at rates the surgeons thought were more fair. Elite professional interests coincided with civil rights aims.

DEMARCATING RELIGION, PUSHING BACK UNCERTAINTY, AND AFFIRMING EXPERTISE

I argued in chapter 4 that conservative opponents of trans health care civil rights have plenty of legal tools and political power behind them. When conditions favor them, they defeat the idea that there is a civil right to gender-affirming care and basic recognition, such as requiring health care providers to use correct pronouns. Judges who support religious conservatives in their rulings tend to see religious freedom as paramount, frame gender-affirming care as uncertain or even dangerous, and broaden the boundaries around appropriate expertise in trans health issues, allowing opponents' expert witnesses to mobilize uncertainty in scientific terms even when they were supported by religious legal organizations. They deny that trans people are a group that should get any heightened scrutiny under the Constitution when laws burden them. They dispute the unity of federal antidiscrimination statutory conceptions of gender identity as part of sex discrimination, arguing that the Title IX educational context affirms gender essentialism and the sex binary through endorsements of things like single-sex dorms, and that this essentialism and binary perspective carries through Section 1557 and fits well in health care. Focusing on children rather than adults heightens emotions and fear. These are the primary pathways to national political and judicial squelching of trans health care civil rights and constitutional rights. I continue the discussion here with a focus on the pro-trans wins, using primary source documents and analysis at a level of generality that pulls out frameworks rather than getting bogged down in the dizzying pace of litigation that these issues have produced.

The conservative legal movement, especially its well-funded evangelical and Catholic groups like Alliance Defending Freedom and the Becket Fund for Religious Liberty, brings heavy hitters and major funding to the social and political movement against gender-identity nondiscrimination. But there are formidable groups on the left that have been successful in mobilizing information and winning lawsuits too. Trans and LGBTQ+ legal advocacy and political action groups have been well organized for several decades, including the Transgender Legal Defense & Education Fund (merged with the National Center for Transgender Equality), the Transgender Law Center, the National Center for Lesbian Rights, Lambda Legal, and the American Civil Liberties Union, among others. The National Women's Law Center has fought against gender discrimination in health for decades, including providing major support in getting Section 1557 included in the ACA and in translating what it means for cisgender and trans people. As state legislators introduced hundreds of anti-trans bills across the country in recent years, a complementary tracking and analysis part of the movement became more prominent. Groups like the Movement Advancement Project take a think tank approach to social change and have become a prominent resource for documenting the dramatic shift against trans rights that came quickly after the media-announced so-called "transgender tipping point" of acceptance around 2015.

A successful legal framework for defending trans civil and constitutional rights in health care relies on legitimizing trans identities and delegitimizing opponents, particularly in trials that pit expert witnesses against each other. The legitimation process involves affirming the reasonableness and scientific credibility of gender-affirming care as a treatment for something real. The delegitimation process involves connecting religious denials of trans people's existence with animus against them as a group and exposing that animus as the real motivation for faux scientific uncertainty. This is, after all, the most infuriating part to religious conservatives: that their religious beliefs are made out to be simple bigotry toward trans people, stirred up relatively recently for political advantage. They see themselves as under attack because the legitimacy of these beliefs as the basis of medical and social policy is precisely the question, and sometimes they lose decisively.

A basic conception of health care civil rights for trans people must include access to gender-affirming medical care, not all of which is about transition. Cutting off and criminalizing gender-affirming transition care is a way to try to stop trans people from existing. At least twenty-two states have passed laws banning gender-affirming care (with some variations).[16] Some federal courts have upheld these bans and others have struck them down. As this book goes to press, a state law that makes providing gender-affirming care to trans youth illegal is before the Supreme Court on Fourteenth Amendment equal protection grounds in *United States v. Skrmetti*. Federal district court judges in both Arkansas and Florida have blocked state laws making gender-affirming care illegal.[17] The fate of gender-affirming care for trans minors (and likely adults too) turns on a combination of the power of professional medical societies and experts to defend it as reasonable and appropriate and on acceptance of the idea that trans people are an oppressed group who deserve to exist both as they are and in the shifting and moving state of gender that transness signifies.

The judge in *Doe v. Ladapo*, the 2023 Florida case challenging the law banning hormone treatments for minors, noted that "the elephant in the room" is whether transgender identity is real and not made up. The state of Florida and those opposed to gender-affirming care are opposed "to transgender status itself." "Gender identity is real," Judge Hinkle, a Clinton appointee, responded.[18] He concluded that "dissuading a person from conforming to the person's gender identity rather than to the person's natal sex is not a legitimate state interest" and found that the prohibitions failed both the intermediate scrutiny *and* rational basis tests under equal protection analysis. Seeing trans people as a group that exists and is oppressed because they violate gender expectations likely leads to legal protection, and here we see it is possible for a judge to declare that forcing people into binary birth sex and the matching lifelong gender identity should not be a goal of the state at all.

It did not help the opponents' cases that the only expert witness who had treated transgender patients and could muster a standard account of medical expertise in the area of gender-affirming care offered opinions that helped the other side. Dr. Stephen B. Levine, a psychiatrist and national go-to expert witness for those supporting anti-trans laws, does not invoke offensive language or religious terms. He presents himself as a reasonable scientific expert with carefully parsed hesitations who has a long professional history in transgender care, mostly dating to the 1990s (he is in his eighties). But the litigation is about criminal bans on providing care enacted in a hot anti-trans environment, no place for this dated middle ground Dr. Levine tries to occupy. Dr. Levine's perspective cannot legitimate all-out criminal bans. In the Arkansas trial, Dr. Levine described being cut off from treatments because of these laws as "shocking" and "devastating" for trans people.[19] Judge Hinkle's Florida ruling noted that Dr. Levine affirmed that transgender identities are real, that he would not ban all treatments himself, and that treatments with safeguards are appropriate. Surely if anti-trans legal advocates could find a doctor who is as mainstream but supports banning treatments, they would have done so. Dr. Levine seems to be the only legitimate expert available, used in case after case, seemingly excusing himself for his own role in assisting "shocking" and "devastating" withdrawals of care.

Trans health care rights win in court when their opponents can be cast as religious zealots who want a world in which trans people do not exist, or at least are neither recognized nor provided for. That was the fate of the other expert witnesses, the new generation selected for this mobilization of anti-trans litigation. Judge James Moody, an Obama appointee, did not credit the expertise of the anti-trans witnesses beyond Dr. Levine in the Arkansas trial. Judge Moody noted that the other experts—Prof. Mark Regnerus, Dr. Paul Hruz, and Dr. Patrick Lappert—were recruited by Alliance Defending Freedom (ADF) at a meeting explicitly aimed at finding experts opposed to gender-affirming care. They are religious conservatives who do not treat gender dysphoria or have any expertise in it. "The ADF," Judge Moody concluded, "is an organization committed to protecting God's design for marriage and family," that is, "not a scientific organization, but a Christian-based legal advocacy group." The experts were chosen for their demonstrated commitments to conservative evangelical Christian and Catholic views of gender identity, in his view, not their expertise in gender-affirming care. The Florida district judge Hinkle cited Dr. Lappert's radio interview comments that "gender-affirming care is a 'lie,' a 'moral violation,' a 'huge evil,' and 'diabolical'" to discredit him.[20] The Arkansas district judge Moody pointed out Prof. Regnerus's previously rejected status as a credible expert on the harms of same-sex marriage ("fringe," "entirely unbelievable and not worthy of serious consideration")[21] to push him beyond the boundary of credible expertise. He found these ADF experts were "testifying more from a religious doctrinal standpoint rather than that required of experts by *Daubert*."[22]

The national legal push to defend the state bans on gender-affirming care is led by Alliance Defending Freedom with explicit religious grounding. Even though I have argued in chapter 4 that our constitutional order and federal laws give religion broad protections, even to discriminate in health care, this analysis shows that the religious framework does not hold up nearly so well in the case of assessing expert witnesses' legitimacy. Religious reasons do not typically count as valid grounds for an expert opinion on a medical or scientific question. Once a legal fact finder assesses trans opponents as primarily religiously motivated it is easy to dismiss their scientific credibility.

But as Joanna Wuest and Briana Last have documented, there are more "agents of uncertainty" than the straightforwardly religious.[23] Organizations that oppose gender-affirming care seem to recognize the benefits of distancing themselves from overtly religious linkages, instead holding conferences and forming think tanks designed to give the impression of a diverse transnational association of concerned parents, detransitioners, experts, and critical thinkers not afraid to ask hard questions about gender. Genspect, a group formed to counter what they see as the wrongly settled consensus in established groups like WPATH, named its conference "The Bigger Picture," describing speakers as "leading lights from across the gender space."[24] These organized groups contain a broader range of perspectives, from people talking about their own lived experience with gender transition and detransition to providers to those more easily characterized as right-wing hacks. They tend to carefully avoid religious frameworks.

As long as Alliance Defending Freedom leads litigation in the United States and relies on religious experts outside the scientific and medical mainstream, however, those efforts will continue to be easily linked to evangelical religious opposition. It may be easier for a more diverse group of opponents to gain traction across Europe and North America by shedding the religious framework in favor of a "question the consensus" approach. Mobilizing shifts in health policies in the UK and Europe to tighten access to gender-affirming care—not places associated with conservative religiosity—could prove useful for advocates in rehabilitating the US anti-trans perspective from religious zealotry to what they prefer to present as sensible caution. The Supreme Court majority may not even need such cover to rule against gender-affirming care. We shall see.

Judicial affirmations of trans health care rights pull trans adults and youth closer into already-protected categories and well-established notions.[25] That is, they affirm that sex discrimination means using sex or ideas about the stability of sex at birth as the governing frame for binary gender to give or withhold benefits. If anyone who is not trans could get access to a procedure or therapy and it is only withheld from trans people because they are trans, how can that not be discrimination? Sex discrimination is punishing gender nonconformity, in other words, and there is no good reason to do it. The winning opinions insist that our civil rights laws share overlapping and similar commitments to equality across the fields of the workplace, education, and healthcare. And they accept that animus toward trans people—a recognizable minority group subjected to subordination across multiple spheres of social and political life—is the same kind of discriminatory animus condemned by our constitutional commitment to basic equality.

All the moments at every level where health care civil rights become intelligible and powerful are nonetheless fragile. At the hospital level, they depend on professionals whose personal perspectives are different from the profile that is elevated by the organization and on changes in the healthcare professions generally (lawyers intervening in patient experience, gay Section 1557 officers who see discrimination because of their own experience). At the insurance level, wins depend on nonexclusionary policies as well as the personal exhaustion of trans people seeking care and the perseverance of their professional allies to argue about medical necessity determinations. At the national level, the arguments in favor of gender-identity protections are strongly rooted in the law but face an uneven and generally hostile judicial branch that has been tilted rightward. And yet, these contingent moments are not random events. They are part of systemic refractions of rights, and in the conclusion, I reflect on ways to strengthen the bits and pieces that scatter about.

Conclusion

How to Strengthen Health Care Civil Rights

Health care civil rights are a product of overlapping structures: the sprawling American healthcare system and our diminished civil rights regime. We can understand why health care civil rights seem hopeful but consistently disappoint by examining how rights refract through the institutions and practices that constitute them.[1] What people do in these structures surely matters, but I have argued that individual-level experiences, opinions, and arguments should be understood not only in terms of those people's deeply held, often conflicting commitments to ideas about gender, equality, medicine, or religion, but also in terms of the incentives that these structures provide. Health does not work well as a framework to motivate sympathy or promote social justice. It merely shifts debates about gender identity and civil rights into one of the most challenging policy settings of the last fifty years: healthcare. It inflects debates about justice and gender identity with concerns about patient satisfaction, for example. It moves conflict into the private control of health insurers, who still hold the power of medical necessity determinations. Health is no answer for those who believe that gender-affirming care is gender ideology gone off on a sinful path.

The most important forces for understanding what health care civil rights have become are the patient safety movement, the rise of managerial, industrialized healthcare, computerization and the rationalization of bureaucratic work in healthcare, the business and (non)regulation of health insurance, and the far-right religious Republican mobilization against health care rights for reproductive and gender-affirming care. These are forces that have arisen and changed, but there is also a recession and a weakening in the patchwork of civil rights. A conservative Supreme Court has removed remedies and weakened enforcement powers even more, and Democratic majorities that could shore up civil rights statutes have been gerrymandered away or withered to tiny margins. The conservative legal movement has destabilized the ability of government to regulate and enforce laws generally across all sectors. There are many other important factors, of course. Social movement mobilization, litigation, election outcomes, and the COVID-19 pandemic all help shape what health care civil rights are today. The politics of the contemporary United States are critical because our slide into ever-more undemocratic rule because of the electoral college, equal Senate representation of wildly differently populated states, and Supreme Court appointments with life tenure has meant that conservative Republicans and religious traditionalists hold disproportionate power.[2] These forces all shape what gender identity can be and determine possibilities for transgender lives.

I argue that we should not remain within what political scientists call the "Overton window" of policy plausibility (that is, policies with a real chance of being enacted under current conditions) as we consider what different options might accomplish. In this conclusion, I reflect on what it would take to achieve a significantly different world for health care civil rights. My aim is to convince readers that precisely because our healthcare and civil rights systems are failing in so many ways, there many options for improvement. The options begin at the microlevel of the patient interaction in the healthcare setting but quickly move to the broader structures of health insurance and the national- and state-level political and legal orders. Most possible solutions require change at all levels, so my recommendations cannot stay cabined in our three-level approach for long. The suggestions I make here have been studied, some much more than others, and I offer them as a cascade of options, some much more realistic than others.

FRANK ACKNOWLEDGEMENT OF CONFLICTS OVER PATIENT CIVIL RIGHTS

I argued in chapter 2 that frameworks of patient centeredness and patient experience can refract civil rights into complaint management. The structural placement of these patient experience offices within a relatively powerless, feminized, bean-counting part of the organization means that they cannot really confront rights violations. Only doctors discipline other doctors, and so the most powerful people in healthcare are exempt from consequences when a patient has a bad experience. The separation of clinical wrongs that could lead to lawsuits from the nonclinical has meant that anything racist, sexist, or harassing ("rude treatment by staff") that is interpersonal goes into the less important bucket. Harms beyond the patient's experience are potentially vast but unrecognizable. Patients have no experience while under sedation, for example, and they have no experience of the clinician's decisions, notes, curiosity level, or willingness to think capaciously or sympathetically about their problems, for example. What providers say and do (and forget to do or never consider doing) about patients out of their earshot could add up to a lot of unfairness. Scholars have rightly focused on unconscious bias as a major driver of lower-quality care for patients from subordinated groups or who do not share an affinity with the provider.[3] Health care civil rights refracted through patient experience frameworks lose most of their visibility, redressability, and potential impact. Strategies to make the patient feel better when they complain (fake apologies, listening) do not get at the source of discrimination. It is not surprising that we found that complaint management software often did not have a drop-down menu item to classify a problem as a civil rights violation or discrimination issue. Survey-driven financial incentives have routed these problems into a part of the organization that is not trained to see rights problems and lacks the tools or the power to address them. Even if we measure inequities better, we still need to put more power and money behind accountable change.

One first step, then, would be to change the healthcare organizational structure so that possible rights violations are seen for what they are and taken seriously by people powerful enough to make changes. Civil rights should not be routed to the patient experience department. The patient experience department should not be the first or only filter for patient problems because it diffuses discrimination before it can be fully understood. There must be a way for the organization to see discrimination in its full range of appearances and to name it as a problem. The recipient rights framework for people in mental health treatment, with all its rights language, monitoring committees, specific lists of protections, and transparent reporting structures, offers one model. Perhaps the problem of discrimination should not be handled by anyone who works for the hospital or clinic at all because the drive to bury problems to protect the organization (from lawsuits or bad survey scores) will be very strong. But if a civil rights coordinator were an attorney and reported to someone high enough in the hospital who valued antidiscrimination and health equity enough to confront problems rather than refract them—including taking the risk of attracting the Department of Health and Human Services (HHS) Office for Civil Rights interventions or lawsuits—then perhaps that inclination could be overcome. Let's first consider what it might look like to reform within the hospital or clinic structure.

I found that the one Section 1557 coordinator who had been a civil rights attorney and investigator and who was placed outside the experience department was able to challenge physicians and to see rights problems as the adversarial challenge that they are. (He did not seem to have a lot of success because overall the organization had not changed around him to make his approach effective, but it was notable all the same.) Acknowledging the pressures of rights denialism and being comfortable with adversarialism between the patient and the organization is critical. Hospitals should hire someone who starts with the assumption that patients have civil rights and that staff at all levels may violate them and thus create a direct conflict that requires uncomfortable, reparative action. Most people currently in grievance handling roles have backgrounds in nursing, which is likely not sufficiently rights-focused and does not make them legally knowledgeable, comfortable managing and even amplifying adversarialism, or empowered to discipline physicians. Hiring a different kind of professional could start to turn the patient experience framework entirely on its head: name harassment and discrimination rather than downgrade them to rudeness or miscommunication, start by believing that rights violations or discrimination happened rather than start by disbelieving, dig into the possibility of harm and learn about it rather than soothe it over, and make civil rights violations as important as clinical harms to patient safety. Give the person in that role the power to recommend discipline for physicians as well as other staff. Success in this role would be defined by the ability to surface conflict and resolve it though changes that benefit disempowered patients.

One specific change organizations should make is to alter their reporting structures to dismantle the division between the clinical and the interpersonal. If these divisions are baked into software reporting programs, then the biggest hospitals need to lead the way in demanding a new product or creating their own version. It is absurd to separate clinical problems from discrimination when so much of what trans people describe as discrimination occurs during clinical time, i.e., during care with providers. Section 1557 regulations have explicitly raised the possibility of clinical care as a site of discrimination, such as if a doctor refused to provide surgical or medical services to someone on the basis of their gender identity (transgender status). Discrimination must be able to be captured at all levels of the patient's engagement with the healthcare providers and staff, including contexts where there is no "patient experience" at all: in clinical decision-making, in records the patient does not see, in care provision under anesthesia or when the patient cannot experience what is happening, and in moments of exclusion or denial of care when discrimination means the person cannot become a patient at all. The professional handling the possible cases must have access to tools and status in the hierarchy needed to probe all these contexts.

Current Section 1557 regulations take this integration even further, requiring that any use of patient care decision support tools, such as clinical algorithms, be nondiscriminatory. Algorithms are rules for a computer to put together bits of information and give the user something back out, like a clinical-decision support recommendation based on the patient's symptoms and traits and run through a database of similar cases. Algorithmic discrimination is a critical issue in health care civil rights because information about traits like race, income, and gender are built into algorithms, and then one might say the outputs are laundered as neutral when the algorithms reproduce the same inequalities that they are built from. The algorithm and the decisions it prompts are completely beyond the patient experience. No system that relies on patient complaints or patient-initiated lawsuits will confront algorithmic discrimination because these algorithms operate within clinical care guidelines, behind electronic medical records logins, and underneath screening criteria that patients know nothing about.[4]

Concerned experts have pointed out that adding discrimination in patient care decision support tools to Section 1557 is well-intentioned and necessary but that it is difficult to task working providers with knowing whether the tools that they use such as algorithms are biased.[5] The Food and Drug Administration regulates medical devices, and software is part of that scope. When HHS passes the civil rights regulations but the Food and Drug Administration holds the power to regulate algorithms and the software that uses them, it is clear that governance matters and that a much broader approach is required here. The burden should be on software creators to prove that their products are nondiscriminatory before sale to healthcare systems. We need open, consultative processes to understand how technologies can become racist and sexist and how to manage their powers in our lives. Democrats have introduced the Algorithmic Accountability Act, which would demand oversight and accountability for algorithmic bias in many areas including housing, credit, and education, as well as health.[6] The complex case of algorithmic discrimination shows yet again how health care civil rights reveal large structural gaps in how we conceptualize, measure, and confront this thing we call health care discrimination. Tackling discriminatory decision tools is tackling disparate impact discrimination in its fastest-growing form. Fighting discrimination on these terms, provided there are enough resources, could be really helpful.

Even the best effort within the organization will require establishing trust with community partners and offering patients who have experienced discrimination direct supports from outside the hospital. The Section 1557 coordinator or office should work directly with community members and advocacy groups in paid, meaningful roles with access to decision-making power so that the perspectives of the patients most likely to experience discrimination are held up and put at the center. This arrangement would need to go beyond the patient advisory boards that may already be in place elsewhere. The Section 1557 office could become a hub for medical-legal partnerships to support the complex array of injustices that vulnerable patients confront, from evictions to criminal justice involvement, centered around real accountability to the community it serves in the form of restorative justice responses, review of problems (with redactions and privacy protections), and funding through an invigorated vision of community benefit obligations for nonprofits. These collaborations would likely be volatile arrangements, bringing together people with different loyalties and interests and vulnerabilities. The strife and vulnerability are already there, though. Leaning into this situation is what democratic engagement with health inequality and systemic discrimination might look like. It would at least be a good way to start. Starting with good faith engagement and then revisioning based on experience is simply a baseline requirement for powerful healthcare entities interested in fighting health inequalities.

ALTERNATE FRAMEWORKS FOR RIGHTS AND REMEDIES

The challenge here is that if this person or office amplifies civil rights problems and helps patients make claims, they are not representing the interests of the hospital in a narrow legal sense. They could raise the litigative risk to the organization or attract bad publicity. If the hospital is for profit or has been bought out by a private equity firm, there will be no duty of community benefit and little interest in burdensome work with difficult patients. How should we understand the pressure of potential lawsuits or HHS investigations in organizational change? The larger issue here is about the role of different parts of the American governance system—the courts and attorneys, the federal agencies and civil servants, and legislative bodies and executives—in creating incentives to drive policy outcomes.[7] Much of this book has been about scrutinizing our hopes for health care civil rights within actually existing incentives, policies, practices, laws, and politics and learning that they fail to hold up well. If increasing private lawsuits from patients is a good answer to civil rights violations, then we would need to use other policy levers to increase the supply of lawyers looking for clients who have suffered health discrimination and make those claims pay enough to be worth pursuing. Whether raising or reducing the risk of being sued increases safety and civil rights compliance are empirical questions, and policies should follow the evidence. The sides on these debates are already arrayed against each other from the medical malpractice and tort reform debates.

If we think of civil rights problems as similar to patient safety and medical errors and place them in that framework, other options emerge. We could adapt some of the patient safety reporting protections for civil rights reporting to drive change from within. The Patient Safety and Quality Improvement Act of 2005 set up a structure for hospitals to report errors that impact patient safety so they could be aggregated and studied without those disclosures being used against the hospital in a lawsuit. Hospitals produce quality-related event reports as part of the protected category of patient safety work product, which are essentially self-studies of mistakes. Patients who suffer harms from these mistakes understandably want to obtain copies of these documents in lawsuits against providers and hospitals. The policy choice is presented as either allowing organizations to air and study their mistakes or allowing patients to gain access to critical information to place blame for their injuries.[8]

Adopting a patient safety framework for civil rights violations would mean following that same dichotomy with the more powerful institutional actor, the hospitals, arguing that they should be free to surface civil rights problems and then protect that information from being used against them in lawsuits. Without much stronger regulation (say, robust recordkeeping and scrutiny plus Office for Civil Rights [OCR] review of these records with significant fines available), it would be hard to tell if hospitals were simply burying or not even trying to find out if they violated Section 1557. It is too early to say how Joint Commission accreditation requirements for health equity will work on the ground or what impacts they will have. We've seen that patients may not experience rights violations as rights violations or may not know how to report them as such, and so such a system would also have far to go to capture and measure what the harms of discrimination are exactly. These are all significant challenges for the healthcare workforce now, where there is little expertise or cultural embrace around rights and discrimination. The patient safety framework would only work for health care civil rights with a throughgoing shift in federal regulations and organizational culture.

The patient safety framework analogizes a civil rights violation to a patient safety error such as giving the wrong medication, and suggests that similar detection, repair, and prevention processes could work on both from within a medical setting. Another option is to analogize civil rights violations to the medical malpractice threat posed by attorneys from outside the hospital walls, who are paid with a percentage of the money damages they win. Unfortunately, comparing the incentives that could attach to civil rights violations to those of medical malpractice lawsuits falters in one big way. The Supreme Court held in the 2022 case of *Cummings v. Premier Rehab Keller* that financial compensation for the emotional harms of discrimination in health care are not allowed under Section 1557 and Section 504 of the Rehabilitation Act.[9] The plaintiff, Jane Cummings, is deaf and legally blind and requested an American Sign Language interpreter to communicate with her physical therapist. The center denied her request and she had to seek care elsewhere.

When the Roberts Court conservative majority ruled against her, they blocked any meaningful remedy for a very common form of discrimination: being treated badly and having to find another provider. When discrimination takes the form of humiliation, contempt, harassment, insults, and disrespect, there may not have been an accompanying physical harm that resulted in financial loss or pain. If the person seeking care is turned away but finds care elsewhere, there may not be any physical harm from not accessing care. There is simply no longer an injury that the law recognizes. Compensation for emotional damages from discriminatory treatment is the main way that victims would be compensated (and that their attorneys would be paid). Without the risk of a jury siding with a humiliated patient and awarding a large emotional-damage award, there is not much risk left for hospitals. Arguably, hospitals and doctors only invest so much in patient safety detection and analysis because the threat of major lawsuits looms (more than they think, sometimes). Without that, would patient civil rights violations be taken seriously?

This lack of a remedy explains why a medical malpractice framework does not bode well, why health care civil rights violations did not seem to concern hospital general counsel offices in the settings I studied, and why housing them in the patient experience department with the low-level problems seems like a good solution. The main threat they pose is to patient satisfaction. Real money attaches to those scores. For problems recognized as civil rights issues, however, HHS Office for Civil Rights investigations are rare and likely to result in an agreement to do more training or change a policy at best, there is no real risk of a damage award for most would-be plaintiffs, and the threat to revoke federal health-care funding seems weak because it is not actually used. Health care civil rights are emblematic of a bigger story in which the rights revolution of the 1960s and 1970s has been beaten back in the courts through undermining the remedial powers attached to private lawsuits and through undermining the regulatory powers of the administrative agencies.[10] This arc is clearly visible when comparing two points of health care civil rights: hospital desegregation and Section 1557 implementation. We saw President Johnson using robust federal legislative carrots and sticks between Title VI and the Medicare rollout in the summer of 1966 (with litigation pulling in the same direction) to force hospitals to formally desegregate in remarkably short order. Now, regulators do not realistically threaten to withhold significant federal funding, there are no more private Title VI lawsuits, and there are no emotional damages under Section 1557 or Section 504. The last two of these three limitations on health care civil rights were all imposed by conservative Supreme Court majorities in rulings that seem arcane or mundane and never attracted much public attention.[11] Undoing these could restore our ability to detect and stop unconscious bias and disparate impacts in healthcare, as Danya Bowen Matthew has argued.[12]

When the Supreme Court interprets statutes passed by Congress, there are political ways to overrule them (unlike in the constitutional context where they have the last word). I have been arguing that the ragtag collection of civil rights laws we have is weak on purpose, and that one way it is weak is that it had to be watered down or silent on potentially controversial details to pass. The ACA was passed so hurriedly that advocates and drafters never got the chance to revise Section 1557 in a conference committee, for example. Their weakness at the macrolevel of national policy shapes incentives and behaviors all the way down, so we see how these three levels of analysis I have created to structure the book interrelate and produce conditions for each other. It is worth imagining what a national political commitment to nondiscrimination might look like.

Congress could pass legislation specifying the full range of discrimination captured under the term sex discrimination, including gender-identity discrimination. We could have full-scale LGBTQ+ civil rights protection legislation across all sectors, from housing to healthcare to employment (and it would not depend on the Supreme Court). Congress could pass legislation specifying disparate impact claims and emotional damages are available under Section 1557 and making sure attorneys' fees are generous.[13] Congress could establish a national fund to pay claims, set up training programs and pay public interest attorneys to take the cases, fund OCR investigations at a much higher rate, and require reporting, transparency, and measurement of progress in reducing discrimination in healthcare, perhaps tied to payments like the patient satisfaction surveys. There are many levers to pull, in other words, from rebalancing incentives to direct legislation to robust enforcement to transparency and public pressure. All these are limp or nonexistent now, and any option is worth trying. Then we might be able to study the empirical questions such as whether risk of lawsuits compels better civil rights compliance, whether hospitals are capable of creating rights cultures on their own, what seeing rights better might look like, whether improved compliance improves health, and whether civil rights compliance reduces inequality. We do not know because we have decided not to create meaningful conditions for any of these changes.

We must rebalance the power relationship between religious control of healthcare and patients' civil rights. Our laws and constitutional interpretations have gone too far in protecting religious discrimination, which has been allowed to push aside other important values like equality and access. We should pull back towards patients' rights to receive nondiscriminatory care that is judged appropriate by scientific and medical authorities rather than religious authorities. We have large sectors of our federally funded health and welfare system run by religious entities that deny care to LGBT people and cisgender women. This situation is no longer compatible (if it ever was) with democratic equality or any conception of health care rights. It has become an openly disrespectful and expanding two-tier system of inclusion and exclusion driven by a coalition of religious partisans and supported by our tax dollars. One option would be to narrow the conception of religious objection to the individual level; that is, a person, not an institution, holds religious views and is protected from having to do anything in their healthcare work that would violate their religious convictions.[14] At the hospital or system level, however, there could not be policies against anyone providing care or firing someone for providing care. Conscience protections would apply equally to providers whose conscience or religion compels them to *provide* care as well as those who claim the right to *withhold* it, and the institution must respect their choices either way. Right now, entire religious hospital systems that cover large geographic areas or care networks are permitted to ban their providers from offering care (abortion, contraception, fertility, and gender-affirming care) that their church objects to. If religious hospitals gain an exemption from having to use a trans person's correct pronouns, providers could be fired for using the pronouns that respect a trans patient's gender identity. (One question will be how many providers, many of whom do not share this virulent anti-trans politics, would put up with such an employer.) A shift to an individual provider-level exercise of conscience, by contrast, would be likely to allow variation.

The Catholic Church would not agree to such a compromise, however, and so pushing this option legislatively (assuming it could pass, a nonstarter with the current Congress) would end with the church pulling out of healthcare or securing a Supreme Court ruling that the legislation paring back institutional religious rights was unconstitutional. The current Supreme Court would undoubtedly side with the religious entity on this question, as they consistently uphold conservative religious interests over nondiscrimination. Yet, it is worth imagining the changes such a new approach would bring. Religious healthcare operators could theoretically pull out of their markets or refuse all federal funding and operate free of any civil rights regulations. Healthcare is significantly federally funded through Medicare and other payments, though, so anything beyond a few small care settings is financially impossible. Hospitals would be sold, broken up, or merged, consistent with any other legislation passed at the time to manage that process.

Perhaps in this alternate political universe, religious entities would agree to a provider-level conscience policy only. Health care consumers would need to know at the provider level what care they could expect to get. Every provider profile should include a statement of what care will not be provided if the provider plans to invoke it, and patients should be informed at every visit if there are objections in place. OCR should require periodic filings of percentages of objecting providers in aggregate so they can track the ability of the public to receive nondiscriminatory care. That data should be publicly available and broken down by geography and insurance details such as provider networks and carrier. Each healthcare entity should have to prove that they can provide care to everyone in their insurance networks and in the geographic area or that they have sufficient referrals in place to meet patients' needs. Insurers should not be able to construct provider networks without proving that there is sufficient nondiscriminatory care available in it.

Even now, we could have much greater transparency about religious interferences with health care than we have. Currently, Section 1557 requires entities to post a notice saying they do not discriminate on the basis of sex, while at the same time they can pursue an exception from the duty of nondiscrimination, and they can refuse to offer a wide range of common services from placing an IUD to monitoring gender-affirming hormones. It's well established that ordinary people do not know about these restrictions and the Section 1557 regulations arguably require misrepresentation ("We don't discriminate" to the public and "We would like to discriminate" to OCR, simultaneously). Civil rights regulations should at the very least require any religiously affiliated healthcare entity to post information about the care it withholds or has an exemption not to provide in the same place and manner that it posts its nondiscrimination assurances. But instead, the most recent 1557 regulations only weakly note that it is a "best practice" to reveal that the hospital is in fact exempt from the very nondiscrimination rules that it posts. There is no duty to inform patients of this complete contradiction.

INSURANCE REFORM FOR CIVIL RIGHTS

I have argued that the mesolevel of insurance refracts health care civil rights into a complex and even bizarre world of private employer regulation, ruled over by a confusing federal statute from the 1970s that was not supposed to govern health care, supplemented by a variable state insurance antidiscrimination landscape with laws that often do not even apply because of that federal statute, and topped off by generous deference in federal civil rights law that permits health insurance companies to use medical necessity determinations to slow down or deny care even when it is supposedly required by civil rights provisions. More than half of seniors in Medicare have Medicare Advantage plans run by commercial insurers, exemplifying a blur between government-run health care and privately-run health care. To make this refraction even messier, state laws criminalizing the provision of trans care have turned rights into crimes, leaving insurance companies in the untenable position of extending coverage as required by federal antidiscrimination law that is a crime to provide. On top of that, private companies are also religious believers, claiming religious protections against covering basic health needs for their employees. Our situation here is a total mess. At least that means there are plenty of ways in to start fixing it.

If a federal health care civil right means everyone having a health insurance plan that upholds civil rights, what does that look like and how do we get it? We need to shift to a universally available healthcare system that requires robust civil rights recognition and insurance coverage provision generally, including for gender-affirming care. The most realistic is introducing an option to buy into an expanded Medicare or other public option (part of the original ACA legislation that did not survive Republican Party and Joe Lieberman's opposition) while leaving employer-sponsored health plans undisturbed. Troyen Brennan argues that incrementally expanding access to Medicare Advantage-type plans (by lowering the age to buy into them) is realistic and will eventually crowd out employer plans because the federal government's power to negotiate prices and control costs is so powerful.[15] Commercial insurers would still sell plans, but subject to much more regulation that could include full-throated civil rights protections. The least realistic—that is, all path dependencies and formidable forces are arrayed against it as far as the eye can see—is a full-scale government single-payer health system in which employers and private insurers play no role or limited roles. States could run their own single-payer systems or the federal government could run it. A public option plan could simply cover gender-affirming care and anyone could buy it and receive a subsidy to afford it. A national care system could shift what we as employees pay in premiums and lower wages to taxes to fund benefits for everyone.

Expanding health care for everyone creates new questions about what the federal government would consider civil rights-based health care and perhaps just moves those debates elsewhere.[16] We already see major disagreements in Congress over federal health care coverage questions around abortion access for members of our armed forces, for example. In an alternate world in which some version of a universal healthcare option could gain political support, however, we could also expect gender-affirming care alongside abortion access as provisions of equal citizenship and nondiscrimination on the basis of sex, gender, pregnancy, or a reinvigorated integration of all three. We could also meaningfully address the other harms to health that providers now just enter as ICD 10 Z codes: lack of transportation, homelessness, and food insecurity. For the first time, we could offer health plan options to everyone that are subject to the same national-level requirements for nondiscrimination in both recognition and provision.

Medicare ("Medicare for all") is the primary option for an expansion point because it is already universal for those over sixty-five. The Veterans Health Administration is the largest health system in the United States, but it is not governed by the specific requirements of the Biden administration's Section 1557 regulations. The administrative rule applies to HHS-administered programs or activities, and Veterans Affairs, Defense, and Personnel Management are different government agencies. The basic clause of the law written into the ACA applies to Veterans Affairs, but implementing regulations to say what nondiscrimination would mean for service members have not been written yet. Public or government health plans are not yet the best examples of civil rights-based healthcare delivery, but why not work to make them so? We need a model health plan or set of plans that could be the basis for a nationally available public plan for anyone to buy into, that is, if we implemented something short of national single-payer system and more like the ACA public option or Medicare Advantage for all.

We could look beyond Medicare or the military health care system to the other complete federal health system as a point of innovation. The Indian Health Service (IHS) is a federal health system for "American Indians and Alaska Natives" that provides health care, including gender-affirming care, to people of all ages. There are IHS facilities in thirty-seven states serving 2.6 million people from the 573 federally recognized tribes.[17] As sovereign nations, the tribes receive federal funding and operate their own hospitals and hundreds of health clinics; other parts of the system are jointly operated.[18] Oklahoma state law makes provision of gender-affirming care to minors a felony, but a federal IHS clinic there has received national recognition for their provision of gender-affirming care.[19] Many IHS clinics do not offer surgical services generally, though the Navajo Area Indian Health Service serves nearly a quarter million people with sites including a comprehensive hospital.[20]

The case of Native and Indigenous health illustrates both the deep inequalities that leave these communities less healthy and more likely to experience violence than non-Native peoples and also the possibilities of a community-led engagement and sovereign empowerment with federal health care.[21] Medicare is focused on the elderly, and the military has distinct health goals for troop readiness. The Employee Retirement Income Security Act of 1974 (ERISA) makes state-level single-payer systems difficult to develop. Why not elevate and invest in the Indian Health Service, making it an enviable example of how our government can deliver comprehensive and equitable health care? Could non-Native health leaders envision "standing with" instead of "giving back," in Kim Tallbear's terms, and collaborate with Indigenous people on such a model?[22] Failing to consider the IHS as the best first site for investment in health equity when we need a national model feels like repeating the settler-colonialist mistake of regarding Indigenous people as stuck in the past or as a tiny sample of the population that is too different to be centrally important.[23] A reparative and justice-informed approach in this already-existing federal health system could yield lessons for policymakers who care about other communities where racism has created poorer health. Instead of or in addition to bringing more people into the public–private partnerships of Medicare Advantage, why not also invest in a community-driven democratic process to develop model plans in IHS?

I am not suggesting that non-Natives take advantage of the IHS to gain access to care that antiabortion and anti-trans state laws have blocked, which would be an extractivist approach that pits vulnerable people against each other rather than solving the underlying injustice. (Recall that the Johnson administration had National Guard helicopters ready to fly Black patients to military hospitals if white supremacist hospital administrators balked at caring for them at the launch of the Medicare program in the summer of 1966. There are other options, though again we would need to fix federal policies for health equality first.) Rather, I am pointing out that we already have a federal direct-care health system that we could invest in to prove that health policy can confront centuries of injustice and current health disparities in compelling ways. Even under current political and legal conditions, tribal sovereignty, federal investment, and the supremacy of federal laws over discriminatory state laws could combine to make gender-affirming care (and many other improvements) through the Indian Health Service a model for future federal health reforms. The IHS has already shown itself capable of innovation as a health system.[24] Centering and empowering gender-diverse and queer Indigenous people who work in and get health care from our IHS facilities to improve federal health policy is a feasible option now. It also builds expertise for a time when the national political climate is more open to health reform.

A truly national healthcare system is one big country-wide insurance risk pool, but once it takes on that scale we typically just call it national healthcare, not health insurance. We would not need all people currently employed in private insurance billing, processing, rate setting, screening, denying, advertising, contract writing, lawyering, and so on. We spend more than other nations on healthcare through these administrative costs (eight percent versus one to three percent), but the main reason why Americans pay more for care is because our prices are much higher for everything, including provider salaries.[25] We would still need determinations of medical necessity, however, and means to decide what treatments are worth paying for and which are not. National healthcare would come with price setting and government salaries for providers, big reasons for its historic unpopularity with the American Medical Association. Other systems like this elsewhere still entertain debates about gender-affirming care and provide care in different ways, as a look at Great Britain and Western Europe shows.[26] Systemic change at this level, though far from easy, is the way to bring a right to health into the United States and to infuse the values behind our weakened civil rights laws back into healthcare. It is the primary way to advance both recognition *and* provision.

We have gotten far from the world of health insurance most of us live in, though. Pulling back to a more realistic world in which the basic parameters of our healthcare system remain in place, there are still major improvements that could improve health care civil rights in our insurance system. An amended Section 1557 could specify that civil rights obligations attach to any entity that provides health care through benefits, including self-insured employers and the plans they write for their employees, and that the tax assistance employers receive counts as federal financial assistance. Passing the Equality Act and specifying the full range of protections from sex discrimination under the ACA would give LGBTQ+ civil rights the firm foundation of explicit congressional approval. The Equality Act states that the Religious Freedom Restoration Act cannot be used as a reason to discriminate, thereby pulling back on conservative expansions of religious shields for discrimination. Religious employers like churches could enjoy special exemptions to discriminate in favor of their own believers, but who counts as a religious employer and which jobs are religious jobs could be more tightly specified to match the spirit of the individual-level conscience exception discussed above. These changes involve legislation as well as turn-arounds in the Supreme Court's interpretations, which have been broadening rather than narrowing religious employers' rights.

ERISA, the pension protection law from the 1970s that focused on insolvent and fraudulently mismanaged pension funds and was never supposed to govern millions of working-age adults' health care, needs reform.[27] Defined benefit pensions have gone the way of the molded Jell-O salad. Self-insured employer health plans are expanding. We could separate the question of what oversight workers' pension plans require from questions about their health benefits. As Elizabeth McCuskey explains, several ERISA reform options are possible.[28] Right now ERISA creates a deregulatory vacuum by sweeping aside state law but only putting a patchwork of protections for health insurance in its place. ERISA preemption waivers (which take away its power to ignore state laws) would permit state laws to have force again. Options from strongest to weakest include repealing the preemption provision in ERISA entirely, closing the loophole for self-funded plans to escape state regulation, allowing HHS to grant waivers if it decides to, or deciding on a list of state laws to exempt from preemption.[29] We could cease allowing stop-loss policies to prop up self-insurance for smaller firms. Understandably, companies did not want the laws of fifty different states to create a maze of rules for them in insurance and benefits when ERISA's federal preemption was created. But the ACA ushered in more federal uniformity in its requirement for large employers to provide health insurance that meets minimum value and affordability standards. There have been many attempts to reform ERISA, but powerful business interest groups currently benefit from these deregulatory, antiquated, and poorly anticipated circumstances and have held off reform so far.

I argued that we simply do not know enough about health insurance plans, what is in them, and how private health insurance companies administer them. ERISA has even thwarted development of an all-payer claims database. We need a fully transparent public data source for all health insurance plans sold in the United States with uniform requirements for clarity, standardization, readability, and accessibility. This obligation to publicly report what is in health plans would be entirely new for private, employer-sponsored plans that cover most working adults and their beneficiaries in the United States. I've already discussed substantive reforms to make what is for sale equitable and open to all, by which I mean offering nondiscriminatory coverage and pricing for gender-affirming care specifically and developing a civil rights-informed healthcare system generally. Transparency on its own does not drive the normative concerns I've raised, and presumably firms could use the information to standardize offerings or even to price fix. But there is also reason to think that unflattering attention to discriminatory or meager plans would influence employees and consumers in ways that could prompt firms to offer better benefits voluntarily. Significant expansions in benefits for same-sex couples in the workplace happened in these ways before marriage equality became law.[30]

NATIONAL STRUCTURAL CHANGES
FOR DEMOCRACY AND HEALTH

Investing in a national model for eventual broad access, establishing federal standards for all health insurance plans, or regulating uses of algorithms are national-level reforms. We could enact wholesale civil rights reforms that document, defend, and remedy sex, gender, and gender-identity discrimination across sectors, both properly recognizing and provisioning for intersectional identities. Major structural reforms for access to care, including funding for those who cannot pay, have been more successful than discrete identity-based protections, but it would be nice not to have to choose. Readers may point out that all these reforms are impossible with our current Congress and Supreme Court (and sometimes the presidency). My response is to concede that, indeed, they are impossible now, but the first step toward change is to articulate a positive vision of an alternative and start convincing others that it is desirable. If we want a better world for the people we count in datasets as health disparity populations, then we must defend why they deserve better and start explaining what it will take to get that for them (and for everybody else too).

I want a world in which people of all ages who experience their gender identity as different than others expect it to be can explore and express their identity without ridicule or injury. I want that because I do not assume that there is a correct distribution and appearance of gender identity in the world. I suspect we all would be better off if many of our current requirements simply went away or became much less important, but a diverse world of beauty pageant contestants, WrestleMania, people whose gender identity is not readily apparent, and pants and makeup everywhere is also benign. The world I want includes access to supportive resources that are appropriate to every individual's situation (a seven year old in a family is differently situated from a twenty-five year old in the workplace, for example) and that they can guide and control as much as possible. When this includes medical interventions, they should be provided according to a well-justified and evidence-based understanding that has been shaped by the people seeking care as well as by professionals with ethically produced and interdisciplinary research expertise. Decisions should be based on informed consent and respecting the autonomy of persons (including individual-level conscience rights for providers to participate or not). Everyone deserves care derived this way, and in an ideal system, efforts to contain costs and avoid overuse (problems I certainly acknowledge) would be comanaged with these aims.

Democratic self-governance requires earnestly trying to convince other people of things, even when it seems like one should not have to defend basic humanity and dignity. Yet clearly we do. Polls suggest that Americans have a range of opinions about trans rights and do not agree about the vision I shared above. I started there, but it should be clear from my approach to gender-identity protections that structural change, not simply persuasive arguments, is essential. We cannot persuade democratically only to continue to fail at enactment. Our institutions have deteriorated to the point that democratic persuasion has been effectively cut off at the pass in some of our heavily gerrymandered state legislatures, for example. The Supreme Court was never supposed to be democratic, but even it has become untethered from its democratic linkage via the Senate appointment process because the Senate is also undemocratically designed and run and has become even more so as US territory and population distributions have increased and skewed.

One way to approach reforming the Supreme Court is to reform its personnel, such as by so-called court packing with additional justices appointed by a Democratic president or by imposing term limits or a partisan balance, but another approach to reforms is to think about disempowering it as an institution that blocks progressive legislation.[31] Legislative goals from health care civil rights to restrictions on guns to campaign spending reforms are effectively blocked for decades by our current Supreme Court, and it is that broader frustration of democratic self-governance that is the problem. Congress has the power to determine the jurisdiction of the federal courts under Article III of the Constitution and to make exceptions and to regulate the Supreme Court's appellate jurisdiction. Disempowering reforms would use this power to take away entire policy areas from Supreme Court reach, giving whoever holds the majority in Congress and holds the presidency the last word instead. Legislatively enacted civil rights, alongside other progressive legislation for health care, environmental protections, and education, have long outpaced Supreme Court protection for rights.[32] Until we reform the Supreme Court and reconsider its role in our democracy, we will not be able to achieve much of anything to advance health care civil rights in even the most narrow sense, let alone achieving a fully integrated approach to health and equality with large-scale investments and strong rights.

Sam checked into the emergency department without health insurance coverage. He had lost access to the regular medications he needed. He had not realized he was pregnant and had no prenatal care. He used the emergency department at a crisis point, as many people without insurance do, because there was nowhere else to go. The health care team did not recognize Sam's gender identity and his health needs fully and accurately as a pregnant man with an obstetrical emergency. Recognition went awry, but provisioning had failed long before that. We can fix provider awareness with training sessions (maybe). We can add organ inventories to medical records. But bringing about the alternate world in which situations like Sam's are nonexistent will take much more. Turning to health may not have any simple power to promote equality or to solve political problems. But studying health and rights through their implementing institutions lets us see their limitations and thus all the opportunities to do better.

NOTES

INTRODUCTION: THE HOPE OF HEALTH CARE CIVIL RIGHTS

1. Daphna Stroumsa et al., "The Power and Limits of Classification—A 32-Year-Old Man with Abdominal Pain," *The New England Journal of Medicine* 380, no. 20 (May 16, 2019): 1885–88, https://doi.org/10.1056/NEJMp1811491.

2. Stroumsa et al., "The Power and Limits of Classification," 1885.

3. Stroumsa et al., "The Power and Limits of Classification," 1885.

4. Stroumsa et al., "The Power and Limits of Classification," 1888.

5. Stroumsa et al., "The Power and Limits of Classification," 1887.

6. Patient Protection and Affordable Care Act, 42 U.S.C. § 18116 (2010).

7. I use the term "trans" throughout this book to mean transgender people who have a different gender identity than the one commonly associated with the sex they were assigned at birth. "Cisgender" means someone who identifies with their sex assigned at birth. I do not assume trans people are moving or have moved from one position in the gender binary to the other. There is a wide range of experience in gender nonconformity that both law and health struggle to represent, and the push to transnormativity (there is a right way to be trans) is strong. Non-binary people can have different needs and experiences in health care than anyone who is clearly situated on one side of the gender binary, though non-binary people sometimes seek similar gender-affirming care as binary-identified trans people do. I sometimes use the phrase "trans or non-binary" despite the opposition of the terms to remind the reader of both possibilities. The research I rely on in this book draws on data from research, activism, and professional work by people with a range of gender identities and expressions who are trans-identified, some also non-binary. I sometimes use "person seeking care" as an alternative to the term "patient." I use the term "health care" when discussing an interaction between a care giver and a person seeking care or the act of care, and the term "healthcare" to mean the healthcare system and institutional structures.

155

8. Jaime M. Grant et al., "Injustice at Every Turn: A Report of the National Transgender Discrimination Survey," 2011, https://www.transequality.org/sites/default/files/docs/resources/NTDS_Report.pdf; Sonny Nordmarken and Reese Kelly, "Limiting Transgender Health: Administrative Violence and Microaggressions in Health Care Systems," in *Health Care Disparities and the LGBT Population*, ed. Vickie L. Harvey et al. (Lanham, MD: Lexington Books, 2014), 120–39; stef m. shuster, *Trans Medicine: The Emergence and Practice of Treating Gender* (New York: New York University Press, 2021), https://nyupress.org/9781479899371/trans-medicine; Shanna K. Kattari et al., "Racial and Ethnic Differences in Experiences of Discrimination in Accessing Health Services Among Transgender People in the United States," *International Journal of Transgenderism* 16, no. 2 (April 3, 2015): 68–79, https://doi.org/10.1080/15532739.2015.1064336.

9. Danya Lagos, "Looking at Population Health Beyond 'Male' and 'Female': Implications of Transgender Identity and Gender Nonconformity for Population Health," *Demography* 55, no. 6 (2018): 2097–117.

10. Jennifer L. Glick et al., "The Role of Discrimination in Care Postponement Among Trans-Feminine Individuals in the U.S. National Transgender Discrimination Survey," *LGBT Health* 5, no. 3 (March 28, 2018): 171–79, https://doi.org/10.1089/lgbt.2017.0093; Calvin Apodaca et al., "Maybe They Had a Bad Day: How LGBTQ and BIPOC Patients React to Bias in Healthcare and Struggle to Speak Out," *Journal of the American Medical Informatics Association* 29, no. 12 (December 1, 2022): 2075–82, https://doi.org/10.1093/jamia/ocac142.

11. Michele Goodwin, *Policing the Womb: Invisible Women and the Criminal Costs of Motherhood* (New York: Cambridge University Press, 2020).

12. Anna Kirkland, "Frameworks and Ideologies for Fat Non-Discrimination Rights," in *The Routledge Handbook of Critical Obesity Studies*, ed. Michael Gard, Darren Powell, and Tenorio Jose (London: Routledge Handbooks Online, 2021), 361–69, https://doi.org/10.4324/9780429344824-45; Anna Kirkland, *Fat Rights: Dilemmas of Difference and Personhood* (New York: New York University Press, 2008).

13. Julia Lynch, *Regimes of Inequality: The Political Economy of Health and Wealth*, (Cambridge, UK: Cambridge University Press, 2019), https://doi.org/10.1017/9781139051576; Julia Lynch, "Reframing Inequality? The Health Inequalities Turn as a Dangerous Frame Shift," *Journal of Public Health* 39, no. 4 (December 1, 2017): 653–60, https://doi.org/10.1093/pubmed/fdw140.

14. Jenna M. Loyd, *Health Rights Are Civil Rights: Peace and Justice Activism in Los Angeles, 1963–1978* (Minneapolis: University of Minnesota Press, 2014).

15. Latoya Hill, Nambi Ndugga, and Samantha Artiga, "Key Data on Health and Health Care by Race and Ethnicity," *Kaiser Family Foundation* (blog), March 15, 2023, https://www.kff.org/racial-equity-and-health-policy/report/key-data-on-health-and-health-care-by-race-and-ethnicity/.

16. Grant et al., "Injustice at Every Turn."

17. Laurel Westbrook, "The Matrix of Violence: Intersectionality and Necropolitics in the Murder of Transgender People in the United States, 1990–2019," *Gender & Society* 37, no. 3 (June 1, 2023): 413–46, https://doi.org/10.1177/08912432231171172.

18. National Council on Disability, "Federal Report Finds Foreseeable, Disproportionate COVID-19 Fatalities, Heavy Toll for People with Disabilities," October 29, 2021, https://ncd.gov/progress%20reports/2021/10/29/federal-report-finds-foreseeable-disproportionate-covid-19-fatalities-heavy-toll-for-people-with-disabilities/.

19. Maritza Vasquez Reyes, "The Disproportional Impact of COVID-19 on African Americans," *Health and Human Rights* 22, no. 2 (December 2020): 299–307.

20. Craig Konnoth, "Medicalization and the New Civil Rights," *Ethics, Medicine and Public Health* 12, SI: Medical Conscience/Medical Rights, (January 1, 2020): 100435, https://doi.org/10.1016/j.jemep.2019.100435.

21. Lynch, *Regimes of Inequality*.

22. Jamila Michener and Tiffany N. Ford, "Racism and Health: Three Core Principles," *The Milbank Quarterly* 101, no. S1 (April 1, 2023): 333–55, https://doi.org/10.1111/1468-0009.12633.

23. Kirkland, "Frameworks and Ideologies for Fat Non-Discrimination Rights."

24. Merlin Chowkwanyun, "What Is a 'Racial Health Disparity'? Five Analytic Traditions," *Journal of Health Politics, Policy and Law* 47, no. 2 (April 1, 2022): 131–58, https://doi.org/10.1215/03616878-9517163.

25. Merlin Chowkwanyun and Adolph L. Reed, "Racial Health Disparities and Covid-19—Caution and Context," *New England Journal of Medicine* 383, no. 3 (July 16, 2020): 201–3, https://doi.org/10.1056/NEJMp2012910.

26. Rob Jackson, "Biblical View on Transgender Identity: A Primer for Parents and Strugglers," Focus on the Family, December 10, 2020, https://www.focusonthefamily.com/parenting/a-biblical-perspective-on-transgender-identity-a-primer-for-parents-and-strugglers/.

27. Department of Health and Human Services, "Nondiscrimination in Health and Health Education Programs or Activities, Delegation of Authority," *Federal Register* Vol. 85 No. 119 (June 19, 2020): 37189, https://www.federalregister.gov/documents/2020/06/19/2020-11758/nondiscrimination-in-health-and-health-education-programs-or-activities-delegation-of-authority.

28. Dean Spade, *Normal Life: Administrative Violence, Critical Trans Politics, and the Limits of Law*, Revised and Expanded Edition (Durham, NC: Duke University Press, 2015), 139, https://www.dukeupress.edu/normal-life-revised.

29. Alondra Nelson, *Body and Soul: The Black Panther Party and the Fight against Medical Discrimination* (Minneapolis: University of Minnesota Press, 2013), https://www.upress.umn.edu/book-division/books/body-and-soul; Steven Epstein, *Impure Science: AIDS, Activism, and the Politics of Knowledge*, Medicine and Society (Berkeley, CA: University of California Press, 1998).

30. Dorothy Roberts, "Reproductive Justice, Not Just Rights," *Dissent* 62, no. 4 (2015): 79–82, https://doi.org/10.1353/dss.2015.0073; Loretta J. Ross, "Reproductive Justice as Intersectional Feminist Activism," *Souls* 19, no. 3 (July 3, 2017): 286–314, https://doi.org/10.1080/10999949.2017.1389634.

31. Khiara Bridges, *Reproducing Race: An Ethnography of Pregnancy as a Site of Racialization* (Berkeley, CA: University of California Press, 2011); Dorothy Roberts, *Torn Apart: How the Child Welfare System Destroys Black Families—and How Abolition Can Build a Safer World* (New York: Basic Books, 2022).

32. Hil Malatino, *Trans Care* (Minneapolis: University of Minnesota Press, 2020), https://www.upress.umn.edu/book-division/books/trans-care; Hil Malatino, "The Promise of Repair: Trans Rage and the Limits of Feminist Coalition," *Signs: Journal of Women in Culture and Society* 46, no. 4 (June 2021): 827–51, https://doi.org/10.1086/713292; Spade, *Normal Life: Administrative Violence, Critical Trans Politics, and the Limits of Law*.

33. Aren Z. Aizura et al., "Thinking with Trans Now," *Social Text* 38, no. 4 (145) (December 1, 2020): 125–47, https://doi.org/10.1215/01642472-8680478. As C. Riley Snorton points

out, the trans subject of law and medicine that we know today is only possible because "sex and gender are racial arrangements" (C. Riley Snorton, *Black on Both Sides: A Racial History of Trans Identity* [Minneapolis: University of Minnesota Press, 2017], 11). My focus here is the subject of liberal legalism, in whom these complexities are rarely recognized, and the patient in the medical organization, who is misrecognized in other ways. The conservative legal movement tries to keep Blackness as heterosexual, cisgender social conservatism in the service of protecting children, as I argue in chapter 4, which whitens transness strategically. They must accomplish this separation to hold at bay the idea that they are dismantling civil rights for everyone, not just trans people. We have seen these patterns before. See Jenny Andrine Madsen Evang, "Is 'Gender Ideology' Western Colonialism?: Anti-Gender Rhetoric and the Misappropriation of Postcolonial Language," *TSQ: Transgender Studies Quarterly* 9, no. 3 (August 1, 2022): 365–86, https://doi.org/10.1215/23289252–9836036.

34. Annabel Kupke, Carmel Shachar, and Christopher Robertson, "Pulse Oximeters and Violation of Federal Antidiscrimination Law," *JAMA* 329, no. 5 (February 7, 2023): 365–66, https://doi.org/10.1001/jama.2022.24976.

35. Daniel Carpenter, "Is Health Politics Different?," *Annual Review of Political Science* 15, no. 1 (2012): 287–311, https://doi.org/10.1146/annurev-polisci-050409–113009.

36. Paula M. Lantz and Sara Rosenbaum, "The Potential and Realized Impact of the Affordable Care Act on Health Equity," *Journal of Health Politics, Policy and Law* 45, no. 5 (2020), https://doi.org/10.1215/03616878–8543298; Sara Rosenbaum et al., "Four Key Takeaways From A Health Care Civil Rights Landmark: The Final Section 1557 Rule," Health Affairs Forefront, June 12, 2024, http://www.healthaffairs.org/do/10.1377/forefront.20240607.491767/full/.

37. "Departments of Justice and Health and Human Services Announce Interim Resolution Agreement in Environmental Justice Investigation of Alabama Department of Public Health," Office for Civil Rights, May 4, 2023, https://www.hhs.gov/about/news/2023/05/04/departments-justice-health-human-services-announce-interim-resolution-agreement-environmental-justice-investigation-alabama-department-public-health.html.

38. Department of Health and Human Services, "Nondiscrimination in Health Programs and Activities," *Federal Register* Vol. 89 No. 88 (May 6, 2024): 37522, https://www.federalregister.gov/documents/2024/05/06/2024-08711/nondiscrimination-in-health-programs-and-activities (codified at 42 *Code of Federal Regulations* § 92.210).

39. The Joint Commission, "R3 Report: New Requirements to Reduce Health Care Disparities," June 20, 2022.

40. "Using Z Codes: The Social Determinants of Health (SDOH) Data Journey to Better Outcomes," Centers for Medicare & Medicaid Services, June 2023, https://edit.cms.gov/files/document/zcodes-infographic.pdf. I am deeply skeptical of the efficacy and beneficence of the push for diagnostic coding for social disadvantage. One of the ICD 10 Z codes for tracking social determinants of health, for example, is Z64, "problems related to unwanted pregnancy." It is grouped as "problems related to psychosocial circumstances" and includes "problems related to multiparity" (giving birth two or more times) and "discord with counselors." One study in a surgical setting found that these Z codes were the most often used, particularly for women of color with public insurance (Rishub K. Das et al., "National Patterns in the Use of International Statistical Classification of Diseases and Health Related Problems, Tenth Revision Z Codes in Ambulatory Surgery from 2016 to 2019," *The American Journal of Surgery* 228 [February 1, 2024]: 54–61, https://doi.org/10.1016/j.amjsurg.2023.06.030). Brochures published by CMS touting the use of Z codes to document social determinants of health do not list out any of the specific Z64 codes, preferring to

publicize the codes about housing and food instead. Coding people with unwanted pregnancies into medical records is dangerous in a post-*Dobbs* world. What seems like sympathetic health-disparities outreach could easily become a literal code for being argumentative, poor, having too many children, and seeking abortion. We know what happens to the people classified like that within powerful systems and it is not receiving helpful resources. It has been sterilization, scapegoating, criminalization, discrimination, and disrespect.

41. David T. Beito, *From Mutual Aid to the Welfare State: Fraternal Societies and Social Services, 1890–1967* (Chapel Hill, NC: University of North Carolina Press, 2000).

42. Jennifer Klein, *For All These Rights: Business, Labor, and the Shaping of America's Public-Private Welfare State* (Princeton, NJ: Princeton University Press, 2006).

43. Anthony S. Chen, *The Fifth Freedom: Jobs, Politics, and Civil Rights in the United States, 1941–1972* (Princeton, NJ: Princeton University Press, 2009), https://press.princeton.edu/books/paperback/9780691139531/the-fifth-freedom.

44. This book is about what happens when the civil rights field pushes into the health care field and its broader law and political economy; that is, can civil rights become part of an already thickly constituted organizational culture in health care settings and what might it take to make it so? Sociolegal studies of law and health care suggest that rights may not be the most powerful force in that setting at all, though legal logics have sometimes worked their way in. See Carol A. Heimer and Arielle W. Tolman, "Between the Constitution and the Clinic: Formal and de Facto Rights to Healthcare," *Law & Society Review* 55, no. 4 (2021): 563–86, https://doi.org/10.1111/lasr.12577; Lauren B. Edelman, *Working Law: Courts, Corporations, and Symbolic Civil Rights* (Chicago: University of Chicago Press, 2016); Elizabeth Chiarello, "Trojan Horse Technologies: Smuggling Criminal-Legal Logics into Healthcare Practice," *American Sociological Review* 88, no. 6 (December 1, 2023): 1131–60, https://doi.org/10.1177/00031224231209445; Carol A. Heimer, "Where Law and Morality Meet: Moral Agency and Moral Deskilling in Organizations," in *Handbook of the Sociology of Morality*, vol. 2, ed. Steven Hitlin, Shai M. Dromi, and Aliza Luft, Handbooks of Sociology and Social Research (Cham, Switzerland: Springer International Publishing, 2023), 43–57, https://doi.org/10.1007/978-3-031-32022-4_3; Carol A. Heimer and Jaimie Morse, "Colonizing the Clinic: The Adventures of Law in HIV Treatment and Research," in *The New Legal Realism. Vol. 2, Studying Law Globally*, ed. H. Klug and S. Engle Merry, 69–95, (New York: Cambridge University Press, 2016), https://doi.org/10.1017/CBO9781139683432.006; Elizabeth Chiarello, *Policing Patients: Treatment and Surveillance on the Frontlines of the Opioid Crisis* (Princeton, NJ: Princeton University Press, 2024), https://press.princeton.edu/books/hardcover/9780691224770/policing-patients; Carol A. Heimer, *Governing the Global Clinic HIV and the Legal Transformation of Medicine* (Chicago: University of Chicago Press, 2025); Angela K Perone, "Constructing Discrimination Rights: Comparisons Among Staff in Long-Term Care Health Facilities," *The Gerontologist* 63, no. 5 (June 1, 2023): 900–9, https://doi.org/10.1093/geront/gnac152.

45. Erving Goffman, *Frame Analysis: An Essay on the Organization of Experience* (Boston: Northeastern University Press, 1986).

46. Valarie K. Blake, "An Opening for Civil Rights in Health Insurance after the Affordable Care Act," *Boston College Journal of Law and Social Justice* 36, no. 2 (2016): 235–86.

47. For example, shuster, *Trans Medicine: The Emergence and Practice of Treating Gender*; Eric Plemons, *Look of a Woman: Facial Feminization Surgery and the Aims of Trans-Medicine* (Durham, NC: Duke University Press, 2017), https://www.dukeupress.edu/the-look-of-a-woman; Spade, *Normal Life: Administrative Violence, Critical Trans*

Politics, and the Limits of Law; Grant et al., "Injustice at Every Turn"; Sari L. Reisner et al., "Discriminatory Experiences Associated with Posttraumatic Stress Disorder Symptoms among Transgender Adults," *Journal of Counseling Psychology* 63, no. 5 (2016): 509–19, https://doi.org/10.1037/cou0000143; Sari L. Reisner et al., "Global Health Burden and Needs of Transgender Populations: A Review," *The Lancet* 388, no. 10042 (July 23, 2016): 412–36, https://doi.org/10.1016/S0140-6736(16)00684-X; Aizura et al., "Thinking with Trans Now"; Jules Gill-Peterson, *Histories of the Transgender Child, Histories of the Transgender Child* (Minneapolis: University of Minnesota Press, 2018).

48. Grant et al., "Injustice at Every Turn"; Glick et al., "The Role of Discrimination in Care Postponement Among Trans-Feminine Individuals in the U.S. National Transgender Discrimination Survey."

49. Anna Kirkland, "Victorious Transsexuals in the Courtroom: A Challenge for Feminist Legal Theory," *Law & Social Inquiry* 28, no. 1 (2003): 1–37.

50. Noah Adams et al., "Guidance and Ethical Considerations for Undertaking Transgender Health Research and Institutional Review Boards Adjudicating This Research," *Transgender Health* 2, no. 1 (October 1, 2017): 165–75, https://doi.org/10.1089/trgh.2017.0012.

51. Florence Ashley, "Accounting for Research Fatigue in Research Ethics," *Bioethics* 35, no. 3 (2021): 270–76, https://doi.org/10.1111/bioe.12829.

52. The personal and intellectual support my family received made some collective thinking possible after our ordeal. Anna Kirkland, David Moran, and Angela Perone, "Child Abuse Evidence: New Perspectives from Law, Medicine, Psychology & Statistics," *University of Michigan Journal of Law Reform* 50, no. 3 (January 1, 2017): 669–76, https://doi.org/10.36646/mjlr.50.3.child. Other scholars have done the work in this area beautifully. Kelley Fong, *Investigating Families: Motherhood in the Shadow of Child Protective Services* (Princeton, NJ: Princeton University Press, 2023); Roberts, *Torn Apart*. The story of the invention and professional consolidation of the job of child abuse pediatrician has yet to be written.

53. I conducted a nationwide search for research assistants and was lucky enough to hire trans, queer, and non-white doctoral students to help with the interviews. Most of our interviews ended up being over the phone. It was not clear how the interviewers' identities may have impacted the data since we did not discuss that with participants.

54. Laura Nader, "Up the Anthropologist: Perspectives Gained From Studying Up," in *Reinventing Anthropology*, ed. Dell Hymes (New York: Vintage Books, 1974), 284–311.

55. The Civil Rights Clearinghouse at the University of Michigan School of Law, directed by Prof. Margo Schlanger, is an accessible resource for documents in trans healthcare access litigation. See https://clearinghouse.net/ and search "Transgender Healthcare Access Cases" under special collections.

1. HEALTH CARE CIVIL RIGHTS: SET UP TO FAIL

1. Charles Kahn and Claudia Salzberg, "The Next Generation Of Measuring Patient Experience," *Health Affairs* (blog), March 8, 2019, https://www.healthaffairs.org/do/10.1377/hblog20190307.766083/full/; Shivan J. Mehta, "Patient Satisfaction Reporting and Its Implications for Patient Care," *AMA Journal of Ethics* 17, no. 7 (July 1, 2015): 616–21, https://doi.org/10.1001/journalofethics.2015.17.7.ecas3-1507.

2. "Hospital Compare," Centers for Medicare & Medicaid Services, accessed January 13, 2020, https://www.medicare.gov/hospitalcompare/search.html?

3. In 2023, the Joint Commission began requiring that organizations appoint leadership to address health care disparities, that they assess patients' health-related social needs, such as housing and food insecurity, that they stratify their patient data on quality and safety by sociodemographic characteristics, and that they track and assess how they are doing to address these disparities (The Joint Commission, "R3 Report: New Requirements to Reduce Health Care Disparities," June 20, 2022). Crunching patient data by demographic group will be widely common, in other words, and at least gathering data about structural problems like housing and transportation will take hold. But it's unclear how much hospitals can do about a lack of housing, food, and transportation for their patients. This approach requires healthcare organizations to use the tools they already have—patient data, survey results, and diagnostic coding—to try to solve another set of vexing social problems. The record of success in endeavors like this is decidedly mixed, especially when criminal justice concerns come in to compete with care provision. Elizabeth Chiarello, *Policing Patients: Treatment and Surveillance on the Frontlines of the Opioid Crisis* (Princeton, NJ: Princeton University Press, 2024), https://press.princeton.edu/books/hardcover/9780691224770 /policing-patients; Jaimie Morse, "Legal Mobilization in Medicine: Nurses, Rape Kits, and the Emergence of Forensic Nursing in the United States since the 1970s," *Social Science & Medicine* 222 (February 1, 2019): 323–34, https://doi.org/10.1016/j.socscimed.2018.12.032. So while Peggy and others could learn a lot from looking more closely at their own data, they will not be able to control all of its uses, and we cannot assume that these initiatives will always be helpful rather than stigmatizing or even criminalizing.

4. Jill Quadagno, "Promoting Civil Rights through the Welfare State: How Medicare Integrated Southern Hospitals," *Social Problems* 47, no. 1 (2000): 68–89, https://doi.org /10.2307/3097152.

5. Ellen Berrey, Robert L. Nelson, and Laura Beth Nielsen, *Rights on Trial: How Workplace Discrimination Law Perpetuates Inequality* (Chicago: University of Chicago Press, 2017); Lauren B. Edelman, *Working Law: Courts, Corporations, and Symbolic Civil Rights* (Chicago: University of Chicago Press, 2016); Frank Dobbin, *Inventing Equal Opportunity* (Princeton, NJ: Princeton University Press, 2009); Frank Dobbin and Alexandra Kalev, "The Civil Rights Revolution at Work: What Went Wrong," *Annual Review of Sociology* 47, no. 1 (July 31, 2021): 281–303, https://doi.org/10.1146/annurev-soc-090820-023615; Michael McCann, "The Unbearable Lightness of Rights: On Sociolegal Inquiry in the Global Era," *Law & Society Review* 48, no. 2 (2014): 245–73, https://doi.org/10.1111/lasr.12075; Michael W. McCann, *Rights at Work: Pay Equity Reform and the Politics of Legal Mobilization*, Language and Legal Discourse (Chicago: University of Chicago Press, 1994).

6. Christina S. Ho, *Normalizing an American Right to Health* (New York: Oxford University Press, 2023).

7. Eleanor D. Kinney and Brian Alexander Clark, "Provisions for Health and Health Care in the Constitutions of the Countries of the World," *Cornell International Law Journal* 37, no. 2 (2004): 285–356.

8. As this book goes to press in 2024, the Supreme Court has agreed to hear *United States v. Skrmetti* to answer whether the equal protection clause permits the state of Tennessee to ban gender-affirming care for minors. The case turns on arguments discussed

in chapter 4: is the ban driven by animus toward trans people (so that cutting off treatments means they cannot exist because they should not exist) or is it sex-neutral protective legislation meant only to protect children from harm? The justices will choose a level of scrutiny (rational basis or intermediate) and apply it to arrive at a decision that aligns with their political and religious preferences about health policy toward trans people.

9. *Dobbs v. Jackson Women's Health Org.*, 597 U.S. 215 (2022).

10. Christopher W. Schmidt, *Civil Rights in America: A History*, Cambridge Studies on Civil Rights and Civil Liberties (Cambridge, UK: Cambridge University Press, 2020), https://doi.org/10.1017/9781108550857.

11. Title VI of the Civil Rights Act of 1964, 42 U.S.C. §§ 2000d et seq. provides that "no person in the United States shall, on the ground of race, color, or national origin, be excluded from participation in, be denied the benefits of, or be subjected to discrimination under any program or activity receiving federal financial assistance." State laws prohibiting unfair discrimination in insurance vary widely, but race, national origin, and religion tend to be the most protected categories. Ronen Avraham, "Discrimination and Insurance," in *The Routledge Handbook of the Ethics of Discrimination*, ed. Kasper Lippert-Rasmussen (Routledge Handbooks Online, 2017), 335–47, https://doi.org/10.4324/9781315681634; Ronen Avraham, Kyle D. Logue, and Daniel Schwarcz, "Towards a Universal Framework for Insurance Anti-Discrimination Laws," *Connecticut Insurance Law Journal*, no. 1 (2015): 1–52; Ronen Avraham, Kyle D. Logue, and Daniel Schwarcz, "Understanding Insurance Antidiscrimination Law," *Southern California Law Review* 87, no. 2 (2014): 195–274.

12. HIPAA Privacy Rule to Support Reproductive Health Care Privacy, 89 Fed. Reg. 32976 (to be codified at 45 C.F.R. pts. 160, 164).

13. "Medicaid Postpartum Coverage Extension Tracker," *Kaiser Family Foundation* (blog), March 28, 2024, https://www.kff.org/medicaid/issue-brief/medicaid-postpartum -coverage-extension-tracker/.

14. "State Overviews | Medicaid," Centers for Medicare & Medicaid Services, accessed April 22, 2024, https://www.medicaid.gov/state-overviews/index.html.

15. Hill-Burton Hospital Survey and Construction Act of 1946, 42 U.S.C. §§ 291 et seq.

16. Karen Kruse Thomas, *Deluxe Jim Crow: Civil Rights and American Health Policy, 1935–1954* (Athens, GA: University of Georgia Press, 2011), 176.

17. Quadagno, "Promoting Civil Rights through the Welfare State."

18. Quadagno, "Promoting Civil Rights through the Welfare State."

19. Thomas, *Deluxe Jim Crow*, 179. Alabama used Hill-Burton funds to build racially segregated hospitals in sixty-five counties of the state. David Barton Smith, "Addressing Racial Inequities in Health Care: Civil Rights Monitoring and Report Cards," *Journal of Health Politics, Policy and Law* 23, no. 1 (February 1, 1998): 81, https://doi.org/10.1215/03616878 -23-1-75.

20. Elizabeth Williams, Robin Rudowitz, and Alice Burns, "Medicaid Financing: The Basics," *Kaiser Family Foundation* (blog), April 13, 2023, https://www.kff.org/medicaid /issue-brief/medicaid-financing-the-basics/.

21. *Brown v. Board of Education*, 347 U.S. 483 (1954).

22. *Simkins v. Moses H. Cone Memorial Hospital*, 323 F.2d 959 (United States Court of Appeals for the Fourth Circuit 1963).

23. *Simkins.*

24. Civil Rights Act of 1964, 42 U.S.C. §§ 2000e-1 et seq.

25. Other federal antidiscrimination legislation also relies on receipt of federal funds to require recipients not to discriminate on the basis of sex (Title IX, passed in 1972), age (Age Discrimination Act, first passed in 1967 as an employment measure but specified to cover recipients of federal funding in 1975) and disability (Section 504, passed in 1973). Title IX was enacted to ban sex discrimination in education, and that limitation to the sphere of education prevented Title IX from having the same reach as Title VI had for race, color, and national origin. These laws rely on the spending clause of the Constitution; that is, Congress may place conditions on the funding it distributes.

26. David Barton Smith, *The Power to Heal: Civil Rights, Medicare, and the Struggle to Transform America's Health Care System* (Nashville, TN: Vanderbilt University Press, 2016), https://muse-jhu-edu.proxy.lib.umich.edu/book/46885.

27. Memo to President Johnson from Lee White, April 26, 1965.

28. P. Preston Reynolds, "The Federal Government's Use of Title VI and Medicare to Racially Integrate Hospitals in the United States, 1963 through 1967," *American Journal of Public Health* 87, no. 11 (November 1997): 1853, https://doi.org/10.2105/ajph.87.11.1850.

29. Smith, *The Power to Heal: Civil Rights, Medicare, and the Struggle to Transform America's Health Care System*, 140.

30. "Contingency Plan for Utilization of Federal Government Hospitals for Medicare Patients," Memo from Philip Lee, M.D., Assistant Secretary for Health and Scientific Affairs to Douglass Cater, June 24, 1966.

31. Dayna Bowen Matthew, *Just Medicine: A Cure for Racial Inequality in American Health Care* (New York: New York University Press, 2015), 25–26, https://muse.jhu.edu/pub/193/monograph/book/76222.

32. Dayna Bowen Matthew, *Just Health: Treating Structural Racism to Heal America* (New York: New York University Press, 2022), 222.

33. *National Federation of Independent Business v. Sebelius*, 567 U.S. 519 (2012).

34. Richard A. Rettig, "Origins of the Medicare Kidney Disease Entitlement: The Social Security Amendments of 1972," in *Biomedical Politics*, ed. Kathi E. Hanna (Washington, DC: National Academies Press, 1991), 176–204, https://www.ncbi.nlm.nih.gov/books/NBK234191/.

35. Section 504 of the Rehabilitation Act of 1973, 29 U.S.C. § 794 (1973), Americans with Disabilities Act of 1990, 42 U.S.C. §§ 12101 et seq.

36. Department of Health and Human Services, "Nondiscrimination in Health Programs and Activities," *Federal Register* Vol. 81 No. 96 (May 18, 2016): 31376, https://www.federalregister.gov/documents/2016/05/18/2016-11458/nondiscrimination-in-health-programs-and-activities; Department of Health and Human Services, "Nondiscrimination in Health Programs and Activities," *Federal Register* Vol. 89 No. 88 (May 6, 2024): 37522, https://www.federalregister.gov/documents/2024/05/06/2024-08711/nondiscrimination-in-health-programs-and-activities (codified at 42 *Code of Federal Regulations* § 92).

37. "Civil Rights and COVID-19," Office for Civil Rights, April 29, 2020, https://www.hhs.gov/civil-rights/for-providers/civil-rights-covid19/index.html.

38. Ari Ne'eman et al., "The Treatment of Disability under Crisis Standards of Care: An Empirical and Normative Analysis of Change over Time during COVID-19," *Journal of Health Politics, Policy and Law* 46, no. 5 (October 1, 2021): 831–60, https://doi.org/10.1215/03616878-9156005.

39. Celeste Watkins-Hayes, *Remaking a Life: How Women Living with HIV/AIDS Confront Inequality* (Oakland, CA: University of California Press, 2019); Steven Epstein, *Impure*

Science: AIDS, Activism, and the Politics of Knowledge, Medicine and Society (Berkeley, CA: University of California Press, 1998).

40. Steven Epstein, *Inclusion: The Politics of Difference in Medical Research* (Chicago: University of Chicago Press, 2008).

41. Theodore E. Schall and Jacob D. Moses, "Gender-Affirming Care for Cisgender People," *Hastings Center Report* 53, no. 3 (2023): 15–24, https://doi.org/10.1002/hast.1486.

42. Elizabeth A. Hoffmann, *Lactation at Work: Expressed Milk, Expressing Beliefs, and the Expressive Value of Law* (New York: Cambridge University Press, 2021), https://doi .org/10.1017/9781108770828.

43. Colleen M. Grogan, *Grow and Hide: The History of America's Health Care State* (New York: Oxford University Press, 2023), https://doi.org/10.1093/oso/9780199812233.001.0001.

44. "Reduce Tax Subsidies for Employment-Based Health Insurance," Congressional Budget Office, December 13, 2018, https://www.cbo.gov/budget-options/54798.

45. "McCarran-Ferguson Act of 1945," 15 U.S.C. §§ 1011–1015 §, accessed May 14, 2020, https://www.law.cornell.edu/uscode/text/15/6701.

46. "Trans Health Project: State Health Insurance Laws and Guidance," Transgender Legal Defense & Education Fund, 2020, https://transhealthproject.org/resources/state -health-insurance-laws-and-guidance/.

47. Employee Retirement Income Security Act of 1974, 29 U.S.C. §§ 1001 et seq.

48. Albert Feuer, "When Do State Laws Determine ERISA Plan Benefit Rights?," *John Marshall Law Review* 47, no. 1 (2013): 145–400; Fred J. Hellinger and Gary J. Young, "Health Plan Liability and ERISA: The Expanding Scope of State Legislation," *American Journal of Public Health* 95, no. 2 (February 1, 2005): 217–23, https://doi.org/10.2105 /AJPH.2004.037895.

49. "History of EBSA and ERISA," Department of Labor, accessed October 27, 2023, http://www.dol.gov/agencies/ebsa/about-ebsa/about-us/history-of-ebsa-and-erisa.

50. *Lange v. Houston County Board of Commissioners*, No. 22–13626, 11th Circuit (May 13, 2024).

51. *Obergefell v. Hodges*, 576 U.S. 644 (2015).

52. Timothy Wang, Elizabeth Kelman, and Sean Cahill, "What the New Affordable Care Act Nondiscrimination Rule Means for Providers and LGBT Patients" (Boston: Fenway Health, 2016); National Center for Transgender Equality, "2015 U.S. Transgender Survey Report," 2015, http://www.ustranssurvey.org.

53. Andrew C. Stevens, "The Future of Healthcare Discrimination Litigation–Section 1557 of the ACA," Arnall Golden Gregory LLP, August 17, 2015, https://www.agg.com/news -insights/publications/the-future-of-healthcare-discrimination-litigationsection-1557-of -the-aca-08-17-2015/.

54. Daniel Carpenter, "Is Health Politics Different?," *Annual Review of Political Science* 15, no. 1 (2012): 287–311, https://doi.org/10.1146/annurev-polisci-050409-113009.

55. Department of Health and Human Services, "Nondiscrimination in Health Programs and Activities," *Federal Register* Vol. 81 No. 96 (May 18, 2016): 31376, https://www.federal register.gov/documents/2016/05/18/2016-11458/nondiscrimination-in-health-programs-and -activities.

56. Kellan Baker, "LGBT Protections in Affordable Care Act Section 1557," *Health Affairs* (blog), June 6, 2016, https://www.healthaffairs.org/do/10.1377/hblog20160606.055155 /full/.

57. Sidney D. Watson, "Section 1557 of the Affordable Care Act: Civil Rights, Health Reform, Race, and Equity," *Howard Law Journal* 55, no. 3 (2012): 855–86.

58. Sharita Gruberg and Frank J. Bewkes, "The ACA's LGBTQ Nondiscrimination Regulations Prove Crucial," Center for American Progress, March 7, 2018, https://www.americanprogress.org/issues/lgbt/reports/2018/03/07/447414/acas-lgbtq-nondiscrimination-regulations-prove-crucial/.

59. US Department of Health and Human Services Office for Civil Rights, "A Civil Rights Training for Health Providers and Employees of Health Programs and Health Insurance Issuers: Presenter's Guide" (Washington, DC, July 2016), www.hhs.gov/sites/default/files/section1557-presenters-guide.pdf.

60. *Franciscan Alliance, Inc. v. Burwell*, 227 F. Supp. 3d 660 (N.D. Tex. 2016).

61. Emma Platoff, "By Gutting Obamacare, Judge Reed O'Connor Handed Texas a Win. It Wasn't the First Time.," *The Texas Tribune*, December 19, 2018, https://www.texastribune.org/2018/12/19/reed-oconnor-federal-judge-texas-obamacare-forum-shopping-ken-paxton/.

62. *Franciscan Alliance, Inc. v. Burwell*, Civil Action No. 7:16-cv-00108-O (December 31, 2016).

63. *Prescott v. Rady Children's Hospital-San Diego*, 265 F. Supp. 3d 1090 (2017); Katie Keith, "More Courts Rule On Section 1557 As HHS Reconsiders Regulation," *Health Affairs* (blog), October 2, 2018, https://www.healthaffairs.org/do/10.1377/hblog20181002.142178.

64. Anna Castro, "Family Settles Suit Against Rady Children's Hospital-San Diego for Discriminatory Treatment of Transgender Teenager," Transgender Law Center, August 30, 2019, https://transgenderlawcenter.org/tlc-mourns-death-of-johana-medina-in-ice-custody-continues-fight-for-trans-migrant-justice-3-3-2/.

65. Department of Health and Human Services, "Nondiscrimination in Health and Health Education Programs or Activities, Delegation of Authority," *Federal Register* Vol. 85 No. 119 (June 19, 2020): 37160, https://www.federalregister.gov/documents/2020/06/19/2020-11758/nondiscrimination-in-health-and-health-education-programs-or-activities-delegation-of-authority; MaryBeth Musumeci and Laurie Sobel, "The Trump Administration's Final Rule on Section 1557 Non-Discrimination Regulations Under the ACA and Current Status," Kaiser Family Foundation, September 18, 2020, https://www.kff.org/racial-equity-and-health-policy/issue-brief/the-trump-administrations-final-rule-on-section-1557-non-discrimination-regulations-under-the-aca-and-current-status/.

66. *Bostock v. Clayton County*, 140 S. Ct. 1731 (2020).

67. Fenway Health, "Fenway Health, Other Groups Sue Federal Government Over Discriminatory Health Care Rule,", July 9, 2020, https://fenwayhealth.org/fenway-health-other-groups-sue-federal-government-over-discriminatory-health-care-rule/; Lambda Legal, "Lambda Legal Sues Trump Administration Over Anti-Transgender Health Care Rule," June 22, 2020, https://www.lambdalegal.org/blog/20200622_lambda-legal-sues-hhs-1557-aca-rule.

68. *Whitman-Walker Health v. U.S. Department of Health and Human Services*, Case No. 1:20-cv-01630, U.S. District Court for the District of District of Columbia (June 22, 2020).

69. Katie Keith, "Court Vacates New 1557 Rule That Would Roll Back Antidiscrimination Protections For LGBT Individuals," *Health Affairs Forefront* (blog), August 18, 2020, https://www.healthaffairs.org/do/10.1377/forefront.20200818.468025/full/.

70. *Loper Bright Enterprises v. Raimondo*, No 22–1219, U.S. Supreme Court (June 28, 2024).

71. Memorandum Opinion and Order Granting Plaintiffs' Motion for Expedited Relief, §705 Relief, and a Preliminary Injunction in *Tennessee v. Becerra*, U.S. District Court for the Southern District of Mississippi, Cause No. 1:24cv161-LG-BWR (July 3, 2024).

72. Out2Enroll, "Summary of Findings: 2020 Marketplace Plan Compliance with Section 1557," 2020, https://out2enroll.org/out2enroll/wp-content/uploads/2019/11/Report-on-Trans-Exclusions-in-2020-Marketplace-Plans-2.pdf.

73. Department of Health and Human Services, "Nondiscrimination in Health Programs and Activities," *Federal Register* Vol. 81 No. 96 (May 18, 2016): 31472, https://www.federalregister.gov/documents/2016/05/18/2016-11458/nondiscrimination-in-health-programs-and-activities.

74. Out2Enroll, "Summary of Findings: 2017 Marketplace Plan Compliance with Section 1557," accessed December 19, 2018, https://out2enroll.org/out2enroll/wp-content/uploads/2015/10/Report-on-Trans-Exclusions-in-2017-Marketplace-Plans.pdf.

75. Out2Enroll, "Summary of Findings: 2018 Marketplace Plan Compliance with Section 1557," accessed December 19, 2018, https://out2enroll.org/out2enroll/wp-content/uploads/2017/11/Overview-of-Trans-Exclusions-in-2018-Marketplace-Plans-1.

76. Out2Enroll, "Plan Information for 2024," 2024, https://out2enroll.org/2024-cocs/.

2. HOW HEALTH CARE CIVIL RIGHTS BECAME PATIENT EXPERIENCE

1. Robert L. Wears and Kathleen M. Sutcliffe, *Still Not Safe: Patient Safety and the Middle-Managing of American Medicine* (New York: Oxford University Press, 2020), 142.

2. Wears and Sutcliffe, *Still Not Safe*, 144.

3. Wears and Sutcliffe, *Still Not Safe*, 150–51.

4. I fully describe the research methods and participants for the study in previously published papers. Overall, my team and I interviewed 109 people and analyzed nearly 1500 insurance plan documents in addition to the primary source and legal research presented here. All names are pseudonyms. See Anna Kirkland, "Dropdown Rights: Categorizing Transgender Discrimination in Healthcare Technologies," *Social Science & Medicine* 289 (November 2021): 114348, https://doi.org/10.1016/j.socscimed.2021.114348; Anna Kirkland and Mikell Hyman, "Civil Rights as Patient Experience: How Healthcare Organizations Handle Discrimination Complaints," *Law & Society Review* 55, no. 2 (2021): 273–95, https://doi.org/10.1111/lasr.12554. These papers are accessible through the publishing journals or in the Deep Blue repository at the University of Michigan.

5. Erin L. Kelly, "Failure to Update: An Institutional Perspective on Noncompliance with the Family and Medical Leave Act," *Law & Society Review* 44, no. 1 (2010): 33–66.

6. Condition of Participation: Patient's Rights. 42 CFR 482.13 (1986).

7. Department of Health and Human Services, "Nondiscrimination in Health Programs and Activities," *Federal Register* Vol. 81 No. 96 (May 18, 2016): 31394, https://www.federalregister.gov/documents/2016/05/18/2016-11458/nondiscrimination-in-health-programs-and-activities.

8. Lauren B. Edelman, *Working Law: Courts, Corporations, and Symbolic Civil Rights* (Chicago: University of Chicago Press, 2016).

9. Lauren B. Edelman, Howard S. Erlanger, and John Lande, "Internal Dispute Resolution: The Transformation of Civil Rights in the Workplace," *Law & Society Review* 27 (1993):

497–534; Frank Dobbin, *Inventing Equal Opportunity* (Princeton, NJ: Princeton University Press, 2009).

10. Department of Health and Human Services, "Nondiscrimination in Health Programs and Activities," *Federal Register* Vol. 81 No. 96 (May 18, 2016): 31395, https://www.federalregister.gov/documents/2016/05/18/2016-11458/nondiscrimination-in-health-programs-and-activities.

11. Edelman, *Working Law*, 26.

12. Richard Bolton Siegrist, "Patient Satisfaction: History, Myths, and Misperceptions," *AMA Journal of Ethics* 15, no. 11 (November 2, 2013): 982–87, https://doi.org/10.1001/virtualmentor.2013.15.11.mhst1–1311.

13. Agency for Healthcare Research and Quality, "The CAHPS Program," accessed May 10, 2023, https://www.ahrq.gov/cahps/about-cahps/cahps-program/index.html.

14. Siegrist, "Patient Satisfaction."

15. Charles Kahn and Claudia Salzberg, "The Next Generation Of Measuring Patient Experience," *Health Affairs Blog* (blog), March 8, 2019, https://www.healthaffairs.org/do/10.1377/hblog20190307.766083/full/.

16. "Our Story—The Beryl Institute—Improving the Patient Experience," The Beryl Institute, accessed May 11, 2023, https://www.theberylinstitute.org/page/OurStory.

17. Johanna Viitanen et al., "Patient Experience from an eHealth Perspective: A Scoping Review of Approaches and Recent Trends," *Yearbook of Medical Informatics* 31, no. 1 (December 4, 2022): 136–45, https://doi.org/10.1055/s-0042–1742515.

18. Barak D. Richman and Kevin A. Schulman, "Are Patient Satisfaction Instruments Harming Both Patients and Physicians?," *Journal of the American Medical Association* 328, no. 22 (December 13, 2022): 2209–10, https://doi.org/10.1001/jama.2022.21677; Alexandra Junewicz and Stuart J. Youngner, "Patient-Satisfaction Surveys on a Scale of 0 to 10: Improving Health Care, or Leading It Astray," *The Hastings Center Report* 45, no. 3 (May 1, 2015): 43–51, https://doi.org/10.1002/hast.453.

19. C. Komal Jaipaul and Gary E. Rosenthal, "Do Hospitals with Lower Mortality Have Higher Patient Satisfaction? A Regional Analysis of Patients with Medical Diagnoses," *American Journal of Medical Quality* 18, no. 2 (March 1, 2003): 59–65, https://doi.org/10.1177/106286060301800203; William Boulding et al., "Relationship between Patient Satisfaction with Inpatient Care and Hospital Readmission within 30 Days," *The American Journal of Managed Care* 17, no. 1 (January 2011): 41–48.

20. "Grievances (Prescription Drugs)," Centers for Medicare & Medicaid Services, March 4, 2019, https://www.cms.gov/Medicare/Appeals-and-Grievances/MedPrescriptDrugApplGriev/Grievances.html; "Grievances (Medicare Managed Care)," Centers for Medicare & Medicaid Services, March 7, 2019, https://www.cms.gov/Medicare/Appeals-and-Grievances/MMCAG/Grievances.html; "CMS Interpretive Guidelines for Hospitals," 2008, §482.13(a)(2).

21. Katherine C. Kellogg, "Brokerage Professions and Implementing Reform in an Age of Experts," *American Sociological Review* 79, no. 5 (2014): 913.

22. Sinha Gaurav, "Patient Safety and Risk Management Software: Global Markets" (BCC Research, October 2020), 124.

23. Scott Regan, "The Merger of RL Solutions and Datix: 11 Things to Know," Becker Hospital Review: Becker's Health IT, February 21, 2019, https://www.beckershospitalreview

.com/healthcare-information-technology/the-merger-of-rl-solutions-and-datix-11-things
-to-know.html.

24. The Joint Commission, "R3 Report: New Requirements to Reduce Health Care Disparities," June 20, 2022.

25. Jane Pryma, "'Even My Sister Says I'm Acting like a Crazy to Get a Check': Race, Gender, and Moral Boundary-Work in Women's Claims of Disabling Chronic Pain," *Social Science & Medicine* 181 (May 1, 2017): 66–73, https://doi.org/10.1016/j.socscimed.2017.03.048; Katrina Kimport, Tracy A. Weitz, and Lori Freedman, "The Stratified Legitimacy of Abortions," *Journal of Health and Social Behavior* 57, no. 4 (December 1, 2016): 503–16, https://doi.org/10.1177/0022146516669970; Elizabeth Chiarello, "Law, Morality, and Health Care Professionals: A Multilevel Framework," *Annual Review of Law and Social Science* 15, no. 1 (October 10, 2019): 117–35, https://doi.org/10.1146/annurev-lawsocsci-101518–042853.

26. Jason A. Wolf, "Patient Experience: The New Heart of Healthcare Leadership," *Frontiers of Health Services Management* 33, no. 3 (Spring 2017): 6, emphasis in original, https://doi.org/10.1097/HAP.0000000000000002.

27. Eduardo Bonilla-Silva, *Racism without Racists: Color-Blind Racism and the Persistence of Racial Inequality in the United States* (Lanham, MD: Rowman & Littlefield Publishers, 2006).

3. HOW INSURANCE COMPANIES BROKER HEALTH CARE CIVIL RIGHTS

1. Department of Health and Human Services, "Nondiscrimination in Health Programs and Activities," *Federal Register* Vol. 89 No. 88 (May 6, 2024): 37522, https://www.federalregister.gov/documents/2024/05/06/2024-08711/nondiscrimination-in-health-programs-and-activities (codified at 42 *Code of Federal Regulations* § 92.207(c)).

2. Miranda Yaver, "Rationing by Inconvenience: How Insurance Denials Induce Administrative Burdens," *Journal of Health Politics, Policy and Law* 49, no. 4 (February 7, 2024): 11186111, https://doi.org/10.1215/03616878–11186111.

3. Tara Gonsalves, "Elaborating Embodied Boundaries: Medical Expertise and (Trans) Gender Classification," *American Journal of Sociology* 129, no. 5 (March 2024): 1317, https://doi.org/10.1086/729505.

4. Anna Kirkland, "Victorious Transsexuals in the Courtroom: A Challenge for Feminist Legal Theory," *Law & Social Inquiry* 28, no. 1 (2003): 1–37; Anna Kirkland, "What's at Stake in Transgender Discrimination as Sex Discrimination?," *Signs: Journal of Women in Culture and Society* 32, no. 1 (2006): 83–111.

5. "Despite High Rates of Insurance, Transgender People More Likely than Cisgender People to Avoid Health Care Due to Cost," UCLA School of Law: Williams Institute, August 18, 2021, https://williamsinstitute.law.ucla.edu/press/transpop-health-cvd-press-release/. When asked their own research priorities, trans people outside the academy list problems with gaining access to and using health insurance as a top concern.

6. National Center for Transgender Equality, "2015 U.S. Transgender Survey Report," 2015, 94, http://www.ustranssurvey.org.

7. Out2Enroll, "Summary of Findings: 2020 Marketplace Plan Compliance with Section 1557," 2020, https://out2enroll.org/out2enroll/wp-content/uploads/2019/11/Report-on-Trans-Exclusions-in-2020-Marketplace-Plans-2.pdf.

8. Ya-Lin A. Huang et al., "HIV Testing and Preexposure Prophylaxis Prescriptions Among U.S. Commercially Insured Transgender Men and Women, 2014 to 2021," *Annals of Internal Medicine* 177, no. 1 (December 19, 2023): 3, https://doi.org/10.7326/M23-2073.

9. Kyla Bender-Baird and Margaret C. Stevenson, "Effects of Medicalization on Case Outcomes in Transgender Employment Discrimination Court Decisions," *Behavioral Sciences & the Law* (June 2024): 1–16, https://doi.org/10.1002/bsl.2685.

10. "47% of Companies Fail to File Form 5500's," *ComplianceBug* (blog), June 12, 2006, https://www.compliancebug.com/47-companies-fail-file-form-5500s/; Marie Leone, "Late ERISA Filers May Number 35,000," CFO: Risk and Compliance, June 12, 2006, https://www.cfo.com/risk-compliance/2006/06/late-erisa-filers-may-number-35000/.

11. Julie A. Su, "Annual Report on Self-Insured Group Health Plans," (Washington, DC: US Department of Labor, March 2024), https://www.dol.gov/agencies/ebsa/about-ebsa/our-activities/resource-center/reports.

12. "2023 Employer Health Benefits Survey," *Kaiser Family Foundation* (blog), October 18, 2023, https://www.kff.org/report-section/ehbs-2023-section-10-plan-funding/.

13. Martin J. Walsh "Annual Report on Self-Insured Group Health Plans" (Washington, DC: US Department of Labor, March 2023), https://www.dol.gov/agencies/ebsa/about-ebsa/our-activities/resource-center/reports.

14. Matthew Bakko and Shanna K. Kattari, "Differential Access to Transgender Inclusive Insurance and Healthcare in the United States: Challenges to Health across the Life Course," *Journal of Aging & Social Policy* 33, no. 1 (June 23, 2019): 67–81 08959420.2019.1632681, https://doi.org/10.1080/08959420.2019.1632681; Ledibabari Ngaage et al., "A Review of Insurance Coverage of Gender-Affirming Genital Surgery," *Plastic and Reconstructive Surgery* 145, no. 3 (March 2020): 803–12, https://doi.org/10.1097/PRS.0000000000006591; Ledibabari Ngaage et al., "Health Insurance Coverage of Gender-Affirming Top Surgery in the United States," *Plastic and Reconstructive Surgery* 144, no. 4 (October 2019): 824–33, https://doi.org/10.1097/PRS.0000000000006012; Ledibabari M. Ngaage et al., "Gender Surgery Beyond Chest and Genitals: Current Insurance Landscape," *Aesthetic Surgery Journal* 40, no. 4 (March 23, 2020): NP202–10, https://doi.org/10.1093/asj/sjz262.

15. "HRC's 2020 Corporate Equality Index," Human Rights Campaign, accessed May 17, 2020, https://www.hrc.org/campaigns/corporate-equality-index/.

16. For example, Huang et al., "HIV Testing and Preexposure Prophylaxis Prescriptions Among U.S. Commercially Insured Transgender Men and Women, 2014 to 2021."

17. Keith Finlay, Michael Mueller-Smith, and Brittany Street, "Children's Indirect Exposure to the U.S. Justice System: Evidence From Longitudinal Links between Survey and Administrative Data," *The Quarterly Journal of Economics* 138, no. 4 (November 1, 2023): 2181–224, https://doi.org/10.1093/qje/qjad021.

18. We used the Department of Labor's study criteria to determine whether plans were self-insured. Most were, although some had mixed coverage and as explained, it's not possible to determine what the mix is given limitations on reporting.

19. Anna Kirkland, Shauhin Talesh, and Angela K. Perone, "Transition Coverage and Clarity in Self-Insured Corporate Health Insurance Benefit Plans," *Transgender Health* 6, no. 4 (September 29, 2020): 207–16, https://doi.org/10.1089/trgh.2020.0067. The dataset and original PDFs of the health plan documents are available at OpenICPSR at the University of Michigan. Anna Kirkland, and Shauhin Talesh, "Health Insurance Contract Analysis (2019:

Corporate, CA, MI)" (Ann Arbor, MI: Inter-university Consortium for Political and Social Research), September 30, 2021, https://doi.org/10.3886/E120901V4.

20. Alex Dubov and Liana Fraenkel, "Facial Feminization Surgery: The Ethics of Gatekeeping in Transgender Health," *The American Journal of Bioethics* 18, no. 12 (December 2018): 3–9, https://doi.org/10.1080/15265161.2018.1531159.

21. Bridget Schaaff, "Using Federal Nondiscrimination Laws to Avoid ERISA: Securing Protection from Transgender Discrimination in Employee Health Benefit Plans," *Duke Journal of Gender Law & Policy* 26, no. 1 (2018): 45–64.

22. Department of Health and Human Services, "Nondiscrimination in Health Programs and Activities," *Federal Register* Vol. 89 No. 88 (May 6, 2024): 37540, https://www.federalregister.gov/documents/2024/05/06/2024-08711/nondiscrimination-in-health-programs-and-activities (codified at 42 *Code of Federal Regulations* § 92.207).

23. Sharita Gruberg and Frank J. Bewkes, "The ACA's LGBTQ Nondiscrimination Regulations Prove Crucial," Center for American Progress, March 7, 2018, https://www.americanprogress.org/issues/lgbt/reports/2018/03/07/447414/acas-lgbtq-nondiscrimination-regulations-prove-crucial/.

24. Transgender Legal Defense & Education Fund, "Medical Organization Statements on Transgender Health Care," Trans Health Project: Working for Transgender Equal Rights, 2020, https://transhealthproject.org/resources/medical-organization-statements/.

25. Christin L. Munsch and C. Elizabeth Hirsh, "Gender Variance in the Fortune 500: The Inclusion of Gender Identity and Expression in Nondiscrimination Corporate Policy," in *Gender and Sexuality in the Workplace*, ed. Christine L. Williams and Kirsten Dellinger, vol. 20, Research in the Sociology of Work (Bingley, UK: Emerald Group Publishing Limited, 2010), 151–77, https://doi.org/10.1108/S0277-2833(2010)0000020010; David M. Hall, *Allies at Work: Creating a Lesbian, Gay, Bisexual and Transgender Inclusive Work Environment* (San Francisco: Out & Equal Workplace Advocates, 2009); Nicole C. Raeburn, *Changing Corporate America from Inside Out: Lesbian and Gay Workplace Rights* (Minneapolis: University of Minnesota Press, 2004).

26. I refer to them as people seeking care rather than as patients to give them more agency in the context of discussing their health insurance issues. Of the people seeking care that we interviewed, sixteen were white, five were Black, ten were transmen, nine were transwomen, and five were non-binary. We gathered interviews from three surgeons who perform gender-confirmation surgeries, two clinical social workers in gender services programs, a surgery scheduler, the office administrator for one of the surgery practices, and a health insurance navigator in a hospital whose job focused on assisting people obtaining gender-affirming care. They all explained how health insurance worked for them in practice, allowing us to see how a right to health insurance is refracted through the industry. We have changed all names to pseudonyms.

27. Cigna's 2019 health plan for Stanley Black & Decker, 63 (on file with the author and available under open access at OpenICPSR).

28. Eric Plemons, "A Capable Surgeon and a Willing Electrologist: Challenges to the Expansion of Transgender Surgical Care in the United States," *Medical Anthropology Quarterly* 33, no. 2 (2019): 282–301, https://doi.org/10.1111/maq.12484.

29. Eric Plemons, "Gender, Ethnicity, and Transgender Embodiment: Interrogating Classification in Facial Feminization Surgery," *Body & Society* 25, no. 1 (March 1, 2019): 3–28, https://doi.org/10.1177/1357034X18812942; Tara Gonsalves, "Gender Identity, the

Sexed Body, and the Medical Making of Transgender," *Gender & Society* 34, no. 6 (December 1, 2020): 1005–33, https://doi.org/10.1177/0891243220965913; Gonsalves, "Elaborating Embodied Boundaries."

30. C. Riley Snorton, *Black on Both Sides: A Racial History of Trans Identity* (Minneapolis: University of Minnesota Press, 2017); Jules Gill-Peterson, *Histories of the Transgender Child, Histories of the Transgender Child* (Minneapolis: University of Minnesota Press, 2018); Sabrina Strings, *Fearing the Black Body: The Racial Origins of Fat Phobia* (New York: New York University Press, 2019), https://nyupress.org/9781479886753/fearing-the-black-body.

31. National Center for Transgender Equality, "2015 U.S. Transgender Survey Report."

32. Amy B. Monahan and Daniel Schwarcz, "Rules of Medical Necessity," *Iowa Law Review* 107, no. 2 (January 2022): 423–94.

33. Sarah L. Schulz, "The Informed Consent Model of Transgender Care: An Alternative to the Diagnosis of Gender Dysphoria," *Journal of Humanistic Psychology* 58, no. 1 (January 2018): 72–92, https://doi.org/10.1177/0022167817745217; Elizabeth Dietz, "More Necessary than Medical: Reframing the Insurance Argument for Transition-Related Care," *IJFAB: International Journal of Feminist Approaches to Bioethics* 13, no. 1 (March 2020): 63–88, https://doi.org/10.3138/ijfab.13.1.04.

34. Shauhin Talesh, "Legal Intermediaries: How Insurance Companies Construct the Meaning of Compliance with Antidiscrimination Laws," *Law & Policy* 37, no. 3 (2015): 209–39, https://doi.org/10.1111/lapo.12037.

35. David A. Brennen, "Tax Expenditures, Social Justice, and Civil Rights: Expanding the Scope of Civil Rights Laws to Apply to Tax-Exempt Charities," *Brigham Young University Law Review* 2001, no. 1 (2001): 167–228. Brennen's argument is that tax breaks are expenditures for charities and that they should trigger federal civil rights obligations just as if the charities took a direct payment from federal funds. Private employers who receive a tax benefit from offering health insurance to employees but do not take any other federal funding arc in a similar position to tax-exempt charities in this analysis.

4. HOW CONSERVATIVES OPPOSE HEALTH CARE CIVIL RIGHTS

1. Joanna Wuest and Briana Last, "Church Against State: How Industry Groups Lead the Religious Liberty Assault on Civil Rights, Healthcare Policy, and the Administrative State," *Journal of Law, Medicine & Ethics* 52, no. 1 (Spring 2024): 151–68.

2. Joanna Wuest and Briana S. Last, "Agents of Scientific Uncertainty: Conflicts over Evidence and Expertise in Gender-Affirming Care Bans for Minors," *Social Science & Medicine* 344, no. 2 (March 2024).

3. Peter J. Levin, "Bold Vision: Catholic Sisters and the Creation of American Hospitals," *Journal of Community Health* 36, no. 3 (June 1, 2011): 343–47, https://doi.org/10.1007/s10900-011-9401-7.

4. Lori Freedman, *Bishops and Bodies: Reproductive Care in American Catholic Hospitals* (New Brunswick, NJ: Rutgers University Press, 2023), https://doi.org/10.36019/9781978828896.

5. I characterize them as white because although Black Americans are a group with relatively high religiosity that also shares Protestantism and some social conservatism with white evangelicals, Black religiosity has different political effects than white religiosity

(Anthea D. Butler, *White Evangelical Racism: The Politics of Morality in America* [Chapel Hill, NC: The University of North Carolina Press, 2021]). Protestant Christians have historically held discriminatory views of Catholics, but in recent decades these two groups have become more politically aligned, and for the purposes of recent debates over health care civil rights for trans people, they adopt nearly identical positions in opposition to them. American Catholics who are leaders in setting anti-LBGTQ policy agendas in this country are also overwhelmingly white, even though Catholicism around the world is more racially diverse, and Latinx Catholics are well represented among US Catholics. Geoffrey Layman, *The Great Divide: Religious and Cultural Conflict in American Party Politics* (New York: Columbia University Press, 2001); John O'Brien and Eman Abdelhadi, "Re-Examining Restructuring: Racialization, Religious Conservatism, and Political Leanings in Contemporary American Life: Social Forces," *Social Forces* 99, no. 2 (December 2020): 474–503; David E. Campbell, James R. G. Kirk, and Geoffrey C. Layman, "Religion and the 2020 Presidential Election: The Enduring Divide," *The Forum* 18, no. 4 (December 30, 2020): 581–605.

6. Melissa May Borja, *Follow the New Way: American Refugee Resettlement Policy and Hmong Religious Change* (Cambridge, MA: Harvard University Press, 2023); Melissa May Borja, "Migration and Modern Religious Pluralism," in *The Oxford Handbook of Religion and Race in American History*, ed. Kathryn Gin Lum and Paul Harvey (New York: Oxford University Press, 2018), 577–96, https://doi.org/10.1093/oxfordhb/9780190221171.013.6.

7. Kim Parker, Juliana Horowitz Manasce, and Anna Brown, "Americans' Complex Views on Gender Identity and Transgender Issues," *Pew Research Center's Social & Demographic Trends Project* (blog), June 28, 2022, https://www.pewresearch.org/social-trends/2022/06/28/americans-complex-views-on-gender-identity-and-transgender-issues/.

8. Neal Hardin, "How Gender Theory Undermines Reality," Alliance Defending Freedom, April 24, 2023, https://adflegal.org/article/how-gender-theory-undermines-reality.

9. Alliance Defending Freedom, "Complaint in *Christian Healthcare Centers, Inc. v. Nessel*" (United States District Court for the Western District of Michigan, August 29, 2022), 2. "Christian Healthcare does not believe that sex is mutable," the complaint elaborates, "so using a pronoun or reference inconsistent with the person's biological sex is untruthful, and being untruthful violates Christian Healthcare's religious beliefs" (18). Christian Healthcare Centers, Inc. is a membership organization for primary care in which doctors do not take any insurance, including Medicare, and instead fund the practice with membership fees. It is not an insurance plan and does not cover prescriptions, surgery, hospital stays, or emergency services (https://www.chcenters.org/insurance/, accessed November 16, 2023). It does not take any government funding and thus would not be covered under Section 1557. The center is an employer and a place open to the public under Michigan civil rights laws, however, and those laws do not exempt religious organizations from antidiscrimination protections for sex, sexual orientation, and gender identity, hence the lawsuit.

10. Catholic Health Care Leadership Alliance, comment in opposition to the proposed rule, *Nondiscrimination in Health Programs and Activities* (HHS), September 30, 2022, 9–10.

11. Christopher F. Rufo, "A Parent's Guide to Radical Gender Theory," May 15, 2023, https://christopherrufo.com/p/a-parents-guide-to-radical-gender-theory.

12. John T. Jost et al., "Are Needs to Manage Uncertainty and Threat Associated With Political Conservatism or Ideological Extremity?," *Personality and Social Psychology Bulletin* 33, no. 7 (July 1, 2007): 989–1007, https://doi.org/10.1177/0146167207301028.

13. United States Conference of Catholic Bishops, "Ethical and Religious Directives for Catholic Healthcare Services, Sixth Edition" (Washington, DC, 2018), 7, https://www.usccb .org/resources/ethical-and-religious-directives-catholic-healthcare-services.

14. Rufo, "A Parent's Guide to Radical Gender Theory."

15. Parker, Horowitz Manasce, and Brown, "Americans' Complex Views on Gender Identity and Transgender Issues."

16. "Bans on Best Practice Medical Care for Transgender Youth," Movement Advancement Project, accessed February 13, 2024, https://www.lgbtmap.org/equality-maps/health care_youth_medical_care_bans; "2024 Anti-Trans Bills," Trans Legislation Tracker, accessed February 13, 2024, https://translegislation.com.

17. Associated Press and Jo Yurcaba, "Alabama Governor Signs Bill Criminalizing Transgender Health Care for Minors," *NBC News*, April 8, 2022, https://www.nbcnews .com/nbc-out/out-politics-and-policy/alabama-governor-signs-bill-criminalizing-trans gender-health-care-mino-rcna23674.

18. Amanda Hollis-Brusky and Joshua C. Wilson, "Playing for the Rules: How and Why New Christian Right Public Interest Law Firms Invest in Secular Litigation," *Law & Policy* 39, no. 2 (2017): 121–41, https://doi.org/10.1111/lapo.12075.

19. Alliance Defending Freedom, "Securing Freedom's Future at the Supreme Court" (Scottsdale, AZ: Alliance Defending Freedom, 2023), https://adflegal.org/us-supreme -court-wins.

20. Amicus brief by Alliance Defending Freedom in *Neese v. Becerra*, Fifth Circuit (June 2, 2023), 9–11.

21. Ibid., 20.

22. Ibid., 28.

23. Ibid.

24. *Religious Sisters of Mercy v. Becerra*, 55 F.4th 583, 601–02 (8th Cir. 2022).

25. Order Granting Motion for Preliminary Injunction in *Christian Employers Alliance v. Becerra*, U.S. District Court for the District of North Dakota, May 16, 2022, Case No. 1:21-cv-195, page 13. Judge Daniel Traynor (a Trump appointee) suggests that parents can demand gender-affirming surgery for infants. He is not referring to intersex surgery here. Advocates for intersex people oppose surgery on infants to make their genitals conform and celebrate inclusion in Section 1557's protections (interACT: Advocates for Intersex Youth, "Federal Healthcare Rule Cements Sex Discrimination Protections to Include Inter-sex Patients," *interACT: Advocates for Intersex Youth* (blog), April 26, 2024, https://interact advocates.org/federal-healthcare-rule-cements-sex-discrimination-protections/). Religi-ous conservatives, through the same legal advocacy organizations, have also claimed that they will be forced to perform abortions despite numerous federal statutes that have pro-tected objectors and their institutions from having to provide abortions for over fifty years. The only possible context that would compel any emergency department to provide an abortion would be the Emergency Medical Treatment and Labor Act in the rare case of a medical emergency in pregnancy requiring an abortion as stabilizing care. In one case, a Catholic hospital approved an abortion of an eleven-week fetus for a woman who would have otherwise died of her complications, and the Catholic bishop overseeing the hospital excommunicated the nun who approved it and revoked its Catholic status, preferring that they had let both the woman and the fetus die. Freedman, *Bishops and Bodies*, 126.

26. *Hammons v. University of Maryland Medical System Corporation*, 649 F. Supp. 3d 104, 107–10, 117 (D. Md. 2023).

27. Anna Kirkland, *Vaccine Court: The Law and Politics of Injury* (New York: New York University Press, 2016); Anna Kirkland, "Credibility Battles in the Autism Litigation," *Social Studies of Science* 42, no. 2 (2012): 237–61.

28. Hollis-Brusky and Wilson, "Playing for the Rules."

29. Becket Fund for Religious Liberty, "Amicus Brief of Little Sisters of the Poor in *Loper Bright Enterprises v. Raimondo*," n.d.

30. Wuest and Last, "Church Against State."

31. *Texas v. EEOC*, 633 F. Supp. 3d 824, 829–31, 833 (N.D. Tex. 2022).

32. Levin, "Bold Vision."

33. Freedman, *Bishops and Bodies*, 18.

34. Kellie E. Schueler et al., "Denial of Tubal Ligation in Religious Hospitals: Consumer Attitudes When Insurance Limits Hospital Choice," *Contraception* 104, no. 2 (August 1, 2021): 194–201, https://doi.org/10.1016/j.contraception.2021.02.011. Women of color are more likely to be treated in a Catholic hospital ("Bearing Faith: The Limits of Catholic Health Care for Women of Color," Columbia Law School Law, Rights, and Religion Project, 2018, https://lawrightsreligion.law.columbia.edu/bearingfaith).

35. Mary E. Homan and Kenneth R. White, "The Changing Landscape of Catholic Hospitals and Health Systems, 2008–2017," *Journal of Healthcare Management* 66, no. 1 (February 2021): 33–45, https://doi.org/10.1097/JHM-D-20-00005.

36. Freedman, *Bishops and Bodies*.

37. Homan and White, "The Changing Landscape of Catholic Hospitals and Health Systems, 2008–2017"; Kenneth R. White, "When Institutions Collide: The Competing Forces of Hospitals Sponsored by the Roman Catholic Church," *Religions* 4, no. 1 (March 2013): 14–29, https://doi.org/10.3390/rel4010014.

38. Jamie Manson, "Little Sisters of the Poor Are the Wealthy Right Wing's Perfect Avatar," *National Catholic Reporter*, July 21, 2020, https://www.ncronline.org/opinion/grace-margins/little-sisters-poor-are-wealthy-right-wings-perfect-avatar.

39. United States Conference of Catholic Bishops, "Ethical and Religious Directives for Catholic Healthcare Services, Sixth Edition," 6.

40. United States Conference of Catholic Bishops, "Ethical and Religious Directives," 8.

41. United States Conference of Catholic Bishops, "Ethical and Religious Directives," 7.

42. United States Conference of Catholic Bishops, "Ethical and Religious Directives," 25.

43. United States Conference of Catholic Bishops, "Ethical and Religious Directives," 26.

44. Catholic Health Care Leadership Alliance, comment in opposition to the proposed rule, *Nondiscrimination in Health Programs and Activities* (HHS), September 30, 2022, 9–10.

45. Eric Plemons, "Not Here: Catholic Hospital Systems and the Restriction Against Transgender Healthcare," *CrossCurrents* 68, no. 4 (December 2018): 533–49, https://doi.org/10.1111/cros.12341.

46. Kate T. Simms et al., "Historical and Projected Hysterectomy Rates in the USA: Implications for Future Observed Cervical Cancer Rates and Evaluating Prevention Interventions," *Gynecologic Oncology* 158, no. 3 (September 2020): 710–18, https://doi.org/10.1016/j.ygyno.2020.05.030.

47. Louise Uttley and Christine Khaikin, "Growth of Catholic Hospitals and Health Systems: 2016 Update of the Miscarriage of Medicine Report" (New York: MergerWatch, 2016), 5, http://www.mergerwatch.org/.

48. Abram Brummett, Meaghan K. Race, and Randall Hilleary, "Catholic Hospitals Should Improve Public Notification of Treatments They Conscientiously Refuse to Provide," *Annals of Internal Medicine* 176, no. 9 (September 19, 2023): 1264–65, https://doi.org/10.7326/M23-1227.

49. Freedman, *Bishops and Bodies*; Jordan Rau, "In Quest to Grow, Catholic Hospital System Pares Religious Ties," *KFF Health News*, January 23, 2012, https://kffhealthnews.org/news/catholic-healthcare-west-pares-religious-ties/; "The Gender Institute," Dignity Health, https://www.dignityhealth.org/bayarea/locations/saintfrancis/services/gender-institute.

50. Elizabeth Sepper and James D. Nelson, "Government's Religious Hospitals," *Virginia Law Review* 109, no. 1 (2023): 61–130.

51. *National Federation of Independent Businesses. v. Sebelius*, 567 U.S. 519, 575–85 (2012).

52. Catholic Health Care Leadership Alliance, comment in opposition to the proposed rule, *Nondiscrimination in Health Programs and Activities* (HHS), September 30, 2022, 5.

53. Memo from William L. Taylor, General Counsel at the United States Commission on Civil Rights to Phillip S. Hughes, Bureau of the Budget, October 3, 1963.

54. People of faith hold many views about health care and LGBTQ+ identities, and for many of them, there are no incompatibilities between full recognition and provision for people of all genders and sexualities and their faith. My point here is simply about the current patterns of political and legal mobilization, in which one very conservative camp in Christianity (or two camps, if you separate evangelicals from Catholics despite their policy agreements here) dominates the law and policy in this area.

55. Justin McCarthy, "U.S. Same-Sex Marriage Support Holds at 71% High," *Gallup*, June 5, 2023, https://news.gallup.com/poll/506636/sex-marriage-support-holds-high.aspx.

56. "Marriage Is the Future," Alliance Defending Freedom, January 27, 2020, https://adflegal.org/issues/marriage. Segregationist senator Robert Byrd also used the language of diversity to defend southern religious all-white private schools set up to evade *Brown v. Board of Education* (Olatunde C. A. Johnson, "The Story of *Bob Jones University v. United States*: Race, Religion, and Congress' Extraordinary Acquiescence," in *Statutory Interpretation Stories*, ed. William N. Eskridge et al. [New York: Foundation Press, 2011], 137).

57. Alliance Defending Freedom, "Marriage Is the Future."

58. Abigail A. Dumes, *Divided Bodies: Lyme Disease, Contested Illness, and Evidence-Based Medicine* (Durham, NC: Duke University Press, 2020); Kirkland, *Vaccine Court*.

59. Transgender Legal Defense & Education Fund, "Medical Organization Statements on Transgender Health Care," Trans Health Project: Working for Transgender Equal Rights, 2020, https://transhealthproject.org/resources/medical-organization-statements/.

60. Timothy Cavanaugh, Ruben Hopwood, and Cei Lambert, "Informed Consent in the Medical Care of Transgender and Gender-Nonconforming Patients," *AMA Journal of Ethics* 18, no. 11 (November 1, 2016): 1147–55, https://doi.org/10.1001/journalofethics.2016.18.11.sect1-1611.; Damien W. Riggs et al., "Transnormativity in the Psy Disciplines: Constructing Pathology in the Diagnostic and Statistical Manual of Mental Disorders and Standards of Care," *American Psychologist* 74, no. 8 (2019): 912–24, https://doi.org/10.1037/amp0000545.

61. Helana Darwin, "Challenging the Cisgender/Transgender Binary: Nonbinary People and the Transgender Label," *Gender & Society* 34, no. 3 (June 1, 2020): 357–80, https://doi.org/10.1177/0891243220912256; Harry Barbee and Douglas Schrock, "Un/Gendering

Social Selves: How Nonbinary People Navigate and Experience a Binarily Gendered World," *Sociological Forum* 34, no. 3 (2019): 572–93, https://doi.org/10.1111/socf.12517; Austin H. Johnson, "Transnormativity: A New Concept and Its Validation through Documentary Film About Transgender Men," *Sociological Inquiry* 86, no. 4 (2016): 465–91, https://doi .org/10.1111/soin.12127.

62. Alliance Defending Freedom, "RE: Nondiscrimination on the Basis of Sex in Education Programs or Activities Receiving Federal Financial Assistance Docket ID ED-2021-OCR-01666," September 11, 2022, 25, 28–29; For additional analysis, see Joanna Wuest, *Born This Way: Science, Citizenship, and Inequality in the American LGBTQ+ Movement* (Chicago: University of Chicago Press, 2023), 17–20 and chapter seven, https://press.uchi cago.edu/ucp/books/book/chicago/B/bo201362155.html; Wuest and Last, "Agents of Scientific Uncertainty: Conflicts over Evidence and Expertise in Gender- Affirming Care Bans for Minors."

63. Alliance Defending Freedom, "RE: Nondiscrimination on the Basis of Sex in Education Programs or Activities Receiving Federal Financial Assistance Docket ID ED-2021-OCR-01666," September 11, 2022, 28.

64. American College of Pediatricians, "Brief of the American College of Pediatricians in *Dekker v. Secretary, Florida Agency for Health Care Administration*" (United States Court of Appeals for the Eleventh Circuit, October 13, 2023), 3.

65. "American College of Pediatricians," Southern Poverty Law Center, accessed November 15, 2023, https://www.splcenter.org/fighting-hate/extremist-files/group/american -college-pediatricians.

66. "Bans on Best Practice Medical Care for Transgender Youth," Movement Advancement Project, December 8, 2023, https://www.lgbtmap.org/equality-maps/healthcare _youth_medical_care_bans.

67. Bench trials occurred in *Brandt v. Rutledge*, No. 4:21CV00450 JM, 2023 U.S. Dist. LEXIS 106517 (E.D. Ark. June 20, 2023) (over the Arkansas Act 626 of 2021, the Arkansas Save Adolescents From Experimentation (SAFE) Act) and in Florida in *Doe v. Ladapo*, 676 F. Supp. 3d 1205 (N.D. Fla. 2023). Both bench trials resulted in strongly worded rulings in favor of the trans youth and their families and against the conservative's expert witnesses. There were a few kinder words for Dr. Stephen Levine in *Doe v. Ladapo*. Levine notably testified that gender identity is real and that treatments help it, in marked contrast to the other experts that conservatives are able to get. I discuss these victories in chapter five.

68. *L.W. v. Skrmetti*, 83 F.4th 460, 479 (6th Cir. 2023). This case is under review at the Supreme Court as this book goes to press.

69. "That many members of the medical community support the plaintiffs is surely relevant. But it is not dispositive for the same reason we would not defer to a consensus among economists about the proper incentives for interpreting the impairment-of-contracts or takings clauses of the U.S. Constitution. At all events, the medical and regulatory authorities are not of one mind about using hormone therapy to treat gender dysphoria. Else, the FDA would by now have approved the use of these drugs for these purposes. That has not happened, however, giving us considerable pause about constitutionalizing an answer they have not given or, best we can tell, even finally studied" (*L.W. v. Skrmetti*, 73 F.4th 408, 416 [6th Cir. 2023]). "[I]t is difficult to maintain that the medical community is of one mind about the use of hormone therapy for gender dysphoria when the FDA is not prepared to put its credibility and careful testing protocols behind the use" (ibid., 418).

70. *L.W. v. Skrmetti*, 83 F.4th 460, 477 (6th Cir. 2023).

71. Alliance Defending Freedom complaint filed in *McComb Children's Clinic v. Becerra* in United States District Court for the Southern District of Mississippi, Western Division on May 13, 2024, Case No. 5:24-cv-48-KS-LGI, p. 2. This case is different from the challenges to the regulation that secured the injunctions against enforcement of the 2024 Section 1557 rule.

72. Anthea D. Butler, *White Evangelical Racism: The Politics of Morality in America* (Chapel Hill, NC: The University of North Carolina Press, 2021).

73. Johnson, "The Story of *Bob Jones University v. United States*: Race, Religion, and Congress' Extraordinary Acquiescence"; "Bob Jones University Drops Interracial Dating Ban," *Christianity Today*, March 1, 2000, https://www.christianitytoday.com/ct/2000/marchweb-only/53.0.html.

5. REALIZING HEALTH CARE CIVIL RIGHTS

1. Michael McCann, "The Unbearable Lightness of Rights: On Sociolegal Inquiry in the Global Era," *Law & Society Review* 48, no. 2 (2014): 245–73, https://doi.org/10.1111/lasr.12075.

2. Neil Gunningham, Robert A. Kagan, and Dorothy Thornton, "Social License and Environmental Protection: Why Businesses Go Beyond Compliance," *Law & Social Inquiry* 29, no. 2 (ed 2004): 307–41, https://doi.org/10.1111/j.1747-4469.2004.tb00338.x.

3. Department of Health and Human Services, "Nondiscrimination in Health Programs and Activities," *Federal Register* Vol. 81 No. 96 (May 18, 2016): 31454, https://www.federalregister.gov/documents/2016/05/18/2016-11458/nondiscrimination-in-health-programs-and-activities.

4. Katherine Wyers, "Health ICTs and Transgender Health Equity: A Research Agenda," *Information Technology for Development* 30, no. 2 (2024): 1–27, https://doi.org/10.1080/02681102.2023.2292740.

5. Institute of Medicine, *The Health of Lesbian, Gay, Bisexual, and Transgender People: Building a Foundation for Better Understanding* (Washington, DC: The National Academies Press, 2011), https://doi.org/10.17226/13128.

6. Department of Health and Human Services, "2015 Edition Health Information Technology (Health IT) Certification Criteria, 2015 Edition Base Electronic Health Record (EHR) Definition, and ONC Health IT Certification Program Modifications," Pub. L. No. 80 FR 62601, §170.315(a)(5) (2015), https://www.federalregister.gov/documents/2015/10/16/2015-25597/2015-edition-health-information-technology-health-it-certification-criteria-2015-edition-base.

7. Tonya Bowers, "Approved Uniform Data System Changes for Calendar Year 2016," US Department of Health and Human Services, March 22, 2016, https://mail.pachc.org/Documents/2016%20UDS%20Training/G1-PAL%202016-2.pdf. The General Social Survey (GSS) also began to ask about gender identity and sex assigned at birth in 2018, creating the first nationally representative survey sample of trans and non-binary people in the US.

8. Elizabeth Brennan and Mark C. Suchman, "Law and Technology in Healthcare Organizations," in *Research Handbook on Socio-Legal Studies of Medicine and Health* (Cheltenham, UK: Edward Elgar, 2020), 169–90.

9. Oliver L. Haimson et al., "Tumblr Was a Trans Technology: The Meaning, Importance, History, and Future of Trans Technologies," *Feminist Media Studies* 21, no. 3 (April 3, 2021): 345–61, https://doi.org/10.1080/14680777.2019.1678505.

10. Rashmee Singh and Dawn Moore, "Bare Death: Femicide, Forensics and the Necropolitics of the Corpse," in *Research Handbook on Socio-Legal Studies of Medicine and Health*, ed. Marie-Andrée Jacob and Anna Kirkland (Cheltenham, UK: Edward Elgar Publishing, 2020), 287–302.

11. Patricia Backlar, "What's in a Name? Mental Health? Behavioral Health?," *Community Mental Health Journal* 32, no. 1 (February 1, 1996): 5–8, https://doi.org/10.1007/BF02249361; Joseph D. Matarazzo, "Behavioral Health and Behavioral Medicine: Frontiers for a New Health Psychology," *American Psychologist* 35, no. 9 (September 1980): 807–17, https://doi.org/10.1037/0003–066X.35.9.807; Steven Findlay, "Managed Behavioral Health Care In 1999: An Industry At A Crossroads," *Health Affairs* 18, no. 5 (September 1999): 116–24, https://doi.org/10.1377/hlthaff.18.5.116.

12. Miranda Yaver, "Rationing by Inconvenience: How Insurance Denials Induce Administrative Burdens," *Journal of Health Politics, Policy and Law* 49, no. 4 (February 7, 2024): 539–65, 11186111, https://doi.org/10.1215/03616878–11186111.

13. Anna Kirkland, Shauhin Talesh, and Angela K. Perone, "Transition Coverage and Clarity in Self-Insured Corporate Health Insurance Benefit Plans," *Transgender Health* 6, no. 4 (August 1, 2021): 207–16, https://doi.org/10.1089/trgh.2020.0067.

14. Melanie M. VanDyke and Ann M. Steffen, "Medication Saving Behaviors of Older Adults: Scale Developed to Assess Family Caregiver Perspectives," *Clinical Gerontologist* 40, no. 4 (August 8, 2017): 258–67, https://doi.org/10.1080/07317115.2016.1276114.

15. stef m. shuster, "Uncertain Expertise and the Limitations of Clinical Guidelines in Transgender Healthcare," *Journal of Health and Social Behavior* 57, no. 3 (September 1, 2016): 319–32, https://doi.org/10.1177/0022146516660343.

16. "Equality Maps: Bans on Best Practice Medical Care for Transgender Youth," Movement Advancement Project, accessed January 19, 2024, www.mapresearch.org/equality-maps/healthcare/youth_medical_care_bans.

17. The bench trial in Florida was *Dekker v. Weida*, filed against the state of Florida for their ban on Medicaid coverage for gender-affirming care. That trial record is what the *Doe v. Ladapo* opinion relies on. The same judge presided over both cases.

18. *Doe v. Ladapo*, 3.

19. *Brandt v. Rutledge*, 50.

20. *Doe v. Ladapo*, 5.

21. *Brandt v. Rutledge*, 58 footnote 11.

22. *Brandt v. Rutledge*, 59.

23. Joanna Wuest and Briana S. Last, "Agents of Scientific Uncertainty: Conflicts over Evidence and Expertise in Gender- Affirming Care Bans for Minors," *Social Science & Medicine* 344, 2024.

24. "Events," Genspect, accessed January 19, 2024, https://genspect.org/category/events/.

25. Petition for a Writ of Certiorari by the United States of America, Petitioner, in *United States v. Skrmetti*, November 2023.

CONCLUSION: HOW TO STRENGTHEN HEALTH CARE CIVIL RIGHTS

1. The relatively new field of implementation science within medical and health research has emerged because researchers can sometimes figure out the best way to solve a

healthcare problem only to see their proposed solution fail to uptake in the organization (Mark S. Bauer and JoAnn Kirchner, "Implementation Science: What Is It and Why Should I Care?" *Psychiatry Research*, VSI: Implementation Science, 283 [January 1, 2020]: 112376, https://doi.org/10.1016/j.psychres.2019.04.025). This entire book could be considered a study of a failure to implement a health reform. Implementation scientists acknowledge the social sciences and policy as offering important context but do not seem to have a full range of critical tools available to understand why things go awry. An interdisciplinary approach with a robust accounting for power relations, hierarchies, professional competition, emotions, political structures, and economic incentives, among other forces, would be helpful. I thank Joanna Wuest for pointing this connection out to me.

2. Thomas M. Keck, "Erosion, Backsliding, or Abuse: Three Metaphors for Democratic Decline," *Law & Social Inquiry* 48, no. 1 (February 2023): 314–39, https://doi.org/10.1017/lsi.2022.43.

3. Dayna Bowen Matthew, *Just Medicine: A Cure for Racial Inequality in American Health Care* (New York: New York University Press, 2015), https://muse.jhu.edu/pub/193/monograph/book/76222.

4. Robert Bartlett et al., "Algorithmic Discrimination and Input Accountability under the Civil Rights Acts," *Berkeley Technology Law Journal* 36, no. 2 (2021): 675–736; Michael P. Cary et al., "Mitigating Racial And Ethnic Bias And Advancing Health Equity In Clinical Algorithms: A Scoping Review," *Health Affairs* 42, no. 10 (October 2023): 1359–68, https://doi.org/10.1377/hlthaff.2023.00553; Katherine E. Goodman, Daniel J. Morgan, and Diane E. Hoffmann, "Clinical Algorithms, Antidiscrimination Laws, and Medical Device Regulation," *JAMA* 329, no. 4 (January 24, 2023): 285–86, https://doi.org/10.1001/jama.2022.23870; Rohan Khazanchi et al., "Leveraging Affordable Care Act Section 1557 To Address Racism In Clinical Algorithms," *Health Affairs Forefront*, accessed August 8, 2023, https://doi.org/10.1377/forefront.20220930.182927.

5. Carmel Shachar and Sara Gerke, "Prevention of Bias and Discrimination in Clinical Practice Algorithms," *JAMA* 329, no. 4 (January 5, 2023): 283–84, https://doi.org/10.1001/jama.2022.23867.

6. Sharona Hoffman and Andy Podgurski, "Artificial Intelligence and Discrimination in Health Care," *Yale Journal of Health Policy, Law and Ethics* 19, no. 3 (2020): 1–49.

7. Jeb Barnes, "Adversarial Legalism and the American Style of Policymaking," in *The Routledge Handbook of Policy Styles*, ed. Michael Howlett and Jale Tosun (New York: Routledge, 2021), 25–37; Sean Farhang, *The Litigation State: Public Regulation and Private Lawsuits in the U.S* (Princeton, NJ: Princeton University Press, 2010); Robert A. Kagan, *Adversarial Legalism: The American Way of Law* (Cambridge, MA: Harvard University Press, 2019).

8. George J. Annas, "The Patient's Right to Safety—Improving the Quality of Care through Litigation against Hospitals," *New England Journal of Medicine* 354, no. 19 (May 11, 2006): 2063–66, https://doi.org/10.1056/NEJMsb053756; "Court Should Respect Privilege Tied to Quality Related Event Report," American Medical Association, December 29, 2021, https://www.ama-assn.org/delivering-care/patient-support-advocacy/court-should-respect-privilege-tied-quality-related-event.

9. Joseph Wardenski, "Supreme Court Slashes Remedies for Victims of Health Care Discrimination," O'Neill Institute for National and Global Health Law, May 12, 2022,

https://oneill.law.georgetown.edu/supreme-court-slashes-remedies-for-victims-of-health
-care-discrimination/.

10. Stephen B. Burbank and Sean Farhang, *Rights and Retrenchment: The Counter-revolution against Federal Litigation* (Cambridge, UK: Cambridge University Press, 2017), https://doi.org/10.1017/9781316480229.

11. Burbank and Farhang, *Rights and Retrenchment*.

12. Matthew, *Just Medicine*.

13. Christine Back, "Civil Rights Remedies in Cummings and Implications for Title VI and Title IX," Legal Sidebar (Washington, DC: Congressional Research Service, June 29, 2022).

14. Elizabeth Sepper, "Conscientious Refusals of Care," in *The Oxford Handbook of U.S. Health Law*, ed. I. Glenn Cohen, Allison K. Hoffman, and William Sage (Oxford University Press, 2017), 354–74, https://doi.org/10.1093/oxfordhb/9780199366521.013.17.

15. Troyen A. Brennan, *The Transformation of American Health Insurance: On the Path to Medicare for All* (Baltimore, MD: Johns Hopkins University Press, 2024), 255–62.

16. Valarie Blake and Elizabeth Y. McCuskey, "Employer-Sponsored Reproduction," *Columbia Law Review* 124, no. 2 (March 2024): 273–359.

17. Indian Health Service, "Indian Health Service Strategic Plan FY 2019–2023: Introduction," accessed February 9, 2024, https://www.ihs.gov/strategicplan/introduction/.

18. Thomas D. Sequist, Theresa Cullen, and Kelly J. Acton, "Indian Health Service Innovations Have Helped Reduce Health Disparities Affecting American Indian And Alaska Native People," *Health Affairs* 30, no. 10 (October 2011): 1965–73, https://doi.org/10.1377/hlthaff.2011.0630.

19. "Nationally Recognized Gender-Affirming Care in Oklahoma," *Indian Country ECHO* (blog), n.d., https://www.indiancountryecho.org/story/nationally-recognized-gender
-affirming-care-in-oklahoma/.

20. "Navajo Area," Indian Health Service, accessed February 9, 2024, https://www.ihs
.gov/navajo/.

21. Sequist, Cullen, and Acton, "Indian Health Service Innovations Have Helped Reduce Health Disparities Affecting American Indian And Alaska Native People"; Timothy M. Westmoreland and Kathryn R. Watson, "Redeeming Hollow Promises: The Case for Mandatory Spending on Health Care for American Indians and Alaska Natives," *American Journal of Public Health* 96, no. 4 (2006): 600–5; Michelle Daigle, "Indigenous Methodologies of Care and Movement," *American Indian Culture and Research Journal* 46, no. 3 (November 6, 2023), https://doi.org/10.17953/A3.1554; Winona LaDuke and Deborah Cowen, "Beyond Wiindigo Infrastructure," *South Atlantic Quarterly* 119, no. 2 (April 1, 2020): 243–68, https://doi.org/10.1215/00382876-8177747.

22. Kim Tallbear, "Standing with and Speaking as Faith: A Feminist-Indigenous Approach to Inquiry," *Journal of Research Practice* 10, no. 2 (2014), https://www-proquest
-com.proxy.lib.umich.edu/docview/2230947090/abstract/3802506105DC4CF8PQ/1.

23. Kim Tallbear, "Caretaking Relations, Not American Dreaming," *Kalfou* 6, no. 1 (Spring 2019): 24–41.

24. Sequist, Cullen, and Acton, "Indian Health Service Innovations Have Helped Reduce Health Disparities Affecting American Indian and Alaska Native People."

25. Irene Papanicolas, Liana R. Woskie, and Ashish K. Jha, "Health Care Spending in the United States and Other High-Income Countries," *Journal of the American Medical Association* 319, no. 10 (March 13, 2018): 1024–39, https://doi.org/10.1001/jama.2018.1150.

26. Ed Kiely et al., "Unequal Geographies of Gender-Affirming Care: A Comparative Typology of Trans-Specific Healthcare Systems across Europe," *Social Science & Medicine*, forthcoming 2024.

27. Elizabeth Y. McCuskey, "ERISA Reform as Health Reform: The Case for an ERISA Preemption Waiver," *The Journal of Law, Medicine & Ethics* 48, no. 3 (October 6, 2020): 450–61, http://journals.sagepub.com/doi/10.1177/1073110520958868.

28. Elizabeth Y. McCuskey, "Reforming ERISA to Help States Control Health Care Costs" (New York: The Commonwealth Fund, February 9, 2023), https://doi.org/10.26099/a10y-0712.

29. McCuskey, "Reforming ERISA to Help States Control Health Care Costs."

30. Nicole C. Raeburn, *Changing Corporate America from Inside Out: Lesbian and Gay Workplace Rights* (Minneapolis: University of Minnesota Press, 2004).

31. Ryan D. Doerfler and Samuel Moyn, "Democratizing the Supreme Court," *California Law Review* 109, no. 5 (2021): 1703–72.

32. Doerfler and Moyn, "Democratizing the Supreme Court."

Adams, Noah, Ruth Pearce, Jaimie Veale, Asa Radix, Danielle Castro, Amrita Sarkar, and Kai Cheng Thom. "Guidance and Ethical Considerations for Undertaking Transgender Health Research and Institutional Review Boards Adjudicating This Research." *Transgender Health* 2, no. 1 (October 1, 2017): 165–75. https://doi.org/10.1089/trgh.2017.0012.

Aizura, Aren Z., Marquis Bey, Toby Beauchamp, Treva Ellison, Jules Gill-Peterson, and Eliza Steinbock. "Thinking with Trans Now." *Social Text* 38, no. 4 (145) (December 1, 2020): 125–47. https://doi.org/10.1215/01642472-8680478.

Annas, George J. "The Patient's Right to Safety—Improving the Quality of Care through Litigation against Hospitals." *New England Journal of Medicine* 354, no. 19 (May 11, 2006): 2063–66. https://doi.org/10.1056/NEJMsb053756.

Apodaca, Calvin, Reggie Casanova-Perez, Emily Bascom, Deepthi Mohanraj, Cezanne Lane, Drishti Vidyarthi, Erin Beneteau, et al. "Maybe They Had a Bad Day: How LGBTQ and BIPOC Patients React to Bias in Healthcare and Struggle to Speak Out." *Journal of the American Medical Informatics Association* 29, no. 12 (December 1, 2022): 2075–82. https://doi.org/10.1093/jamia/ocac142.

Ashley, Florence. "Accounting for Research Fatigue in Research Ethics." *Bioethics* 35, no. 3 (2021): 270–76. https://doi.org/10.1111/bioe.12829.

Avraham, Ronen. "Discrimination and Insurance." In *The Routledge Handbook of the Ethics of Discrimination*, edited by Kasper Lippert-Rasmussen, 335–47. Routledge Handbooks Online, 2017. https://doi.org/10.4324/9781315681634.

Avraham, Ronen, Kyle D. Logue, and Daniel Schwarcz. "Towards a Universal Framework for Insurance Anti-Discrimination Laws." *Connecticut Insurance Law Journal*, no. 1 (2015): 1–52.

———. "Understanding Insurance Anti-Discrimination Laws." *Southern California Law Review* 87, no. 2 (August 24, 2012): 195–274. https://doi.org/10.2139/ssrn.2135800.

Backlar, Patricia. "What's in a Name? Mental Health? Behavioral Health?" *Community Mental Health Journal* 32, no. 1 (February 1, 1996): 5–8. https://doi.org/10.1007/BF02249361.

Bakko, Matthew, and Shanna K. Kattari. "Differential Access to Transgender Inclusive Insurance and Healthcare in the United States: Challenges to Health across the Life Course." *Journal of Aging & Social Policy* 33, no. 1 (June 23, 2019): 67–81, 08959420.2019.1632681. https://doi.org/10.1080/08959420.2019.1632681.

Barbee, Harry, and Douglas Schrock. "Un/Gendering Social Selves: How Nonbinary People Navigate and Experience a Binarily Gendered World." *Sociological Forum* 34, no. 3 (2019): 572–93. https://doi.org/10.1111/socf.12517.

Barnes, Jeb. "Adversarial Legalism and the American Style of Policymaking." In *The Routledge Handbook of Policy Styles*, edited by Michael Howlett and Jane Tosun, 25–37. New York: Routledge, 2021.

Bartlett, Robert, Adair Morse, Nancy Wallace, and Richard Stanton. "Algorithmic Discrimination and Input Accountability under the Civil Rights Acts." *Berkeley Technology Law Journal* 36, no. 2 (2021): 675–736.

Bauer, Mark S., and JoAnn Kirchner. "Implementation Science: What Is It and Why Should I Care?" *Psychiatry Research*, VSI: Implementation Science, 283 (January 1, 2020): 112376. https://doi.org/10.1016/j.psychres.2019.04.025.

Beito, David T. *From Mutual Aid to the Welfare State: Fraternal Societies and Social Services, 1890–1967.* Chapel Hill, NC: University of North Carolina Press, 2000.

Bender-Baird, Kyla, and Margaret C. Stevenson. "Effects of Medicalization on Case Outcomes in Transgender Employment Discrimination Court Decisions." *Behavioral Sciences & the Law*, June 2024, 1–16. https://doi.org/10.1002/bsl.2685.

Berrey, Ellen, Robert L. Nelson, and Laura Beth Nielsen. *Rights on Trial: How Workplace Discrimination Law Perpetuates Inequality.* Chicago: University of Chicago Press, 2017.

Blake, Valarie K. "An Opening for Civil Rights in Health Insurance after the Affordable Care Act." *Boston College Journal of Law and Social Justice* 36, no. 2 (2016): 235–86.

Blake, Valarie, and Elizabeth Y. McCuskey. "Employer-Sponsored Reproduction." *Columbia Law Review* 124, no. 2 (March 2024): 273–359.

Bonilla-Silva, Eduardo. *Racism without Racists: Color-Blind Racism and the Persistence of Racial Inequality in the United States.* Lanham, MD: Rowman & Littlefield Publishers, 2006.

Borja, Melissa May. *Follow the New Way: American Refugee Resettlement Policy and Hmong Religious Change.* Cambridge, MA: Harvard University Press, 2023.

———. "Migration and Modern Religious Pluralism." In *The Oxford Handbook of Religion and Race in American History*, edited by Kathryn Gin Lum and Paul Harvey, 577–96, 2018. https://doi.org/10.1093/oxfordhb/9780190221171.013.6.

Boulding, William, Seth W. Glickman, Matthew P. Manary, Kevin A. Schulman, and Richard Staelin. "Relationship between Patient Satisfaction with Inpatient Care and Hospital Readmission within 30 Days." *The American Journal of Managed Care* 17, no. 1 (January 2011): 41–48.

Brennan, Elizabeth, and Mark C. Suchman. "Law and Technology in Healthcare Organizations." In *Research Handbook on Socio-Legal Studies of Medicine and Health*, 169–90. Cheltenham, UK: Edward Elgar, 2020.

Brennen, David A. "Tax Expenditures, Social Justice, and Civil Rights: Expanding the Scope of Civil Rights Laws to Apply to Tax-Exempt Charities." *Brigham Young University Law Review* 2001, no. 1 (2001): 167–228.

Bridges, Khiara. *Reproducing Race: An Ethnography of Pregnancy as a Site of Racialization.* Berkeley, CA: University of California Press, 2011.

Burbank, Stephen B., and Sean Farhang. *Rights and Retrenchment: The Counterrevolution against Federal Litigation.* Cambridge, UK: Cambridge University Press, 2017. https://doi.org/10.1017/9781316480229.

Butler, Anthea D. *White Evangelical Racism: The Politics of Morality in America.* Chapel Hill, NC: The University of North Carolina Press, 2021.

Campbell, David E., James R. G. Kirk, and Geoffrey C. Layman. "Religion and the 2020 Presidential Election: The Enduring Divide." *The Forum* 18, no. 4 (December 30, 2020): 581–605. https://doi.org/10.1515/for-2020-2104.

Carpenter, Daniel. "Is Health Politics Different?" *Annual Review of Political Science* 15, no. 1 (2012): 287–311. https://doi.org/10.1146/annurev-polisci-050409–113009.

Cary, Michael P., Anna Zink, Sijia Wei, Andrew Olson, Mengying Yan, Rashaud Senior, Sophia Bessias, et al. "Mitigating Racial And Ethnic Bias And Advancing Health Equity In Clinical Algorithms: A Scoping Review." *Health Affairs* 42, no. 10 (October 2023): 1359–68. https://doi.org/10.1377/hlthaff.2023.00553.

Cavanaugh, Timothy, Ruben Hopwood, and Cei Lambert. "Informed Consent in the Medical Care of Transgender and Gender-Nonconforming Patients." *AMA Journal of Ethics* 18, no. 11 (November 1, 2016): 1147–55. https://doi.org/10.1001/journalofethics.2016.18.11.sect1–1611.

Chen, Anthony S. *The Fifth Freedom: Jobs, Politics, and Civil Rights in the United States, 1941–1972.* Princeton, NJ: Princeton University Press, 2009. https://press.princeton.edu/books/paperback/9780691139531/the-fifth-freedom.

Chiarello, Elizabeth. "Law, Morality, and Health Care Professionals: A Multilevel Framework." *Annual Review of Law and Social Science* 15, no. 1 (October 10, 2019): 117–35. https://doi.org/10.1146/annurev-lawsocsci-101518–042853.

———. *Policing Patients: Treatment and Surveillance on the Frontlines of the Opioid Crisis.* Princeton, NJ: Princeton University Press, 2024. https://press.princeton.edu/books/hardcover/9780691224770/policing-patients.

———. "Trojan Horse Technologies: Smuggling Criminal-Legal Logics into Healthcare Practice." *American Sociological Review* 88, no. 6 (December 1, 2023): 1131–60. https://doi.org/10.1177/00031224231209445.

Chowkwanyun, Merlin. "What Is a 'Racial Health Disparity'? Five Analytic Traditions." *Journal of Health Politics, Policy and Law* 47, no. 2 (April 1, 2022): 131–58. https://doi.org/10.1215/03616878-9517163.

Chowkwanyun, Merlin, and Adolph L. Reed. "Racial Health Disparities and Covid-19—Caution and Context." *New England Journal of Medicine* 383, no. 3 (July 16, 2020): 201–3. https://doi.org/10.1056/NEJMp2012910.

Cohen, Cathren. "Surgeries on Intersex Infants Are Bad Medicine." National Health Law Program, July 1, 2021. https://healthlaw.org/surgeries-on-intersex-infants-are-bad-medicine/.

Darwin, Helana. "Challenging the Cisgender/Transgender Binary: Nonbinary People and the Transgender Label." *Gender & Society* 34, no. 3 (June 1, 2020): 357–80. https://doi.org/10.1177/0891243220912256.

Das, Rishub K., Izabela A. Galdyn, Galen Perdikis, Brian C. Drolet, and Kyla P. Terhune. "National Patterns in the Use of International Statistical Classification of Diseases and

Health Related Problems, Tenth Revision Z Codes in Ambulatory Surgery from 2016 to 2019." *The American Journal of Surgery* 228 (February 1, 2024): 54–61. https://doi.org/10.1016/j.amjsurg.2023.06.030.

Dietz, Elizabeth. "More Necessary than Medical: Reframing the Insurance Argument for Transition-Related Care." *IJFAB: International Journal of Feminist Approaches to Bioethics* 13, no. 1 (March 2020): 63–88. https://doi.org/10.3138/ijfab.13.1.04.

Dobbin, Frank. *Inventing Equal Opportunity*. Princeton, NJ: Princeton University Press, 2009.

Dobbin, Frank, and Alexandra Kalev. "The Civil Rights Revolution at Work: What Went Wrong." *Annual Review of Sociology* 47, no. 1 (July 31, 2021): 281–303. https://doi.org/10.1146/annurev-soc-090820-023615.

Doerfler, Ryan D., and Samuel Moyn. "Democratizing the Supreme Court." *California Law Review* 109, no. 5 (2021): 1703–72.

Dubov, Alex, and Liana Fraenkel. "Facial Feminization Surgery: The Ethics of Gatekeeping in Transgender Health." *The American Journal of Bioethics* 18, no. 12 (December 2018): 3–9. https://doi.org/10.1080/15265161.2018.1531159.

Dumes, Abigail Anne. *Divided Bodies: Lyme Disease, Contested Illness, and Evidence-Based Medicine*. Durham, NC: Duke University Press, 2020.

Edelman, Lauren B. *Working Law: Courts, Corporations, and Symbolic Civil Rights*. Chicago: University of Chicago Press, 2016.

Edelman, Lauren B., Howard S. Erlanger, and John Lande. "Internal Dispute Resolution: The Transformation of Civil Rights in the Workplace." *Law & Society Review* 27 (1993): 497–534.

Epstein, Steven. *Impure Science: AIDS, Activism, and the Politics of Knowledge*. Medicine and Society. Berkeley, CA.: Univ. of California Press, 1998.

———. *Inclusion: The Politics of Difference in Medical Research*. Chicago: University of Chicago Press, 2008.

Evang, Jenny Andrine Madsen. "Is 'Gender Ideology' Western Colonialism?: Anti-Gender Rhetoric and the Misappropriation of Postcolonial Language." *TSQ: Transgender Studies Quarterly* 9, no. 3 (August 1, 2022): 365–86. https://doi.org/10.1215/23289252-9836036.

Farhang, Sean. *The Litigation State: Public Regulation and Private Lawsuits in the U.S.* Princeton, NJ: Princeton University Press, 2010.

Feuer, Albert. "When Do State Laws Determine ERISA Plan Benefit Rights?" *John Marshall Law Review* 47, no. 1 (2013): 145–400.

Finlay, Keith, Michael Mueller-Smith, and Brittany Street. "Children's Indirect Exposure to the U.S. Justice System: Evidence From Longitudinal Links between Survey and Administrative Data." *The Quarterly Journal of Economics* 138, no. 4 (November 1, 2023): 2181–224. https://doi.org/10.1093/qje/qjad021.

Freedman, Lori. *Bishops and Bodies: Reproductive Care in American Catholic Hospitals*. New Brunswick, NJ: Rutgers University Press, 2023. https://doi.org/10.36019/9781978828896.

Gill-Peterson, Jules. *Histories of the Transgender Child*. Minneapolis: University of Minnesota Press, 2018.

Glick, Jennifer L., Katherine P. Theall, Katherine M. Andrinopoulos, and Carl Kendall. "The Role of Discrimination in Care Postponement Among Trans-Feminine Individuals in the U.S. National Transgender Discrimination Survey." *LGBT Health* 5, no. 3 (March 28, 2018): 171–79. https://doi.org/10.1089/lgbt.2017.0093.

Goffman, Erving. *Frame Analysis: An Essay on the Organization of Experience.* Boston: Northeastern University Press, 1986.

Gonsalves, Tara. "Elaborating Embodied Boundaries: Medical Expertise and (Trans) Gender Classification." *American Journal of Sociology* 129, no. 5 (March 2024): 1311–58. https://doi.org/10.1086/729505.

———. "Gender Identity, the Sexed Body, and the Medical Making of Transgender." *Gender & Society* 34, no. 6 (December 1, 2020): 1005–33. https://doi.org/10.1177/0891243220965913.

Goodman, Katherine E., Daniel J. Morgan, and Diane E. Hoffmann. "Clinical Algorithms, Antidiscrimination Laws, and Medical Device Regulation." *JAMA* 329, no. 4 (January 24, 2023): 285–86. https://doi.org/10.1001/jama.2022.23870.

Goodwin, Michele. *Policing the Womb: Invisible Women and the Criminal Costs of Motherhood.* New York: Cambridge University Press, 2020.

Grant, Jaime M., Lisa A. Mottet, Justin Tanis, Jack Harrison, Jodi L. Herman, and Mara Keisling. "Injustice at Every Turn: A Report of the National Transgender Discrimination Survey." Washington, DC: National Center for Transgender Equity and National Gay and Lesbian Task Force, 2011. https://www.transequality.org/sites/default/files/docs/resources/NTDS_Report.pdf.

Grogan, Colleen M. *Grow and Hide: The History of America's Health Care State.* New York: Oxford University Press, 2023. https://doi.org/10.1093/oso/9780199812233.001.0001.

Gunningham, Neil, Robert A. Kagan, and Dorothy Thornton. "Social License and Environmental Protection: Why Businesses Go Beyond Compliance." *Law & Social Inquiry* 29, no. 2 (April 2004): 307–41. https://doi.org/10.1111/j.1747-4469.2004.tb00338.x.

Haimson, Oliver L., Avery Dame-Griff, Elias Capello, and Zahari Richter. "Tumblr Was a Trans Technology: The Meaning, Importance, History, and Future of Trans Technologies." *Feminist Media Studies* 21, no. 3 (April 3, 2021): 345–61. https://doi.org/10.1080/14680777.2019.1678505.

Hall, David M. *Allies at Work: Creating a Lesbian, Gay, Bisexual and Transgender Inclusive Work Environment.* San Francisco: Out & Equal Workplace Advocates, 2009.

Heimer, Carol A. *Governing the Global Clinic HIV and the Legal Transformation of Medicine.* Chicago: University of Chicago Press, 2025.

———. "Where Law and Morality Meet: Moral Agency and Moral Deskilling in Organizations." In *Handbook of the Sociology of Morality*, Volume 2, edited by Steven Hitlin, Shai M. Dromi, and Aliza Luft, 43–57. Handbooks of Sociology and Social Research. Cham, Switzerland: Springer International Publishing, 2023. https://doi.org/10.1007/978-3-031-32022-4_3.

Heimer, Carol A., and Arielle W. Tolman. "Between the Constitution and the Clinic: Formal and de Facto Rights to Healthcare." *Law & Society Review* 55, no. 4 (2021): 563–86. https://doi.org/10.1111/lasr.12577.

Heimer, Carol A., and Jaimie Morse. "Colonizing the Clinic: The Adventures of Law in HIV Treatment and Research," in *The New Legal Realism*. Vol. 2, *Studying Law Globally*, edited by H. Klug and S. Engle Merry, 69–95. New York: Cambridge University Press, 2016. https://doi.org/10.1017/CBO9781139683432.006.

Hellinger, Fred J., and Gary J. Young. "Health Plan Liability and ERISA: The Expanding Scope of State Legislation." *American Journal of Public Health* 95, no. 2 (February 1, 2005): 217–23. https://doi.org/10.2105/AJPH.2004.037895.

Hill, Latoya, Nambi Ndugga, and Samantha Artiga. "Key Data on Health and Health Care by Race and Ethnicity." *Kaiser Family Foundation* (blog), March 15, 2023. https://www.kff.org/racial-equity-and-health-policy/report/key-data-on-health-and-health-care-by-race-and-ethnicity/.

Ho, Christina S. *Normalizing an American Right to Health.* New York: Oxford University Press, 2023.

Hoffmann, Elizabeth A. *Lactation at Work: Expressed Milk, Expressing Beliefs, and the Expressive Value of Law.* New York: Cambridge University Press, 2021. https://doi.org/10.1017/9781108770828.

Hoffman, Sharona, and Andy Podgurski. "Artificial Intelligence and Discrimination in Health Care." *Yale Journal of Health Policy, Law and Ethics* 19, no. 3 (2020): 1–49.

Hollis-Brusky, Amanda, and Joshua C. Wilson. "Playing for the Rules: How and Why New Christian Right Public Interest Law Firms Invest in Secular Litigation." *Law & Policy* 39, no. 2 (2017): 121–41. https://doi.org/10.1111/lapo.12075.

Huang, Ya-Lin A., Asa Radix, Weiming Zhu, Anne A. Kimball, Evelyn J. Olansky, and Karen W. Hoover. "HIV Testing and Preexposure Prophylaxis Prescriptions Among U.S. Commercially Insured Transgender Men and Women, 2014 to 2021." *Annals of Internal Medicine* 177, no. 1 (December 19, 2023). https://doi.org/10.7326/M23-2073.

Institute of Medicine. *The Health of Lesbian, Gay, Bisexual, and Transgender People: Building a Foundation for Better Understanding.* Washington, DC: The National Academies Press, 2011. https://doi.org/10.17226/13128.

interACT: Advocates for Intersex Youth. "Federal Healthcare Rule Cements Sex Discrimination Protections to Include Intersex Patients." *interACT: Advocates for Intersex Youth* (blog), April 26, 2024. https://interactadvocates.org/federal-healthcare-rule-cements-sex-discrimination-protections/.

Jaipaul, C. Komal, and Gary E. Rosenthal. "Do Hospitals With Lower Mortality Have Higher Patient Satisfaction? A Regional Analysis of Patients With Medical Diagnoses." *American Journal of Medical Quality* 18, no. 2 (March 1, 2003): 59–65. https://doi.org/10.1177/106286060301800203.

Johnson, Olatunde C.A. "The Story of Bob Jones University v. United States: Race, Religion, and Congress' Extraordinary Acquiescence." In *Statutory Interpretation Stories*, edited by William N. Eskridge, Philip P. Frickey, Elizabeth Garrett, and James J. Brudney, 127–63. New York: Foundation Press, 2011.

Jost, John T., Jaime L. Napier, Hulda Thorisdottir, Samuel D. Gosling, Tibor P. Palfai, and Brian Ostafin. "Are Needs to Manage Uncertainty and Threat Associated With Political Conservatism or Ideological Extremity?" *Personality and Social Psychology Bulletin* 33, no. 7 (July 1, 2007): 989–1007. https://doi.org/10.1177/0146167207301028.

Junewicz, Alexandra, and Stuart J Youngner. "Patient-Satisfaction Surveys on a Scale of 0 to 10: Improving Health Care, or Leading It Astray." *The Hastings Center Report* 45, no. 3 (May 1, 2015): 43–51. https://doi.org/10.1002/hast.453.

Kagan, Robert A. *Adversarial Legalism: The American Way of Law.* Cambridge, MA: Harvard University Press, 2019.

Kattari, Shanna K., N. Eugene Walls, Darren L. Whitfield, and Lisa Langenderfer-Magruder. "Racial and Ethnic Differences in Experiences of Discrimination in Accessing Health Services Among Transgender People in the United States." *International Journal of*

Transgenderism 16, no. 2 (April 3, 2015): 68–79. https://doi.org/10.1080/15532739.2015.1064336.

Keck, Thomas M. "Erosion, Backsliding, or Abuse: Three Metaphors for Democratic Decline." *Law & Social Inquiry* 48, no. 1 (February 2023): 314–39. https://doi.org/10.1017/lsi.2022.43.

Kellogg, Katherine C. "Brokerage Professions and Implementing Reform in an Age of Experts." *American Sociological Review* 79, no. 5 (2014): 912–41.

Kelly, Erin. "Failure to Update: An Institutional Perspective on Noncompliance with the Family and Medical Leave Act." *Law & Society Review* 44, no. 1 (2010): 33–66.

Kiely, Ed, Nessa Millet, Asher Baron, Baudewijntje P.C. Kreukels, and David Matthew Doyle. "Unequal Geographies of Gender-Affirming Care: A Comparative Typology of Trans-Specific Healthcare Systems across Europe." *Social Science & Medicine,* forthcoming 2024.

Kimport, Katrina, Tracy A. Weitz, and Lori Freedman. "The Stratified Legitimacy of Abortions." *Journal of Health and Social Behavior* 57, no. 4 (December 1, 2016): 503–16. https://doi.org/10.1177/0022146516669970.

Kinney, Eleanor D., and Brian Alexander Clark. "Provisions for Health and Health Care in the Constitutions of the Countries of the World." *Cornell International Law Journal* 37, no. 2 (2004): 285–356.

Kirkland, Anna. "Credibility Battles in the Autism Litigation." *Social Studies of Science* 42, no. 2 (2012): 237–61.

———. "Dropdown Rights: Categorizing Transgender Discrimination in Healthcare Technologies." *Social Science & Medicine* 289 (November 2021): 114348. https://doi.org/10.1016/j.socscimed.2021.114348.

———. *Fat Rights: Dilemmas of Difference and Personhood.* New York: New York University Press, 2008.

———. "Frameworks and Ideologies for Fat Non-Discrimination Rights." In *The Routledge Handbook of Critical Obesity Studies,* edited by Michael Gard, Darren Powell, and Tenorio Jose, 361–69. London: Routledge Handbooks Online, 2021. https://doi.org/10.4324/9780429344824-45.

———. *Vaccine Court: The Law and Politics of Injury.* New York: New York University Press, 2016.

———. "Victorious Transsexuals in the Courtroom: A Challenge for Feminist Legal Theory." *Law & Social Inquiry* 28, no. 1 (2003): 1–37.

———. "What's at Stake in Transgender Discrimination as Sex Discrimination?" *Signs: Journal of Women in Culture and Society* 32, no. 1 (2006): 83–111.

Kirkland, Anna, and Mikell Hyman. "Civil Rights as Patient Experience: How Healthcare Organizations Handle Discrimination Complaints." *Law & Society Review* 55, no. 2 (2021): 273–95. https://doi.org/10.1111/lasr.12554.

Kirkland, Anna, Shauhin Talesh, and Angela K. Perone. "Health Insurance Rights and Access to Health Care for Trans People: The Social Construction of Medical Necessity." *Law & Society Review* 55, no. 4 (2021): 539–62. https://doi.org/10.1111/lasr.12575.

———. "Transition Coverage and Clarity in Self-Insured Corporate Health Insurance Benefit Plans." *Transgender Health* 6, no. 4 (September 29, 2020): 207–16. https://doi.org/10.1089/trgh.2020.0067.

Klein, Jennifer. *For All These Rights: Business, Labor, and the Shaping of America's Public-Private Welfare State*. Princeton, NJ: Princeton University Press, 2006.

Konnoth, Craig. "Medicalization and the New Civil Rights." *Ethics, Medicine and Public Health*, SI: Medical Conscience/Medical Rights, 12 (January 1, 2020): 100435. https://doi.org/10.1016/j.jemep.2019.100435.

Kupke, Annabel, Carmel Shachar, and Christopher Robertson. "Pulse Oximeters and Violation of Federal Antidiscrimination Law." *JAMA* 329, no. 5 (February 7, 2023): 365–66. https://doi.org/10.1001/jama.2022.24976.

LaDuke, Winona, and Deborah Cowen. "Beyond Wiindigo Infrastructure." *South Atlantic Quarterly* 119, no. 2 (April 1, 2020): 243–68. https://doi.org/10.1215/00382876-8177747.

Lagos, Danya. "Looking at Population Health Beyond 'Male' and 'Female': Implications of Transgender Identity and Gender Nonconformity for Population Health." *Demography* 55, no. 6 (2018): 2097–117.

Lane, Megan, Anna R. Kirkland, and Daphna Stroumsa. "Protecting Care for All—Gender-Affirming Care in Section 1557 and Beyond." *New England Journal of Medicine* 387, no. 21 (November 24, 2022): 1916–18. https://doi.org/10.1056/NEJMp2212586.

Lantz, Paula M., and Sara Rosenbaum. "The Potential and Realized Impact of the Affordable Care Act on Health Equity." *Journal of Health Politics, Policy and Law* 45, no. 5 (2020). https://doi.org/10.1215/03616878-8543298.

Layman, Geoffrey. *The Great Divide: Religious and Cultural Conflict in American Party Politics*. New York: Columbia University Press, 2001.

Levin, Peter J. "Bold Vision: Catholic Sisters and the Creation of American Hospitals." *Journal of Community Health* 36, no. 3 (June 1, 2011): 343–47. https://doi.org/10.1007/s10900-011-9401-7.

Loyd, Jenna M. *Health Rights Are Civil Rights: Peace and Justice Activism in Los Angeles, 1963–1978*. Minneapolis: University of Minnesota Press, 2014.

Lynch, Julia. "Reframing Inequality? The Health Inequalities Turn as a Dangerous Frame Shift." *Journal of Public Health* 39, no. 4 (December 1, 2017): 653–60. https://doi.org/10.1093/pubmed/fdw140.

———. *Regimes of Inequality: The Political Economy of Health and Wealth*. Cambridge, UK: Cambridge University Press, 2019. https://doi.org/10.1017/9781139051576.

Malatino, Hil. "The Promise of Repair: Trans Rage and the Limits of Feminist Coalition." *Signs: Journal of Women in Culture and Society* 46, no. 4 (June 2021): 827–51. https://doi.org/10.1086/713292.

———. *Trans Care*. Minneapolis: University of Minnesota Press, 2020. https://www.upress.umn.edu/book-division/books/trans-care.

Matarazzo, Joseph D. "Behavioral Health and Behavioral Medicine: Frontiers for a New Health Psychology." *American Psychologist* 35, no. 9 (September 1980): 807–17. https://doi.org/10.1037/0003-066X.35.9.807.

Matthew, Dayna Bowen. *Just Health: Treating Structural Racism to Heal America*. New York: New York University Press, 2022. https://doi.org/10.18574/nyu/9781479802685.001.0001.

———. *Just Medicine: A Cure for Racial Inequality in American Health Care*. New York: NYU Press, 2015. https://muse.jhu.edu/pub/193/monograph/book/76222.

McCann, Michael W. *Rights at Work: Pay Equity Reform and the Politics of Legal Mobilization*. Language and Legal Discourse. Chicago: University of Chicago Press, 1994.

———. "The Unbearable Lightness of Rights: On Sociolegal Inquiry in the Global Era." *Law & Society Review* 48, no. 2 (2014): 245–73. https://doi.org/10.1111/lasr.12075.

McCuskey, Elizabeth Y. "ERISA Reform as Health Reform: The Case for an ERISA Preemption Waiver." *The Journal of Law, Medicine & Ethics* 48, no. 3 (October 6, 2020): 450–61. http://journals.sagepub.com/doi/10.1177/1073110520958868.

———. "Reforming ERISA to Help States Control Health Care Costs." New York: The Commonwealth Fund, February 9, 2023. https://doi.org/10.26099/a10y-0712.

Mehta, Shivan J. "Patient Satisfaction Reporting and Its Implications for Patient Care." *AMA Journal of Ethics* 17, no. 7 (July 1, 2015): 616–21. https://doi.org/10.1001/journalofethics.2015.17.7.ecas3–1507.

Michener, Jamila, and Tiffany N Ford. "Racism and Health: Three Core Principles." *The Milbank Quarterly* 101, no. S1 (April 1, 2023): 333–55. https://doi.org/10.1111/1468–0009.12633.

Monahan, Amy B., and Daniel Schwarcz. "Rules of Medical Necessity." *Iowa Law Review* 107, no. 2 (January 2022): 423–94.

Morse, Jaimie. "Legal Mobilization in Medicine: Nurses, Rape Kits, and the Emergence of Forensic Nursing in the United States since the 1970s." *Social Science & Medicine* 222 (February 1, 2019): 323–34. https://doi.org/10.1016/j.socscimed.2018.12.032.

Munsch, Christin L., and C. Elizabeth Hirsh. "Gender Variance in the Fortune 500: The Inclusion of Gender Identity and Expression in Nondiscrimination Corporate Policy." In *Gender and Sexuality in the Workplace*, edited by Christine L. Williams and Kirsten Dellinger, 20:151–77. Research in the Sociology of Work. Bingley, UK: Emerald Group Publishing Limited, 2010. https://doi.org/10.1108/S0277–2833(2010)0000020010.

Nader, Laura. "Up the Anthropologist: Perspectives Gained From Studying Up." In *Reinventing Anthropology*, edited by Dell Hymes, 284–311. New York: Vintage Books, 1974.

Ne'eman, Ari, Michael Ashley Stein, Zackary D. Berger, and Doron Dorfman. "The Treatment of Disability under Crisis Standards of Care: An Empirical and Normative Analysis of Change over Time during COVID-19." *Journal of Health Politics, Policy and Law* 46, no. 5 (October 1, 2021): 831–60. https://doi.org/10.1215/03616878–9156005.

Nelson, Alondra. *Body and Soul: The Black Panther Party and the Fight against Medical Discrimination*. Minneapolis: University of Minnesota Press, 2013. https://www.upress.umn.edu/book-division/books/body-and-soul.

Ngaage, Ledibabari, Brooks Knighton, Caroline Benzel, Katie McGlone, Erin Rada, Devin Coon, Rachel Bluebond-Langner, and Yvonne Rasko. "A Review of Insurance Coverage of Gender-Affirming Genital Surgery." *Plastic and Reconstructive Surgery* 145, no. 3 (March 2020): 803–12. https://doi.org/10.1097/PRS.0000000000006591.

Ngaage, Ledibabari, Brooks Knighton, Katie McGlone, Caroline Benzel, Erin Rada, Rachel Bluebond-Langner, and Yvonne Rasko. "Health Insurance Coverage of Gender-Affirming Top Surgery in the United States." *Plastic and Reconstructive Surgery* 144, no. 4 (October 2019): 824–33. https://doi.org/10.1097/PRS.0000000000006012.

Ngaage, Ledibabari M., Katie L. McGlone, Shan Xue, Brooks J. Knighton, Caroline A. Benzel, Erin M. Rada, Devin Coon, Jens Berli, and Yvonne M. Rasko. "Gender Surgery Beyond Chest and Genitals: Current Insurance Landscape." *Aesthetic Surgery Journal* 40, no. 4 (March 23, 2020): NP202–10. https://doi.org/10.1093/asj/sjz262.

Nordmarken, Sonny, and Reese Kelly. "Limiting Transgender Health: Administrative Violence and Microaggressions in Health Care Systems." In *Health Care Disparities and the LGBT Population*, edited by Vickie L. Harvey, Teresa Heinz Housel, Gary L. Kreps, and Allan D. Peterkin, 120–39. Lanham, MD: Lexington Books, 2014.

O'Brien, John, and Eman Abdelhadi. "Re-Examining Restructuring: Racialization, Religious Conservatism, and Political Leanings in Contemporary American Life: Social Forces." *Social Forces* 99, no. 2 (December 2020): 474–503. https://doi.org/10.1093/sf/soaa029.

Papanicolas, Irene, Liana R. Woskie, and Ashish K. Jha. "Health Care Spending in the United States and Other High-Income Countries." *Journal of the American Medical Association* 319, no. 10 (March 13, 2018): 1024–39. https://doi.org/10.1001/jama.2018.1150.

Perone, Angela K. "Constructing Discrimination Rights: Comparisons Among Staff in Long-Term Care Health Facilities." *The Gerontologist* 63, no. 5 (June 1, 2023): 900–9. https://doi.org/10.1093/geront/gnac152.

Plemons, Eric. "A Capable Surgeon and a Willing Electrologist: Challenges to the Expansion of Transgender Surgical Care in the United States." *Medical Anthropology Quarterly* 33, no. 2 (2019): 282–301. https://doi.org/10.1111/maq.12484.

———. "Gender, Ethnicity, and Transgender Embodiment: Interrogating Classification in Facial Feminization Surgery." *Body & Society* 25, no. 1 (March 1, 2019): 3–28. https://doi.org/10.1177/1357034X18812942.

———. *Look of a Woman: Facial Feminization Surgery and the Aims of Trans-Medicine*. Durham, NC: Duke University Press, 2017. https://www.dukeupress.edu/the-look-of-a-woman.

———. "Not Here: Catholic Hospital Systems and the Restriction Against Transgender Healthcare." *CrossCurrents* 68, no. 4 (December 2018): 533–49. https://doi.org/10.1111/cros.12341.

Pryma, Jane. "'Even My Sister Says I'm Acting like a Crazy to Get a Check': Race, Gender, and Moral Boundary-Work in Women's Claims of Disabling Chronic Pain." *Social Science & Medicine* 181 (May 1, 2017): 66–73. https://doi.org/10.1016/j.socscimed.2017.03.048.

Quadagno, Jill. "Promoting Civil Rights through the Welfare State: How Medicare Integrated Southern Hospitals." *Social Problems* 47, no. 1 (2000): 68–89. https://doi.org/10.2307/3097152.

Raeburn, Nicole C. *Changing Corporate America from Inside Out: Lesbian and Gay Workplace Rights*. Minneapolis: University of Minnesota Press, 2004.

Reisner, Sari L., Tonia Poteat, JoAnne Keatley, Mauro Cabral, Tampose Mothopeng, Emilia Dunham, Claire E. Holland, Ryan Max, and Stefan D. Baral. "Global Health Burden and Needs of Transgender Populations: A Review." *The Lancet* 388, no. 10042 (July 23, 2016): 412–36. https://doi.org/10.1016/S0140-6736(16)00684-X.

Reisner, Sari L., Jaclyn M. White Hughto, Kristi E. Gamarel, Alex S. Keuroghlian, Lauren Mizock, and John E. Pachankis. "Discriminatory Experiences Associated with Posttraumatic Stress Disorder Symptoms among Transgender Adults." *Journal of Counseling Psychology* 63, no. 5 (2016): 509–19. https://doi.org/10.1037/cou0000143.

Rettig, Richard A. "Origins of the Medicare Kidney Disease Entitlement: The Social Security Amendments of 1972." In *Biomedical Politics*, edited by Kathi E. Hanna, 176–204. Washington, DC: National Academies Press, 1991. https://www.ncbi.nlm.nih.gov/books/NBK234191/.

Reynolds, P. Preston. "The Federal Government's Use of Title VI and Medicare to Racially Integrate Hospitals in the United States, 1963 through 1967." *American Journal of Public Health* 87, no. 11 (November 1997): 1850–58. https://doi.org/10.2105/ajph.87.11.1850.

Richman, Barak D., and Kevin A. Schulman. "Are Patient Satisfaction Instruments Harming Both Patients and Physicians?" *Journal of the American Medical Association* 328, no. 22 (December 13, 2022): 2209–10. https://doi.org/10.1001/jama.2022.21677.

Riggs, Damien W., Ruth Pearce, Carla A. Pfeffer, Sally Hines, Francis White, and Elisabetta Ruspini. "Transnormativity in the Psy Disciplines: Constructing Pathology in the Diagnostic and Statistical Manual of Mental Disorders and Standards of Care." *American Psychologist* 74, no. 8 (2019): 912–24. https://doi.org/10.1037/amp0000545.

Roberts, Dorothy. "Reproductive Justice, Not Just Rights." *Dissent* 62, no. 4 (2015): 79–82. https://doi.org/10.1353/dss.2015.0073.

———. *Torn Apart: How the Child Welfare System Destroys Black Families—and How Abolition Can Build a Safer World*. New York: Basic Books, 2022.

Rosenbaum, Sara, MaryBeth Musumeci, Kian Azimpoor, and Josemiguel Rodriguez. "Four Key Takeaways from A Health Care Civil Rights Landmark: The Final Section 1557 Rule." *Health Affairs Forefront*, June 12, 2024. http://www.healthaffairs.org/do/10.1377/forefront.20240607.491767/full/.

Ross, Loretta J. "Reproductive Justice as Intersectional Feminist Activism." *Souls* 19, no. 3 (July 3, 2017): 286–314. https://doi.org/10.1080/10999949.2017.1389634.

Schaaff, Bridget. "Using Federal Nondiscrimination Laws to Avoid ERISA: Securing Protection from Transgender Discrimination in Employee Health Benefit Plans." *Duke Journal of Gender Law & Policy* 26, no. 1 (2018): 45–64.

Schall, Theodore E., and Jacob D. Moses. "Gender-Affirming Care for Cisgender People." *Hastings Center Report* 53, no. 3 (2023): 15–24. https://doi.org/10.1002/hast.1486.

Schmidt, Christopher W. *Civil Rights in America: A History*. New York: Cambridge University Press, 2021.

Schulz, Sarah L. "The Informed Consent Model of Transgender Care: An Alternative to the Diagnosis of Gender Dysphoria." *Journal of Humanistic Psychology* 58, no. 1 (January 2018): 72–92. https://doi.org/10.1177/0022167817745217.

Sepper, Elizabeth. "Conscientious Refusals of Care." In *The Oxford Handbook of U.S. Health Law*, edited by I. Glenn Cohen, Allison K. Hoffman, and William Sage, 354–74. Oxford University Press, 2017. https://doi.org/10.1093/oxfordhb/9780199366521.013.17.

Shachar, Carmel, and Sara Gerke. "Prevention of Bias and Discrimination in Clinical Practice Algorithms." *JAMA* 329, no. 4 (January 5, 2023): 283–83. https://doi.org/10.1001/jama.2022.23867.

shuster, stef m. *Trans Medicine: The Emergence and Practice of Treating Gender*. New York: New York University Press, 2021. https://nyupress.org/9781479899371/trans-medicine.

———. "Uncertain Expertise and the Limitations of Clinical Guidelines in Transgender Healthcare." *Journal of Health and Social Behavior* 57, no. 3 (September 1, 2016): 319–32. https://doi.org/10.1177/0022146516660343.

Siegrist, Richard Bolton. "Patient Satisfaction: History, Myths, and Misperceptions." *AMA Journal of Ethics* 15, no. 11 (November 2, 2013): 982–87. https://doi.org/10.1001/virtualmentor.2013.15.11.mhst1-1311.

Singh, Rashmee, and Dawn Moore. "Bare Death: Femicide, Forensics and the Necropolitics of the Corpse." In *Research Handbook on Socio-Legal Studies of Medicine and Health*, edited by Marie-Andrée Jacob and Anna Kirkland, 287–302. Cheltenham, UK: Edward Elgar Publishing, 2020.

Smith, David Barton. *The Power to Heal: Civil Rights, Medicare, and the Struggle to Transform America's Health Care System.* Nashville, TN: Vanderbilt University Press, 2016. https://muse-jhu-edu.proxy.lib.umich.edu/book/46885.

Snorton, C. Riley. *Black on Both Sides: A Racial History of Trans Identity.* Minneapolis: University of Minnesota Press, 2017.

Spade, Dean. *Normal Life: Administrative Violence, Critical Trans Politics, and the Limits of Law.* Revised and Expanded Edition. Durham, NC: Duke University Press, 2015. https://www.dukeupress.edu/normal-life-revised.

Strings, Sabrina. *Fearing the Black Body: The Racial Origins of Fat Phobia.* New York: New York University Press, 2019. https://nyupress.org/9781479886753/fearing-the-black-body.

Stroumsa, Daphna, and Anna R. Kirkland. "Health Coverage and Care for Transgender People—Threats and Opportunities." *New England Journal of Medicine* 383, no. 25 (December 12, 2020): 2397–99. https://doi.org/10.1056/NEJMp2032453.

Stroumsa, Daphna, Elizabeth F.S. Roberts, Hadrian Kinnear, and Lisa H. Harris. "The Power and Limits of Classification—A 32-Year-Old Man with Abdominal Pain." *The New England Journal of Medicine* 380, no. 20 (May 16, 2019): 1885–88. https://doi.org/10.1056/NEJMp1811491.

Talesh, Shauhin. "Legal Intermediaries: How Insurance Companies Construct the Meaning of Compliance with Antidiscrimination Laws." *Law & Policy* 37, no. 3 (2015): 209–39. https://doi.org/10.1111/lapo.12037.

Tallbear, Kim. "Caretaking Relations, Not American Dreaming." *Kalfou* 6, no. 1 (Spring 2019): 24–41.

———. "Standing With and Speaking as Faith: A Feminist-Indigenous Approach to Inquiry." *Journal of Research Practice* 10, no. 2 (2014). https://www-proquest-com.proxy.lib.umich.edu/docview/2230947090/abstract/3802506105DC4CF8PQ/1.

Thomas, Karen Kruse. *Deluxe Jim Crow: Civil Rights and American Health Policy, 1935–1954.* Athens, GA: University of Georgia Press, 2011.

———. "The Hill-Burton Act and Civil Rights: Expanding Hospital Care for Black Southerners, 1939–1960." *The Journal of Southern History* 72, no. 4 (2006): 823–70. https://doi.org/10.2307/27649234.

VanDyke, Melanie M., and Ann M. Steffen. "Medication Saving Behaviors of Older Adults: Scale Developed to Assess Family Caregiver Perspectives." *Clinical Gerontologist* 40, no. 4 (August 8, 2017): 258–67. https://doi.org/10.1080/07317115.2016.1276114.

Vasquez Reyes, Maritza. "The Disproportional Impact of COVID-19 on African Americans." *Health and Human Rights* 22, no. 2 (December 2020): 299–307.

Viitanen, Johanna, Paula Valkonen, Kaisa Savolainen, Nina Karisalmi, Sini Hölsä, and Sari Kujala. "Patient Experience from an eHealth Perspective: A Scoping Review of Approaches and Recent Trends." *Yearbook of Medical Informatics* 31, no. 1 (December 4, 2022): 136–45. https://doi.org/10.1055/s-0042-1742515.

Wailoo, Keith. *Dying in the City of the Blues: Sickle Cell Anemia and the Politics of Race and Health.* Chapel Hill, NC: University of North Carolina Press, 2001.

Watkins-Hayes, Celeste. *Remaking a Life: How Women Living with HIV/AIDS Confront Inequality.* Oakland, CA: University of California Press, 2019.

Watson, Sidney D. "Section 1557 of the Affordable Care Act: Civil Rights, Health Reform, Race, and Equity." *Howard Law Journal* 55, no. 3 (2012): 855–86.

Wears, Robert L., and Kathleen M. Sutcliffe. *Still Not Safe: Patient Safety and the Middle-Managing of American Medicine.* New York: Oxford University Press, 2020.

Westbrook, Laurel. "The Matrix of Violence: Intersectionality and Necropolitics in the Murder of Transgender People in the United States, 1990–2019." *Gender & Society* 37, no. 3 (June 1, 2023): 413–46. https://doi.org/10.1177/08912432231171172.

Westmoreland, Timothy M., and Kathryn R. Watson. "Redeeming Hollow Promises: The Case for Mandatory Spending on Health Care for American Indians and Alaska Natives." *American Journal of Public Health* 96, no. 4 (2006): 600–5.

Wuest, Joanna. *Born This Way: Science, Citizenship, and Inequality in the American LGBTQ+ Movement.* Chicago: University of Chicago Press, 2023. https://press.uchicago.edu/ucp/books/book/chicago/B/bo201362155.html.

Wuest, Joanna, and Briana S. Last. "Agents of Scientific Uncertainty: Conflicts over Evidence and Expertise in Gender- Affirming Care Bans for Minors." *Social Science & Medicine* 344, no. 2 (2024).

———. "Church Against State: How Industry Groups Lead the Religious Liberty Assault on Civil Rights, Healthcare Policy, and the Administrative State." *Journal of Law, Medicine & Ethics* 52, no. 1 (Spring 2024): 151–68.

Wyers, Katherine. "Health ICTs and Transgender Health Equity: A Research Agenda." *Information Technology for Development* 30, no. 2 (2024): 1–27. https://doi.org/10.1080/02681102.2023.2292740.

Yaver, Miranda. "Rationing by Inconvenience: How Insurance Denials Induce Administrative Burdens." *Journal of Health Politics, Policy and Law* 49, no. 4 (August 1, 2024): 539–65. https://doi.org/10.1215/03616878-11186111.

Founded in 1893,
UNIVERSITY OF CALIFORNIA PRESS
publishes bold, progressive books and journals
on topics in the arts, humanities, social sciences,
and natural sciences—with a focus on social
justice issues—that inspire thought and action
among readers worldwide.

The UC PRESS FOUNDATION
raises funds to uphold the press's vital role
as an independent, nonprofit publisher, and
receives philanthropic support from a wide
range of individuals and institutions—and from
committed readers like you. To learn more, visit
ucpress.edu/supportus.

9 780520 416109